TRUE TO LIFE

STARTER

Stephen Slater
Simon Haines

TEACHER'S BOOK

CAMBRIDGE
UNIVERSITY PRESS

PUBLISHED BY THE PRESS SYNDICATE OF THE UNIVERSITY OF CAMBRIDGE
The Pitt Building, Trumpington Street, Cambridge, United Kingdom

CAMBRIDGE UNIVERSITY PRESS
The Edinburgh Building, Cambridge CB2 2RU, UK
40 West 20th Street, New York, NY 10011–4211, USA
477 Williamstown Road, Port Melbourne, VIC 3207, Australia
Ruiz de Alarcón 13, 28014 Madrid, Spain
Dock House, The Waterfront, Cape Town 8001, South Africa

http://www.cambridge.org

© Cambridge University Press 1998

First published 1998
Fourth printing 2004

Printed in Dubai by Oriental Press

ISBN 0 521 59578 9 Class Book
ISBN 0 521 59577 0 Personal Study Workbook
ISBN 0 521 59576 2 Teacher's Book
ISBN 0 521 59575 4 Class Cassette Set
ISBN 0 521 59574 6 Personal Study Workbook Cassette
ISBN 0 521 59573 8 Personal Study Audio CD

CONTENTS

INTRODUCTION

The True to Life series

True to Life is a five-level course taking learners from beginner through to upper-intermediate level. It is designed specifically for adult learners.

The series combines structured language input with plentiful opportunities to use the language naturally with other learners in a wide variety of ways. Topics have been chosen for their interest and relevance to adults around the world and the activities have been designed to provide adults with the opportunity to talk about their experiences, express opinions and exchange ideas.

Who is the Starter level for?

The Starter level is designed for learners in any country who have not learned English before and who want to understand basic English and build confidence to speak English from the start. It is also for learners who, although they may have learned some English before, wish to start a course again from beginner level. It is for learners who like to learn and communicate with other learners and for learners who like variety of activity when they learn something new.

The Starter level provides at least 40–60 hours of classroom material, depending on the time available and the options used.

Key features

Learner engagement and personalisation

A guiding principle of the series is the belief that learning is most effective when learners are actively engaged in tasks which they find motivating and challenging. It is essential for learners to see the relevance of new language to themselves. Learning a language is also a social experience. The course therefore draws on the lives and experiences of the learners as a springboard for natural language use, inviting their involvement, their views and experience of life.

Ready-made lessons

Each Class Book unit contains three ready-made lessons, A, B and C, each designed to take 45–60 minutes. Each lesson has been designed as a self-contained, logical sequence of varied activities, which can be used as they stand. (Alternative ways of using the material are indicated in the Teacher's Book.)

Recycling

Learners and teachers like to have regular revision and the importance of constant recycling is acknowledged in *True to Life*. The fourth lesson of every unit, section D, is Review and development. This section revises and sometimes extends the language taught in the previous two units.

Speaking and listening

The *True to Life* series puts particular emphasis on listening and speaking in the classroom. It has been our experience that adult learners place great emphasis on oral/aural practice in the classroom, often because it is their only opportunity to obtain such practice.

The Starter level has a strong focus on listening in particular. Of course, speaking is encouraged from the start, but it is acknowledged that adult beginners often need time to tune their ears to a new language, above all during the very early stages of learning.

Dual-level listening

An innovative feature of the series is the dual-level listening. Two versions of a listening text are provided – one simpler, the other more challenging. Teachers can select the listening material that best suits the needs of their particular learners or they can choose to use both versions.

At the Starter level the language in the first version of the text is very carefully controlled to make it accessible for beginners.

Reading and writing

The Starter level includes simple reading and writing tasks from the very beginning of the course. It provides regular written practice of grammar and vocabulary in order to help learners to memorise the formal aspects of the new language system they are using when they speak or listen.

A particular feature is the serialised story in the Workbook, which recycles the key language from each unit in an enjoyable and motivating way.

Vocabulary

Vocabulary development is a key aspect of the series and has been deliberately emphasised. A wide range of active vocabulary development tasks is included throughout the course. Great importance is attached to the spoken practice of new vocabulary so that learners have an early opportunity to use new words to express their own ideas and opinions.

At the Starter level the vocabulary load is carefully controlled for beginner learners.

Grammar

Grammar is important and needs to be visible. *True to Life* Starter maintains the view that adults like to see the grammar and work with it in its own right while at the same time having opportunities to use language naturally with others. A guiding principle of the course has been to make grammar prominent without allowing it to be over-intrusive or an inhibition to natural language use.

International content

The topic and thematic content has a broad international appeal, reflecting the learning of English in the learners' own context overseas rather than just in Britain.

Progess tests

There is a progress test after every three units of the Class Book. These four photocopiable tests are included at the back of the Teacher's Book.

Components

Each level consists of a Class Book and Class Cassette Set, a Teacher's Book, a Personal Study Workbook and Personal Study Cassette or Audio CD. There are Videos and Video Activity Books for the Elementary, Pre-intermediate and Intermediate levels.

The Class Book

The Class Book contains 12 units, each one providing three to four hours of classroom activity. The first three lessons contain the main language input. This consists of:
- a clear grammatical syllabus
- an emphasis on lexical development
- key functional exponents
- listening and reading practice
- speaking and writing activities.

The final section of each unit provides review and development activities based on the previous two units; e.g. The Review and development in Unit 3 revises Units 1 and 2; Unit 4 revises Units 2 and 3 etc.

Aims of each activity

Each activity in each lesson is clearly labelled with a brief indication of the skill or area of language that the activity is aiming to develop.

Quick Checks

There are Quick Check exercises in every unit, at the end of Lessons A, B and C. The Quick Checks offer learners a range of simple exercises on the grammar and vocabulary learned in each lesson. They can be done as homework or as revision at the beginning of class, and are ideal for busy adults.

In conversation

Each unit contains an 'In conversation' activity, which provides a short but realistic conversation using natural and useful language for learners to adapt to situations in which they may find themselves using English with native speakers.

Regular pronunciation

Alongside an extensive range of listening activities, the Starter level contains a good range of pronunciation tasks which explore areas such as stress in words, difficult sounds, question intonation and linking. These tasks are often to be found in the Review and Development sections (Lesson D). The Personal Study Workbook also includes regular pronunciation exercises.

Personal Study Workbook activities

At the end of Lesson C in each Unit there is a brief description of some of the linked language practice activities in the corresponding unit of the Personal Study Workbook.

Grammar Reference section

At the back of the Class Book there is an illustrated grammar summary, giving explanations and examples of the areas of grammar covered in each unit.

The Personal Study Workbook

Each unit in the Personal Study Workbook mirrors in broad terms the topics or themes of the corresponding unit in the Class Book, giving related language consolidation and extension. Wherever appropriate, practice activities ask the learner for personalised information.

Serialised story

The power of a narrative to structure and sustain reading or listening in a new language is acknowledged as a powerful motivation to read. *Lost in time*, a twelve-part story in the Personal Study Workbook and on the Personal Study Workbook Cassette/Audio CD provides a valuable and enjoyable reading and listening experience for the beginner learner of English. Each episode is carefully graded and reviews the key language from the unit.

Visual dictionary

The Personal Study Workbook has a visual dictionary at the back of the book. This provides an illustrated page for each unit for learners to compile their own personal dictionary.

The Teacher's Book

The Teacher's Book is interleaved with the Class Book pages for ease of use. It contains suggested steps for each activity, guidance on potential language difficulties, plus a wide range of options for linked activities or for different types of learning group. Tapescripts and answers to exercises are included in the Unit notes.

At the back of the book there is a section of extra resource material for the teacher to use in class:
- a photocopiable worksheet for every unit
- four photocopiable progress tests.

COURSE OVERVIEW

Unit	Language focus	Vocabulary	Topics	Review
1 HI AND BYE **Page 4**	pronouns: *I, you, he, she, it, we, they* verb *to be* questions: *How are you? Am I late?* introductions: *I'm ..., this is ...* saying hello and goodbye	places numbers 1–10 alphabet *Mr, Ms, Mrs* adjectives *Yes/No*	meeting people introductions making invitations	Classroom language
2 WELCOME! **Page 12**	*What's this/that? It's a/the* *this is / that is (that's)* *Is it ...? Yes, it is. / No, it isn't.* *Where's ...?* prepositions of place: *in, from, on, at* possessive adjectives: *my, your* plural nouns	numbers 11–30; *first–tenth* places: countries, cities, buildings, hotels	countries and cities giving personal details at a hotel asking about facilities in hotels room service	Unit 1
3 PEOPLE AND THINGS IN MY LIFE **Page 19**	possessive adjectives *Who is this/that?* *Where ... from?* questions about age (*How old is ...?*) questions (*to be*) short answer forms *there is/are* saying thank you / responding	numbers 31–100 describing people personal possessions	talking about people and things identifying people	Unit 1 Unit 2
4 ABOUT TOWN **Page 28**	*Is there ...? / Are there (any) ...?* showing uncertainty: *perhaps / I think* showing interest: *Really? / Is it really? / That's interesting* talking about age: *How old is it?*	numbers over 100 buildings in towns *north, south, east, west*	towns and features of towns descriptions of buildings	Unit 2 Unit 3
5 I'VE GOT ONE ON THE WALL **Page 35**	*has/have got, What have you got?* *some/any* *How many ...? Where ...?*	rooms and things on walls people in family colours *see you* expressions	rooms and things in them families	Unit 3 Unit 4
6 DON'T FORGET YOUR SUNGLASSES **Page 42**	imperative forms prepositions (*to, for, in, on, under, by*)	holidays and travel countries and places days of the week	travel and tourism	Unit 4 Unit 5
7 TIME FOR WORK **Page 51**	present simple: statements, questions, short answers asking for and giving the time: *What's the time? / It's 6 o'clock.* showing enthusiasm: *It's fantastic!*	jobs work places	time routines jobs	Unit 5 Unit 6
8 INTERNATIONAL FOOD **Page 60**	expressing likes and dislikes: *like(s) / don't (doesn't) like* asking about likes and expressing agreement: *Do you like ...? So do I. Me too.* conjunctions: *and* and *but* question forms: *How long ...? How many ...?* expressing lack of knowledge or information: *I don't know. I've no idea.* possessives: *'s*	food months language skills	food and restaurants food likes and dislikes English courses	Unit 6 Unit 7
9 MONEY! MONEY! MONEY! **Page 68**	talking about prices: *How much?* asking for things in shops: *I'd like ...* asking someone to repeat something: *Pardon? Sorry?*	presents money and currencies electrical goods	shopping for souvenirs currencies and prices asking prices in shops shopping by telephone	Unit 7 Unit 8
10 CLOTHES FOR WORK AND PLAY **Page 76**	questions: *whose/which* possessive *'s* *too* + adjective compliments: *I like your ... It suits you.*	clothes jobs	clothes for work and leisure time uniforms talking about possessions compliments	Unit 8 Unit 9
11 ARE YOU THE RIGHT PERSON FOR YOUR JOB? **Page 84**	*can, can't* for ability questions forms: *Why (not)? because What about?* use of impersonal pronoun *you* apologies and excuses	applying for jobs work skills	job skills and abilities working abroad making excuses	Unit 9 Unit 10
12 LET'S HAVE A PARTY **Page 92**	suggestions: *Let's ... What about ...?* saying *yes* and *no* to suggestions *here/there*	parties	planning a party sending invitations conversations at parties writing thank you letters	Unit 10 Unit 11

Grammar Reference   **Page 99**   **Tapescripts**   **Page 106**

1

HI AND BYE

Language focus:
pronouns: *I, you, he, she, it, we, they*
verb *to be*
questions: *How are you? Am I late?*
introductions: *I'm ..., this is ...*
saying hello and goodbye

Vocabulary:
places
numbers 1–10
alphabet
Mr, Ms, Mrs
adjectives
Yes/No

A   HELLO, AM I LATE?

1 Hi!   Hello/Hi, how are you? (I'm) fine, thanks.

A 📼 Listen. Match 1, 2, 3, 4, 5 with a, b, c, d, e.

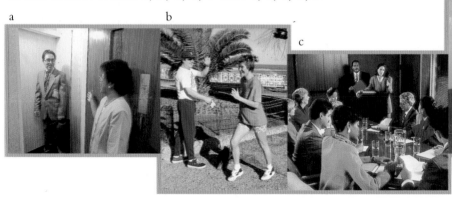

B 📼 Listen. Guess the pictures for the greetings.

Greetings
Good morning. I'm Gloria Jones.
Hi, nice day.
Hello, Juan.
Hello, I'm Jill Smith. Are you Kemal Caglar?
Hi, Maria. How are you?

Replies
Hello, Ryoko.
Yes, pleased to meet you.
Hi, Phil, fine thanks.
... morning.
Oh, hi, yes ... beautiful.

C 📼 Listen. Match greetings and replies.

2 Pleased to meet you   I, you

📼 Listen to the examples. Make conversations.

Example 1:   *Hello, I'm .... Pleased to meet you.*
              Hello, pleased to meet you. I'm ....
Example 2:   *Hi, how are you?*
              Hello, fine thanks, and you?
              Fine, thanks.

HELP	In your language?
Pardon?	....

HI AND BYE

Introduction to the unit

This first unit presents simple greetings and introductions and enables pronouns and the verb *to be* to occur in short, natural exchanges. There is plentiful listening to ease your learners into the new language but also some manageable, spoken questions and responses for them to practise. The activities of Unit 1 of the Personal Study Workbook give related practice.

In Lesson A the language of greetings and introductions is presented and practised. Lesson B continues the personal theme with the question *How are you?* with its various answers. The alphabet is also introduced here. In Lesson C, learners practise simple informal conversations and learn 1–10 in the context of telephone numbers. Because this is the first unit, Lesson D, Review and development is replaced by a focus on classroom language.

A HELLO AM I LATE?

Breaking the ice

If this is your first lesson with your learners, you may be using a shared first language to make initial contact, to talk about your approach to learning and to negotiate preferred styles of teaching and learning. Part of this negotiation may involve deciding when to use English and when to use the shared first language.

If you prefer to start off in English before using the first activity in Lesson A, greet each of your learners with: *Hello, I'm …* . Shake hands if that is culturally comfortable. If anyone is willing to repeat *hello* back to you, give encouragement. It's probably better not to insist on a response at this stage as this is a vulnerable time for some learners.

1 Hi! ▭

Suggested steps

This is a graded listening activity.

The first listening activity involves matching the sounds that go with each place illustrated. This establishes the context in which greetings are being used. The numbers 1–5 will be heard on the recording so you may want to write those up on a board together with a, b, c, d, e and teach the pronunciation of these letters and numbers.

Control the listening so that you stop after each one and ask for the matching picture. Model the vocabulary for each place, e.g. *an airport, a park* and use *is*, e.g. *1 is a …; Yes, 2 is a …* .

The second part of the listening combines the sounds and the different greetings. Learners guess the pictures for the greetings. There is no need to ask learners to repeat each greeting. Again stop the recording after each greeting for matching. Ask: *Is it A? Is it B?* etc.

Tapescript

B
1.	WOMAN:	Hello, Juan.
2.	WOMAN:	Good morning. I'm Gloria Jones.
3.	WOMAN:	Hi, nice day.
4.	MAN:	Hi, Maria. How are you?
5.	WOMAN:	Hello, I'm Jill Smith. Are you Kemal Caglar?

The final part of the listening asks learners to match greetings and replies. You may not want learners to write in the books, so prepare a copy or write the greetings and replies on the board.

If you prefer, let learners listen to the final part again with no task, just to take in sounds and meaning.

Tapescript

C
1.	WOMAN:	Good morning. I'm Gloria Jones.
	CHORUS:	Morning.
2.	WOMAN JOGGER:	Hi, nice day.
	MAN WALKING DOG:	Oh, hi, yes … beautiful.
3.	RYOKO:	Hello, Juan.
	JUAN:	Hello, Ryoko.
4.	JILL:	Hello. I'm Jill Smith. Are you Kemal Caglar?
	KEMAL:	Yes, pleased to meet you.
5.	PHIL:	Hi, Maria. How are you?
	MARIA:	Hi, Phil, fine thanks.

Answer key

A
1b 2d 3e 4c 5a
B
a. Hello, Juan.
b. Hi, nice day.
c. Good morning … I'm Gloria Jones.
d. Hello, I'm Jill Smith. Are you Kemal Caglar?
e. Hi, Maria, how are you?
C
See tapescript for C.

2 Pleased to meet you ▭

Suggested steps

This activity follows on from Exercise 1. It models simple exchanges for greetings. Use the recording to model the greetings and pronunciation. Circulate and model: *Hello, I'm …, pleased to meet you* moving from learner to learner. Encourage responses. Encourage learners to move around, greeting each other. Monitor and assist but don't over-correct at this point, let learners build their confidence.

Do any intensive pronunciation practice afterwards, especially practice of rhythm and intonation.

If this has gone well, try the second conversation in a similar way. This is a slightly extended exchange, so do it in stages if your learners are finding it difficult to string the utterance together.

Tapescript

1. JUAN: Hello, I'm Juan. Pleased to meet you.
   PATRICIA: Hello, pleased to meet you. I'm Patricia.
2. WOMAN: Hi, how are you?
   MAN: Hello, fine thanks, and you?
   WOMAN: Fine, thanks.

HELP boxes

These offer additional vocabulary or expressions that may be helpful to the activity. For this first Help box we have introduced *Pardon?* so that learners have a polite expression to use when they don't hear or don't understand something. You might like to encourage learners to think about the expression they use in their own language in similar situations. Remember that *Pardon?* has a rising intonation to indicate it is questioning what was said before. It is best spoken gently.

3 Am I late? ▭

Suggested steps

This listening activity involves ticking and writing.

Make sure your learners are clear about the context by using the illustrations to elicit *airport*.

Check that your learners are clear about the task. Demonstrate *tick*, *a man*, *a woman* and *late*. It may help to play the first conversation and then stop to check understanding of the task. Then play the second and third conversations uninterrupted.

Prepare for the writing task for the second listening. Teach *write* by showing a pen moving across paper. Let learners listen to each conversation and stop after each one to give time to complete the writing. When you check the answers, teach pronunciation of *Mr/Mrs/Ms*. You may want to explain the differences between these forms in your own language (see Language Point below).

If you practise the conversations, set up the room to simulate an airport counter with staff and passengers. Model the passenger role with a learner behind the counter so they know what their task is and focus on asking questions with rising intonation.

Monitor for rising intonation when learners are using question forms but don't over-correct during the activity as these early activities need to build learners' confidence to speak in the new language. Do further practice later or in a follow-up lesson devoted to tricky areas of pronunciation.

The worksheet on page 205 offers an interactive, extension activity for these mini conversations.

The table completion activity offers a chance to change pace and enjoy a little quiet consolidation of some of the written versions of the forms used so far.

Language Point

Mr/Mrs/Ms are used in formal situations to address adults. *Mr* is used for adult men. *Mrs* is used for adult married women, or women who have been married. *Ms* (/məz/) has become popular as a replacement for *Mrs* and is used by adult women (women who use *Ms* may or may not be married or in relationships). *Miss*, though still used as a title for an unmarried woman, is now considered by many to be old fashioned.

Answer key

Ms Tanaka: a woman   Mr James: a man
Mrs Sukova: a woman
Ms Tanaka: late? No   Mr James: late? Yes
Mrs Sukova, late? No

Tapescript

1. WOMAN: Are you Ms Tanaka?
   MS TANAKA: Yes, I am. Am I late?
   WOMAN: No.
   MS TANAKA: Good.
2. WOMAN: Are you Mr James?
   MR JAMES: Yes, I am. Am I late?
   WOMAN: Yes, you are.
   MR JAMES: I'm sorry.
3. MAN: Are you Mrs Petrovna?
   MRS SUKOVA: No, I'm not, I'm Mrs Irina Sukova. Am I late?
   MAN: No, you're not.
   MRS SUKOVA: Oh, good.

4 Introducing ... ▭

This is the final listening activity for this lesson and it provides more language for introductions. You might like to model the language first using a learner as the person you wish to introduce with: *This is ... .*

Model *What's your name?* by saying: *I'm (Pierre/Jana)*, pointing to yourself and then *What's your name?*, pointing to a learner. In your own language you might want to talk about when you use first names only and when you use full names (first and family name), before listening.

If your learners have a shared first language, use the three pictures to establish the setting and whether it is formal or informal. Ask learners to guess what Jacques is saying in each picture.

3 Am I late?

> Am I/Are You ...? Yes, you are/No, you're not; Mr/Mrs/Ms

Listen and tick the box.

Is Ms Tanaka:

a man ♂ ☐ a woman ♀ ☐?

late? Yes ☐ No ☐

Is Mr James:

a man ♂ ☐ a woman ♀ ☐?

late? Yes ☐ No ☐

Is Mrs Sukova:

a man ♂ ☐ a woman ♀ ☐?

late? Yes ☐ No ☐

Listen again and complete 1–3.

1. Are you Ms Tanaka?
   Yes, I am.

   .... late?

   ....

   ....

2. Are you Mr James?
   Yes, I am.

   .... late?

   ....

   I'm sorry.

3. Are you Mrs Petrovna?
   No, I'm not, I'm Mrs Irina Sukova.

   .... late?

   ....

Practise the conversations.

4 Introducing ...

> I'm ... and this is ...; What's your name?

Hello. I'm Jacques Leotard; this is Maria Gasso.

1

What's your name?

2

Hi!

3

Listen to 1, 2 and 3. Write the words.

Ask and answer, like this:

What's your name?

I'm .... *and this is* ....

HELP	In your language?
first name	....
family name	....

A Complete 1–3.

1. ANDREW: Hi, I'm Andrew.
   JENNIFER: Hello, ... Jennifer.
   ANDREW: Pleased to .... you.

2. What's your name?
   Jacques, and .... is Elsa.
   I'm Peter. Pleased .... meet you.

3. Hi, how .... you?
   Fine, thanks, Santo, and ....?
   Fine, ...

B Complete this:

Short	Long	Question
I'm	I	Am ....?
You're	You are	.... you?

Man	Woman
....	Ms
	....

C Write the short forms.

Long	Short
I am Alessandre.	.... Alessandre.
What is your name?	.... your name?

D Mark 3 strong sounds in a, and 3 in b.

Example: *Are you **pleased**? **Yes, I am**.*

  a. Are you Juan? Yes, I am.
  b. Am I late? No, you're not.

E Correct sentences a and b.

a. How are you? Fine, thank.
b. Are you Maria? Yes, I'm.

B HOW ARE YOU?

1 How are you? Fine [responding to *How are you?*]

📼 Listen to 1, 2, 3 and 4. Is the answer from a man or a woman?

	Man?	Woman?
1	☐	☐
2	☐	☐
3	☐	☐
4	☐	☐

Practise like this:

Hello, how are you?

(I'm) fine/OK/all right/not bad, thanks/thank you.

Play the recording and stop after each one to give time for writing and checking.

Tapescript

1. JACQUES: Hello. I'm Jacques Leotard; this is Maria Gasso.
2. WOMAN: What's your name?
   JACQUES: I'm Jacques Leotard and this is Maria Gasso.
3. JACQUES: Hi, I'm Jacques, this is Maria.
   PEOPLE AT BARBECUE: Hi!

Option

If time allows you could use this activity to practise intonation using the same language. Make up some more name cards with famous people from English speaking countries on them. Distribute name cards and put learners in pairs. Let them move around introducing themselves. Clap your hands when you want the other one of the pair to take over the introductions.

Quick Check

There is a Quick Check at the end of Lessons A, B and C of each unit.
The aims are:
to enable learners to practise the structures or the language learnt in a quick, simple way;

to get learners to think about language forms that have been practised, but perhaps not highlighted during the interactive activities. For example, the Quick Check often gives examples, then asks learners to make deductions about items such as long forms and short forms;

to help learners build their confidence in actually using the language. For this reason, this kind of exercise is not usually very difficult.

The Quick Check can be used for personal practice after the interactive practice of the lesson. Learners can be allowed to do it by themselves, perhaps as homework. This helps them to take responsibility for their own learning. Alternatively, you may wish to use some of them as short tests of the material learnt in the lesson or the unit.

Answer key

A.
1. ANDREW: Hi, I'm Andrew.
   JENNIFER: Hello, **I'm** Jennifer.
   ANDREW: Pleased to **meet** you.
2. What's your name?
   Jacques, and **this** is Elsa.
   I'm Peter. Pleased **to** meet you.
3. Hi, how **are** you?
   Fine, thanks, Santo, and **you**?
   Fine, **thanks**.

B
Short	Long	Question	Man	Woman
I'm	I am	Am I?	Mr	Ms
You're	You are	Are you?		Mrs

C
I'm Alessandre.
What's your name?
D
a. Are you **Juan**? **Yes**, I **am**.
b. Am I **late**? **No**, you're **not**.
E
a. How are you? Fine, **thanks**.
b. Are you Maria? Yes, I **am**.

Personal Study Workbook

1: writing responses to greetings
2: listening; ellipsis in greetings

1 How are you? Fine

Suggested steps

This activity provides more responses to the question, *How are you?* You can get learners accustomed to the different responses by getting them to ask you: *How are you?* and responding with different answers starting with *fine*, then *OK*, *all right*, and *not bad*.

Use the board to show that *fine* is the most positive reply and so on down to *not bad* (probably the least positive).

Use the picture to clarify that the task for listening is merely to say whether the speakers 1, 2, 3, 4 who are replying to *How are you?*, are men or women.

Answer key

1. man   2. woman   3. man   4. woman

Tapescript

1.
WOMAN ARTIST: Hello. How are you?
OLDER MAN: Hello. I'm fine, thanks.
2.
WOMAN ARTIST: Hello. How are you?
YOUNG WOMAN: Hello. I'm OK, thanks.
3.
WOMAN ARTIST: Hello. How are you?
YOUNG MAN: Hi. All right, thanks.
4.
WOMAN ARTIST: Hello. How are you?
OLDER WOMAN: Hello, not bad, thank you.

2 They're all right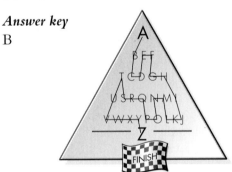

reading; *she's, he's, we're, they're, it's*

Suggested steps

Use the photo to establish the word *family* and the names Eli and Josef (Mr and Mrs Bosnic), Goran, Nick (sons); Vesna, Anna (daughters).
Say: *Mr Bosnic is a man; Mrs Bosnic is a woman* to establish vocabulary for the activity after reading. Ask: *Is Vesna a woman?; Is Nick a man?*

Clarify that the text is a letter from the family in `Australia to Alex, a friend in London.

Write the names of the family members, *coffee shop* and *Brisbane*, on one side of the board and these expressions *fine / OK / all right / busy / beautiful* on the other. Tell learners to read the letter and to match the names and nouns with the adjectives and other expressions.

Help learners with any unknown expressions, then ask them to complete the table in the book.

Use the recorded material to do some pronunciation work on contracted forms.

Move into the classroom question and answer sequence so that learners can use the forms realistically.

Option

Let learners ask as well as answer questions, perhaps by putting them in pairs and asking them to list the names of four people in the class and then to ask/answer the question *How's ...?* about the four people on the list.

Answer key

Column 2: a place
Column 3: He's; they are; We're; it is; It's (it is)

Tapescript

Example:
MAN:	How's Vesna?
WOMAN:	She's fine.
NARRATOR:	Now you.
WOMAN:	She's fine.

1. MAN: How's Vesna?
   WOMAN: She's fine.
   NARRATOR: Now you.
   WOMAN: She's fine.
2. MAN: How's Goran?
   WOMAN: He's OK.
   NARRATOR: Now you.
   WOMAN: He's OK.
3. MAN: How are Anna and Nick?
   WOMAN: They're all right.
   NARRATOR: Now you.
   WOMAN: They're all right.
4. MAN: How are you and Josef?
   WOMAN: We're fine.
   NARRATOR: Now you.
   WOMAN: We're fine.
5. MAN: How's the coffee shop?
   WOMAN: It's busy.
   NARRATOR: Now you.
   WOMAN: It's busy.
6. MAN: How's Brisbane?
   WOMAN: It's beautiful.
   NARRATOR: Now you.
   WOMAN: It's beautiful.

3 Is that an *e* or a *c*?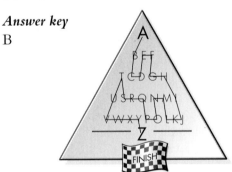

This activity introduces the alphabet through sound and symbol recognition.

Suggested steps

Let learners try to guess the sounds before playing the recording or saying the letters yourself. You might try remaining silent and letting learners attempt to make the sounds themselves. Reward any close attempts with a positive gesture.

Let the learners repeat chorally the letters grouped in threes (a, b, c) or twos (y, z).

The follow-up activity also tests learners' ability to match sound and symbol by asking them to draw a line from one letter to the next as they listen.

Option

After learners have repeated the correct pronunciation, let one learner say a letter and another point to the appropriate symbol as a check. Or use acronyms to test memory (e.g. NATO, UN, BMW). The next activity uses hand-written signatures as a basis for learners to try to read out the letters correctly, and the names. It could be done as a pair dictation.

Answer key
B

C
Charles Dickens
William Shakespeare

Tapescript
C
The names are:
1. Charles Dickens.
   Spelt CHARLES DICKENS.
2. William Shakespeare.
   Spelt WILLIAM SHAKESPEARE.

2 They're all right

[reading; she's, he's, we're, they're, it's]

The Bosnic family, from Croatia, is in Australia.
Read a letter to Alex, a friend in London.

Complete 2 and 3.

Vesna is in Sydney, and she's fine. Goran is in Brisbane. He's OK. (Brisbane is a city – it's beautiful.)
Anna and Nick are in Tokyo, for a meeting. They're all right.
And Josef and I? We're fine – and the coffee shop is fine. It's busy in the morning.
How are you, Alex? Are you busy? How about a letter from you?
It's late! Goodbye for now.
Write please!
Love
Eli and Josef

1	2	3
Vesna	a woman	She's (she is) fine.
Goran	a man	H.............. (he is) OK.
Anna and Nick	a man and a woman	They're (they ....) all right.
Josef and I	a man and a	We.......... (we are) fine.
the coffee shop	a shop	It's (it ....) busy.
Brisbane	a	It.......... (.......... is) beautiful.

Listen to Alex. Repeat the expressions in 3.

Ask your teacher about people in your class.

Examples: A: *How's Marisa?*   A: *How's Carlos?*   A: *How are Melina and Stavros?*
B: *She's fine, thanks.*   B: *He's OK.*   B: *They're all right, thanks.*
C: *Good.*   C: *Good.*

3 Is that an *e* or a *c*?   [alphabet]

A Listen and repeat the letters.

A B C	D E F	G H I	J K L	M N O	P Q R	S T	U V	W X	Y Z
a b c	d e f	g h i	j k l	m n o	p q r	s t	u v	w x	y z

B Listen and join the letters.

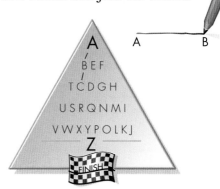

A ————— B

C What are the letters and names?

Listen and write.

A Look at the names for the meeting. Write *He's a man* or *She's a woman*.

> ── MEMO ──
>
> Ms E Ahmad ....
>
> Mr G Smith ....
>
> Mrs A Etvos ....

B Answer the questions.

1. How's Goran? .... fine.
2. How's Vesna? .... OK.
3. How are Anna and Nick? .... not bad.
4. How's your teacher? ....
5. How's the meeting? .... all right.

C Look at the letters of the alphabet.

A B C D F G H I J K M N O P Q R S T U V X Y Z

Three letters are not there.
Write the three letters. ....

C   HOW ABOUT A DRINK? OK

1   In conversation

📖 Listen and read.

FRIEND: Hell**o**.
JOHN: **Hi**, is **An**na there?
FRIEND: Just a **min**ute.
ANNA: Hell**o**.
JOHN: **Hi**, **An**na, it's **John**.
ANNA: Oh, **hi**. How are **you**?
JOHN: I'm **fine**. Are you **bus**y?
ANNA: **No**, not **rea**lly.
JOHN: **Grea**t ... How about a **cof**fee?
ANNA: Mm, **OK**.

Answer 1–4.

1. Is Anna there? Yes, she is. ☐ No, she isn't. ☐

2. Is John OK?   Yes, he is. ☐ No, he isn't. ☐

3. Is Anna busy? Yes, she is. ☐ No, she isn't. ☐

4. Picture 4 is: a. ☐ b. ☐

        a   b

Practise the telephone conversation. Choose questions from the box.

How about a drink?   How about a beer?

How about a coffee?   How about a tea?

Quick Check

Answer key

A

Ms E Ahmad:	She's a woman.
Mr G Smith:	He's a man.
Mrs A Etvos:	She's a woman.

B

1. He's fine.   2. She's OK.   3. They're not bad.
4. She's/He's … .   5. It's all right.

C

The three letters are: E, L, W

Personal Study Workbook

3: vocabulary
5: writing a note to a friend
4: writing questions
6: vocabulary

---

1 In conversation 🔲

This is the first of a range of simple, fairly natural conversations throughout the book which aim to help learners get a feel for conversational English, and provide a framework for oral practice or simple role play.

Suggested steps

Use the pictures in the book to set the scene. Clarify the listening task. Ask learners to listen and read the conversation and decide which parts of the conversation go with pictures 1, 2 and 3. Learners can answer the questions 1–4 in pairs orally. Monitor pronunciation of *she/he*.

Explain that a back-to-back conversation helps to simulate a phone conversation.

Model, *tea, beer, drink* using the pictures. Practise pronunciation. Explain that *drink* is the general word and the others are examples (*Tea is a drink; coffee is a drink; beer is a drink*). Ask learners to have telephone conversations back-to-back but to use their own names and to choose a different word from *coffee*. Let them read the conversations first but encourage them to talk without the books after a few tries.

Option

To build confidence you can divide the class into two halves and let one half be John and the other half be Anna (you can be the friend). This choral work will help to build rhythm and stress.

Monitor pronunciation for later practice; at this stage allow confidence to be built with lots of positive encouragement and gentle, limited correction.

Answer key

1. Yes, she is.
2. Yes, he is.
3. No, she isn't.
4. Picture b.

2 What's your number?

This activity provides modelling and practice of numbers 1–10.

Suggested steps

This is a variant on presenting the numbers from *one* to *ten*, with the numbers on the recording going from *ten* to *one* followed by the sound of an explosion. If you prefer, teach the numbers *one* to *ten* first, perhaps with flash cards to show spelling and meaning. Hold up different numbers of things to elicit a correct number, e.g. pens, books, keys.

Use the recording as an amusing consolidation and have choral repetition followed by the sound of the explosion.

Use the recording of telephone numbers for practice in listening and writing numerals. The Help box enables you to show learners before listening that the same number occurring twice in a phone number is pronounced *double six; double four*.

> **Language Point**
> The number '0' is sometimes pronounced *zero* and sometimes pronounced the same as the letter 'o' when giving phone numbers.

As a final, realistic practice, ask learners to move around the class and ask at least two people in English for their phone numbers. Model the activity first by asking two learners: *What's your number?* and writing their numbers on the board.

Answer key

a. 801 25466   b. 635 12449   c. 199 72680

Tapescript

A
Ten, nine, eight, seven, six, five, four, three, two, one, zero.
B
Repeat the numbers.

C
a
A: What's your number?
B: It's 801 25466.
b
A: What's your number?
B: It's 635 12449.
c
A: What's your number?
B: It's 199 72680.
d
A: What's your number?
B: Write your number.

3 Thanks for a nice day 🔲

This activity models and introduces expressions for *thank you* and *goodbye*; it is helpful to do it at the end of your class session.

Suggested steps

Use the picture to establish that the couples are returning to their hotel after having been taken out for the day by the couple in the car. Ask learners what they would say in their language in such a situation.

Clarify the listening task. Learners are to listen to the couples and to write the numbers 1, 2, 3 and 4 next to the appropriate speech balloon.

Check answers and indicate to learners that *thank you* is more formal than *thanks* and *goodbye* is more formal than *bye*. Most people are comfortable with *bye* and *thanks*.

If this is the final activity for your class, ask them to say *goodbye* and *thank you* as they leave. Answer with *Bye. You're welcome.*

Answer key

See tapescript.

Tapescript

1. MAN: Thanks, goodbye.
   WOMAN: Bye.
2. WOMAN: Bye, thanks.
   MAN: Bye bye.
3. MAN: Goodbye and thank you.
   WOMAN: Goodbye.
4. WOMAN: Bye and thanks for a nice time.
   MAN: You're welcome.

2 What's your number? | numbers 1–10

A Listen.

10 (ten)	9 (nine)	8 (eight)	7 (seven)	6 (six)	5 (five)
4 (four)	3 (three)	2 (two)	1 (one)	0 (zero)	

B Repeat the numbers.

C Listen and complete the telephone numbers:

a   80 _ 25 _ _ _

b   6 _ _ 1 _ _ _ _

c   1 _ _ _ 2 _ _ _

d   your telephone number   - - - - - - - - - - - - -

Ask two learners: *What's your number?*
Write two telephone numbers.

1. Name ....   Number ....
2. Name ....   Number ....

HELP	In your language?
66 = double six	....
44 = double four	....
99 = double nine	....
0 = zero	....

3 Thanks for a nice day | goodbye and thank you

> Thanks, good bye. ☐

> Goodbye and thank you. ☐

> Bye.

> Bye bye.

> Bye, thanks. ☐

> Goodbye.

> You're welcome.

> Bye and thanks for a nice time. ☐

 Listen. Write 1, 2, 3 and 4 in the boxes ☐.

Is it the end of your class? Say goodbye to your teacher.

A Match numbers and words.

6	four
2	seven
8	six
4	five
9	nine
1	three
3	two
10	eight
7	one
5	ten

C Circle Yes or No.

1. You're = You are   Yes/No
2. You're = Your   Yes/No
3. Hi = Hello   Yes/No
4. Goodbye = Bye bye   Yes/No
5. Thank you = Thanks   Yes/No
6. 88 = double five   Yes/No
7. What's ...? = What is ...?   Yes/No

B Rewrite the conversation.

GUY: you how are Hi?
JANE: you fine. busy Are I'm?
GUY: really Not
JANE: drink Good a about how?
GUY: KO Yes

PERSONAL STUDY WORKBOOK

- greetings
- writing a note
- pronunciation of final sounds
- visual dictionary – letters and numbers 1–10
- reading – episode 1 of *Lost in time*

D **CLASSROOM ENGLISH**

1 Classroom English   [questions with *can*]

Listen and tick 7 boxes.

Quick Check

Answer key

A

6: six   2: two   8: eight   4: four   9: nine   1: one
3: three   10: ten   7: seven   5: five

B

GUY: Hi, how are you?
JANE: I'm fine. Are you busy?
GUY: Not really.
JANE: Good, how about a drink?
GUY: Yes, OK.

C

1. Yes   2. No   3. Yes   4. Yes   5. Yes   6. No   7. Yes

Personal Study Workbook

7: alphabet and numbers
8: final consonant sounds; pronunciation
9: visual dictionary

D CLASSROOM ENGLISH

1 Classroom English

This lesson introduces some common expressions that learners can use in the classroom in English. They are not part of the progression through the core language in the units but can be learnt if you use English most of the time in the classroom.

Suggested steps

Use the picture to establish the context. It is a classroom; learners are asking questions and the teacher is giving instructions or encouragement. Clarify the meaning of *write, spell, listen, repeat.*

Clarify the listening task. Learners listen and tick the box next to each sentence they hear on the recording.

Check answers and model intonation for *Can* questions with *please.*

Answer key

Can you spell 'welcome' please? is the only box with no tick.

Tapescript

TEACHER: Can you spell 'busy', please? ... er ... Juan.
JUAN: B-U-S-Y.
TEACHER: Good ... . 'Busy'. Repeat please, ... er ... Mira.
MIRA: Busy.
TEACHER: Very good. OK ... er ... . Can you write 'busy', please? Good. Listen, please. 'Welcome to New York'.
JUAN: Can you write 'welcome', please?
TEACHER: Yes, OK.

2 Practise classroom language in English ▭

Suggested steps

The next listening task requires learners to carry out the action (either saying the spelling of a word or writing it). It could be done in a language lab or individually. The answers are on the recording as a check.

The final activity provides pair practice with classroom English. Learners choose words from the box and ask either: *Can you spell …?* or *Can you write …?* The box shows learners that double letters are pronounced 'double e' or 'double f' not e, e, or f, f.

If time allows, ask learners to write other English words down and to test another learner's spelling or writing using the same question forms.

Tapescript

A
1. Can you spell 'beautiful'?
2. Can you write 'coffee'?
3. Can you write 'welcome'?
4. Can you spell 'fine'?

B
Can you spell 'beautiful'?
Yes, 'beautiful', b-e-a-u-t-i-f-u-l.
Good.

Can you spell 'fine'?
Yes, 'fine', f-i-n-e.
Very good.

3 What's 'ejemplo' in English?

This is an extension option when learners ask for a translation into or from their own language, or the main language in the classroom.

Suggested steps

Let learners write the translations of the common expressions listed to get used to looking for corresponding expressions in their own language.

Listen to the examples in the recording and practise asking the question: *What's … in English?* using a word from the first language. Let learners ask you a few *What's … in …?* questions.

Put learners in pairs. Use dictionaries, or let them choose expressions from the first unit of the Class Book to practise *What's … in …?* questions and answers. Remind them of the question: *Can you spell …?*

Unit 1 Worksheet

Suggested steps

The teacher models pronunciation of all the names and asks for repitition. Establish which is a woman's and which is a man's name.

The teacher then photocopies the sheet of names and dictates ten of the similar sounding names one by one saying: *one, John; two, Joan,* etc. The learners put the number next to the name they hear.

Each person in the class is assigned a different name on a card from the list, and given a list of three names from the above box that have been assigned to other learners.

The learners get up and try to find the three people on their list.
Example:

       A: *Hello, are you …?*
       B: *No, sorry, I'm not.*
       A: *OK, thanks.*
OR

       B: *Yes, I am.*
       A: *Oh, good. Pleased to meet you.*

At the end, each person introduces their three people (or one person or two people if you want to make it quicker and easier), like this:
Hello, I'm …, this is …, … and … .
(and then checks that they are right by asking each learner to reveal their name card to check spelling and pronunciation).

2 Practise classroom language in English

listening for *can* questions

A 🎧 Listen and answer questions 1–4.

1. 🖊️
2. 🖊️ ....
3. 🖊️ ....
4. 🖊️

B 🎧 Listen to 1 and 4 again. Check your answers.

With a partner, ask and answer questions about:

busy	late	fine	m<u>ee</u>ting (double *e*)	park	co<u>ff</u><u>ee</u> (double *f*, double *e*)
beer	city	tea			

Can you spell ....? Can you write ....?
(in English)

3 What's 'ejemplo' in English?

classroom questions with *what*

Complete.

Word in English	question (?)	example	tick (✓)	check	answer
In your language	....	....	....	....	....

🎧 Listen. Ask and answer, like this:

1.
   A: What's 'example' in (Spanish)?
   B: Ejemplo.
   A: Thank you.

2.
   A: What's 'pregunta' in English?
   B: Question.
   A: Thanks.

WELCOME!

Language focus:
What's this/that? It's a/the
this is / that is (that's)
Is it ...? Yes, it is / No, it isn't.
Where's ...?
prepositions of place: *in, from, on, at*
possessive adjectives: *my, your*
plural nouns

Vocabulary:
numbers 11–30
first – tenth
places: countries, cities, buildings, hotels

A COUNTRIES AND CITIES

1 Welcome   listening and speaking

Listen and match numbers 1, 2, 3, 4 with pictures A, B, C, D.

A Rome

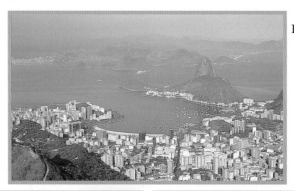

B Rio

C Istanbul

D Moscow

Write the name of a country and two cities in this country.

Example: *USA: New York / Los Angeles*

2 Conversation   speaking

Partner A: You are a tourist guide. Welcome a visitor to one of your cities from Exercise 1.

Partner B: You are a visitor. Say thank you and say who you are.

Make a conversation like this:

Example: A: *Hello/Hi, I'm ..... Welcome to ......*   B: *Thanks. I'm pleased to be here. I'm ......*

Now B is the guide and A is the visitor.

WELCOME!

The topic focus of this unit is places and the most important language points relate to asking and answering questions about places: *What's this? Where's the …?*, prepositions of place and place vocabulary.

In Lesson A a couple arrive in a city, take a taxi to their hotel and talk about what they can see on the way. An international hotel is the setting for Lesson B and this provides a context for giving addresses, and talking about hotel facilities. The main focuses of Lesson C are conversational language of use to a hotel guest and writing an e-mail.

Warm-up

Using a map of the world, find out which countries learners know and/or have visited. If the class is interested, continue by paying particular attention to one or two large countries, perhaps those known to most learners, and find out how many cities in these countries they can name. Do not spend more than ten minutes on this warm-up.

Note: In these warm-up activities, allow learners to use their own language or a mixture of this and English if they wish. At this very elementary level, learner involvement is a key consideration. If they manage to use English, do not spend time correcting mistakes at this stage, but make it clear that you welcome and value all contributions from the class. It is important in these early stages to establish that learner participation is an integral feature of your methodology as a language teacher.

1 Welcome 🎧

Suggested steps

Elicit the names of the four cities. Correct pronunciation of names and give choral repetition practice if necessary.

Clarify the activity. Learners will hear four short statements by speakers welcoming people to these four cities. Learners listen for the name of the city and match the statements with the photos. Elicit the answers.

Answer key

1: Rio (de Janeiro) 2: Rome 3: Moscow 4: Istanbul

Now ask learners to write the name of one country and the names of two cities in that country. Go round the room checking that they have understood and are doing this correctly, but do not ask them to say the names of their places aloud.

Tapescript

1. Good morning, ladies and gentlemen. Welcome to Rio. Thank you for flying with Varig Airlines.
2. Hello, everybody. I'm Gina – welcome to Rome.
3. Hi! I'm Alexei. We're in Moscow and I'm your guide today.
4. Hello and welcome. I'm Jacqueline and I'm from the Sheraton Hotel in Istanbul.

2 Conversation

This is a simple role play in which learners practise introducing themselves and welcoming their partners to the cities they have just noted down.

Suggested steps

Explain the activity, getting the class as a whole to repeat the sample exchange in their books. Point out that learners now use the cities they wrote down at the end of Exercise 1.

Monitor conversations, correcting pronunciation. Elicit sample conversations from a few pairs of learners.

Option

This could be continued as a mingling exercise. Learners walk around the class having conversations with several partners.

3 Look! 🔲

Suggested steps

Before looking at the photos in the book, stick one or two pictures of objects learners know on the board, point to each and ask: *What's that?* and *Is that a ...?* Get learners to repeat these questions several times.

Draw a man and a woman on the board. Point to them and say: *That is Paul. That is Sue. They are visitors to New York. Maybe tourists, maybe business people.*

Say and get the class to repeat the names of the places in the photographs. Don't spend long on this, but insist on correct pronunciation of *the* /ðə/ and *a* /ə/.

Clarify the listening activity. Learners listen for the names of the places mentioned by Paul and Sue in their taxi conversation. Play the recording, once or twice as necessary. Check answers.

Answer key

(places are mentioned in this order) The Plaza Hotel
The Statue of Liberty   The World Trade Centre
Penn Station   A restuarant   Central Park

Learners now work in pairs and make conversations like the first example. Do an example with the class.

Monitor learners' conversations, correcting where necessary. Repeat procedure for the second conversation, making sure you elicit a negative answer to the question: *Is that ...?* Again monitor pair work.

Tapescript

PAUL:	Taxi! Taxi!
TAXI DRIVER:	Hi. Where to?
SUE:	The Plaza Hotel, please.
TAXI DRIVER:	The Plaza. Sure.
PAUL:	Look Sue, the Statue of Liberty.
SUE:	It's beautiful! And what's that? Is it the Empire State Building?
PAUL:	No, it isn't. It's the World Trade Centre.
SUE:	Fantastic! Where is the Empire State Building?
PAUL:	I don't know.
SUE:	Is that a station?
TAXI DRIVER:	Yeah, it's Penn Station.
SUE:	Thanks.
PAUL:	That's a nice restaurant.
TAXI DRIVER:	Yeah, it's a very popular restaurant.
SUE:	Is this Central Park?
TAXI DRIVER:	Yeah. That's right.
SUE:	Look, the hotel.
PAUL:	Great!
TAXI DRIVER:	Twenty dollars, please.
PAUL:	Thank you.
TAXI DRIVER:	Thanks. Have a nice day.
SUE:	Bye.

> ### Language Point
>
> You may be asked a question about, or you may decide to deal with the difference between *a* and *the*, both of which appear in the photo captions to Exercise 3. We suggest that you do not attempt detailed explanations here, especially since no articles are used with *Central Park* and *Penn Station*, but you could point out that *the* is often used when there is only ONE of something, and *a* is used when this is one of many.

4 Capital cities 🔲

Suggested steps

Check learners understand *capital city* by using an example they are familiar with: *Paris is a city. It's a capital city. Paris is the capital of France.*

Learners do this matching exercise individually, then compare answers with a partner.

Play the first version of the recording to allow learners to check their answers. (This first version has long-form verbs; Example: *Ankara is in Turkey.*)

Answer key

Ankara – Turkey   Cairo – Egypt   Tokyo – Japan
Moscow – Russia   Athens – Greece   Warsaw – Poland

Play the second version of the recording and ask learners to repeat each sentence. (This has contracted verb forms; Example: *Ankara's in Turkey.*)

Elicit more city names and write these on the board. Point to one of these to model the *Where?* question. Elicit the answer: *It's in* (+ country name).

Learners ask their own questions using cities from the list on the board. Monitor their conversations.

Use examples from the list in the book to introduce and practise: *Yes, it is / No, it isn't* answers. Then ask a question which the class cannot possibly answer. Example: *Is Newtown in The United States?* This will give you the opportunity to introduce: *I don't know.*

Learners then ask each other more questions about cities and countries to practise the answers: *Yes, it is / No, it isn't / I don't know.* Monitor their conversations.

Tapescript

A and B
1. Ankara is in Turkey. (Ankara's)
2. Cairo is in Egypt. (Cairo's)
3. Tokyo is in Japan. (Tokyo's)
4. Moscow is in Russia. (Moscow's)
5. Athens is in Greece. (Athens is)
6. Warsaw is in Poland. (Warsaw's)

Quick Check

Answer key

A
1. A: Hello, I'm John. Welcome **to** Rio.
   B: Thanks. It's good to **be** here.

3 Look!

listening; *Is that ...? What's that?*

Paul and Sue are in a taxi in New York. They are visitors.

Central Park

The Plaza Hotel

The Statue of Liberty

Penn Station

Restaurant

The World Trade Centre

A New York taxi

📼 What do they see? Listen. Find the photos and the names.

Point to the photos and make conversations like this:

A: *What's that?*   B: *It's the Statue of Liberty.*

Now point to the photos and make conversations, like this:

A: *Is that a restaurant?*   B: *No, it isn't. It's a station.*

4 Capital cities

Where's ...? It's in ... Yes, it is. No, it isn't.

A Match the capital cities with the countries.

Capital cities		*Countries*	
Ankara	Moscow	Japan	Egypt
Cairo	Athens	Greece	Russia
Tokyo	Warsaw	Turkey	Poland

📼 Listen and check your answers.

B 📼 Now listen and repeat.

Think of more cities and countries. With a partner ask and answer questions, like this:

A: *Where's Rio?*   B: *It's in Brazil.*

Now ask and answer questions, like this:

A: *Is Istanbul in Turkey?*   B: *Yes, it is.*
A: *Is New York in England?*   B: *No, it isn't.*

HELP	In your language?
I don't know	....

✔ Quick Check

A Finish the conversations.

1. a: Hello, I'...... John. Welcome .... Rio.
   b: Thanks. It's good to .... here.
2. a: Where .... they?
   b: They're .... Moscow.
3. a: ....'s that?
   b: ....'s a station.
4. a: .... that the Empire State Building?
   b: No, it ....

B Correct these sentences.

1. My name Paul.
2. Cairo is Egypt.
3. A: Is the Statue Liberty in Ankara?
   B: No, it is.
4. A: Are London in France?
   B: Yes, it isn't.
5. Hello. Welcome Rome.

1 Ten plus   numbers 11–30

A ⟳ Choose five of the numbers 11–30. Listen for your numbers.

B ⟳ Now read, listen and repeat the numbers 11–30.

eleven	twelve	thirteen	fourteen	fifteen	sixteen	seventeen	eighteen
nineteen	twenty	twenty-one	twenty-two	twenty-three	twenty-four		
twenty-five	twenty-six	twenty-seven	twenty-eight	twenty-nine	thirty		

C ⟳ Look at these pictures. Say the numbers. Listen and find the numbers in the pictures.

⟳ Listen again and write the numbers. Which numbers are not in the picture?

2 What's your address?   listening; numbers

⟳ Listen to some conversations at the Royal Hotel. Write the numbers and names.

What's your address, please, Mr Jones?

It's 25, York Avenue, Liverpool, L14 2PR.

FAMILY NAME	FIRST NAME	ADDRESS
1 Jones	Peter	.........., York Avenue, Liverpool, L .... PR
2 Smith	....	.........., Exeter Gardens, Manchester, M .... AG
3 Procter	....	.........., New Road, Melbourne .... Australia
4 Harriman	Dorothy	.........., Central Avenue, Washington DC, USA
5 Collins	Angela	.........., Barrack Street, Cape Town, ... South Africa
6 Charles	....	.........., Park Road, Perth .... Western Australia

Write the names and addresses of three other learners. Ask: *What's your address?*

2. A: Where **are** they?
   B: They're **in** Moscow.
3. A: **What's** that?
   B: **It's** a station.
4. A: **Is** that the Empire State Building?
   B: No, it **isn't**.

B
1. My name **is** Paul. / My name's Paul.
2. Cairo is **in** Egypt.
3. A: Is the Statue of Liberty in Ankara?
   B: No, it **isn't**.
4. A: **Is** London in France?
   B: **No**, it isn't.
5. Hello. Welcome **to** Rome.

Personal Study Workbook
7: reading and vocabulary

B NUMBERS AND ADDRESSES

1 Ten plus ▭

Before introducing numbers 11 – 30, revise numbers 1 – 10.

Suggested steps

Before learners open their books, ask them to write five numbers between 11 and 30. Tell them they are going to listen to all the numbers between 11 and 30 in the normal sequence. They should tick 'their' numbers as they hear them.

Play the recording once or twice as necessary. Learners now open their books and read, listen and repeat numbers 11 – 30.

In pairs, learners now look at the pictures and say the numbers they can see.
11 the number of a bus route; **12** part of a car number plate; **13** a taxi number; **15** house number (on the door); **17** a price tag/ticket (in dollars); **19** a train number; **20** a floor indicator in a lift; **22** number on a classroom door; **23** departure gate at an airport; **27** number of racing car; **30** price tag/ticket (in pounds)

Learners now listen to the recording and tick each picture as they hear the relevant numbers. In this recording the numbers are not in the normal sequence, but are read in five different logical sets. The idea of this is to get learners used to recognising numbers out of their normal sequence.

Tapescript
C
twenty, twenty-five, thirty, twelve, fourteen, sixteen, eighteen, eleven, thirteen, fifteen, seventeen, nineteen, twenty-one, twenty-nine, twenty-eight, twenty-seven, twenty-six, twenty-two, twenty-three, twenty-four

Get learners to repeat these sets of numbers. Learners listen again, write the five sets of numbers and work out which numbers on the recording are not in the picture.

Answer key
(including some numbers which continue the sequences)
- 20; 25; 30
- 12; 14; 16; 18   (20; 22; 24; 26)
- 11; 13; 15; 17; 19; 21   (23; 25; 27; 29)
- 29; 28; 27; 26   (25; 24; 23; 22)
- 22; 23; 24
Numbers not in picture: 14; 16; 18; 21; 24; 25; 26; 28; 29

Option

Get learners to say the next few numbers in each of sets 2, 3 and 4. (See Answer key.)

2 What's your address? ▭

This is a listening activity which provides learners with practice in picking out numbers from normal conversation. The conversations also introduce addresses and spelling.

Suggested steps

Ask learners to look at the picture and say what they can see: a hotel reception and a computer screen with details of guests.

Clarify the activity: learners listen to hotel reception conversations and fill in the missing information; a mixture of names and numbers.

You may prefer to get learners to listen for numbers on the first listening and names on the second, or vice versa. Play the recording, pausing after each conversation to allow learners time to think and write their answers. Play once or twice more as necessary. Learners may compare their answers before a final listening. Check answers.

Answer key

Family name	First name	Address
1 Jones	Peter	**25**, York Avenue, Liverpool, **L14 2PR**
2 Smith	**Julie**	**24**, Exeter Gardens, Manchester **M17 2AG**
3 Procter	**Simon**	**16**, New Road, Melbourne **3001** Australia
4 Harriman	Dorothy	**21**, Central Avenue, Washington DC, USA
5 Collins	Angela	**28** Barrack Street, Cape Town, **8000** South Africa
6 Charles	**William**	**18**, Park Road, Perth **6026** W. Australia.

Practise asking and answering the question: *What's your address?* with the whole class, then ask learners to find out and write down each other's addresses. Monitor conversations.

Tapescript
See page 128.

3 Where's my room? 📖

There are two versions of the recording for this listening activity which introduces ordinal numbers in the context of the floors of a hotel.

Suggested steps

Check that learners understand the word *lift*, explain the activity, then play the first or the second version of the recording.

Learners repeat each 'floor' phrase: *tenth floor, ninth floor*, etc. Correct pronunciation, especially of the *-th* endings. If you started with the easier listening, go on to the second. Get learners to match the cardinal numbers 1 – 10 with the figures and the ordinal numbers. Elicit answers.

Answer key

one	1	first	six	6	sixth
two	2	second	seven	7	seventh
three	3	third	eight	8	eighth
four	4	fourth	nine	9	ninth
five	5	fifth	ten	10	tenth

Tapescript

See page 128.

Clarify the next listening task, then play the recording of five hotel conversations involving numbers. Elicit answers.

Answer key

	Name	Room	Floor
a.	Mrs Smith	232	second
b.	Mr Procter	473	fourth
c.	Ms Harriman	591	fifth
d.	Miss Collins	740	seventh
e.	Mr Charles	193	first

Learners each think of their own room number (three figures) and floor number, then go round the class asking and answering questions.

> ### Language Point
>
> Tell the class to pronounce these room numbers as three individual figures; e.g. *two-three-two*, rather than a single large number *two hundred and thirty-two*. (Larger numbers are dealt with in Unit 4.)

Monitor and correct.

4 Where's the restaurant?

The first matching activity introduces the vocabulary of hotel facilities.

Suggested steps

Explain the activity and let learners do it together in pairs. Check answers.

Answer key

a Restaurant   b Swimming pool   c Rest room
d Gym   e Bar   f Sauna   g Conference room
h Coffee bar   i Disco

> ### Language Point
>
> Point out that *Rest room* is American English. Common British English equivalents are *toilet* or, in informal speech, *loo*.

Individual learners now decide for themselves where these various facilities are in an imaginary hotel. They could simply write a floor number (first – tenth) next to each place on the list.

The many different resulting combinations provide the information gap necessary for the conversations which follow.

Read through the sample conversation with the class, then monitor as pairs take it in turns to work through their lists of facilities and floor numbers.

Option

Continue this activity by getting the class to think about facilities in a building they are familiar with, e.g. a college or workplace.

Quick Check
Answer key

A
1. What's your first name?
2. What's your family name?
3. What's your address?
4. What's your telephone number?
B
1. **What's** your address?
2. My room's on **the** fourth floor.
3. You're **in** Room 591. Here's your key.
4. Is my room **on** the first floor?
5. **What's** your telephone number, please?

Personal Study Workbook

1: prepositions
6: numbers and letters
8: writing

3 Where's my room? `listening; numbers`

A  You are in a hotel lift. Listen and repeat the numbers of the floors.

Match the words with the numbers.

eight	1	fourth
five	2	tenth
four	3	second
nine	4	sixth
one	5	eighth
seven	6	fifth
six	7	third
ten	8	seventh
three	9	first
two	10	ninth

B Listen to more conversations. Write the numbers of the rooms and the floors.

	Room	Floor
a. Mrs Smith	....	....
b. Mr Procter	....	....
c. Ms Harriman	....	....
d. Miss Collins	....	....
e. Mr Charles	....	....

HELP	In your language?
family name	....
first name	....
Here's (is)	....
That's right.	....

Choose a floor and room at the hotel. Make conversations like this:

A: *Where's your room?*   B: *I'm in Room 657. It's on the sixth floor.*

4 Where's the restaurant? `reading; speaking`

These are places in a hotel. Match the words and the pictures.

Bar   Coffee bar   Conference room   Disco   Gym
Restaurant   Rest room   Sauna   Swimming pool

Where are these places? Decide and write the floor number.

Example: Restaurant – *fourth*

Make conversations in pairs, like this:

A: *Excuse me. Where's the restaurant?*   B: *It's on the fourth floor.*   A: *Thanks a lot.*

✔ Quick Check

A Write the questions for these answers.

1. My first name's Pete.
2. My family name's Bogart.
3. It's 23, Pool Road, London.
4. It's 0171 234 8351.

B Correct the mistakes.

1. What your address?
2. My room's on fourth floor.
3. You're on Room 591. Here your key.
4. Is my room in the first floor?
5. That's your telephone number, please?

1 Enquiries | listening and speaking; *Can I have?*

A 🔊 Listen and read.

CLARE: Hello. Room Service. This is Clare.
CARTER: Hello, Mr Carter here. Room 504.
CLARE: How can I help?
CARTER: Can I have a beer, please?
CLARE: Of course, Mr Carter.

🔊 Listen again and repeat.

Now make conversations in pairs. Take turns.

Partner A: You are Room Service.
Partner B: You are a hotel guest.
Ask for a drink.

B 🔊 Listen and read this conversation.

MATTHEW: Hello, Reception. Matthew here.
BOUTON: Hi, this is Room 613. This is Miss Bouton.
MATTHEW: How can I help?
BOUTON: Where's the gym, please?
MATTHEW: It's on the first floor, Miss Bouton.
BOUTON: Thank you.
MATTHEW: You're welcome.

🔊 Listen again and repeat.

Make conversations. Take turns.

Partner A: You are Reception.
Partner B: You are a hotel guest.
Ask where a place is in the hotel.

HELP	In your language?
How can I help?	....
Can I have a beer?	....

2 Hi from Brussels | reading and writing

Read the e-mail. Who is it from? Who is it to?

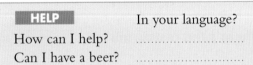

```
Normal   FILE PRINT SAVE DELETE ENCL CLIP SPELL RECEIPT SEND

Sent: 4/11/97 9.02 am
Received: 4/11/97 11.22 am
From: Mike Carter, KAN79@dial.pipex.com
To: Susi Carter, carter@compuserve.com

Subject: Hotel

Hi Susi
I'm at the Hotel Metropole in Brussels. I'm on the fifth floor –
Room 504. It's a beautiful old hotel in the centre of the city.
The address is Place de Brouckere 31, B-1000 Brussels, Belgium.
The telephone number is 32-2-217-2300.
Bye
Mike
```

modern

old

You are in a hotel in a city in another country. Write an e-mail to a friend.

1 Enquiries ⊂⊃

Suggested steps

Before learners open their books, find out how many of the class have stayed in a hotel. If it is a significant number, ask them who they would phone in the hotel if they wanted a drink or a snack. If they are not familiar with the term *room service*, teach it.

Learners open their books and read the first conversation to themselves.

Play the recording while learners follow the text. Play again and get the class to repeat. Make sure that *can* in *How can I help?* and *Can I have a beer …?* is pronounced /kən/. Explain the role play activity to the class. In pairs, learners make conversations between room service and a hotel guest who wants one of the drinks illustrated.

> #### Language Point
>
> Although the words: *tea, coffee* and *beer* were introduced in Unit 1 and learners will already know *Cola*, you could introduce *wine* and the expressions *a cup of* (*tea, coffee*) and *a glass of* (*wine, beer, Cola*). In this context *Can I have a cup of tea, please?* is more appropriate than *Can I have a tea, please?* although both versions are acceptable with *beer, Coca-Cola* and *coffee*.

Repeat steps above with this second hotel conversation.

Using the symbols, learners take turns to ask and answer questions about places in a hotel. Monitor conversations, correcting as necessary.

2 Hi from Brussels

Before starting this activity, find out how many of the class use e-mail. When do they use e-mail in preference to the phone or a normal letter?

Suggested steps

Pre-teach the words *old* and *modern* using the illustrations. Draw attention to the reading questions and elicit answers.

Answer key

The e-mail is from Mike Carter to Susi Carter.

Get learners to read the e-mail, then ask further comprehension questions.
1. Where's Mike?   2. What's his room number?
3. Is it on the first floor? 4. What's the address?
5. What's the telephone number?

Answer key

1. At the Hotel Metropole in Brussels.
2. It's room 504.
3. No, it's on the fifth floor.
4. (The address is/It's) Place de Brouckere, 31, B – 1000, Brussels, Belgium.
5. (The telephone number is / It's) 32–2–217 23 00.

Learners now write their own e-mails to friends. They should model their writing closely on the e-mail in the book, but replacing all names.

Option

Having finished writing, learners could exchange e-mails, then read and maybe correct each other's work.

REVIEW OF UNIT 1

1 How do you spell that? | alphabet

Write five English words.   Example: *morning coffee meet …*

Choose one word.   Example: *meet*

Ask your partner: *How do you spell 'meet'?*

2 Matching | questions and answers

Match the questions with the answers.

Questions	Answers
1. Are you Hitomi?	Fine, thanks.
2. What's your name?	Yes, OK.
3. How are you?	No, she isn't.
4. Is Julia in?	She's OK.
5. How's Renate?	Frederic Paris.
6. How about a coffee?	Yes, I am.

3 Words | vocabulary

Write three words with double letters.

Example: *meet*

Write three words ending in *y*.

Example: *really*

Write the opposites.

Example: good – *bad*

1. Yes – ....   4. Hi – ....

2. question – ....   5. is – ....

3. Hello – ....

Find five groups of three words.

| beer | day | eight | fine | Good morning | coffee | Hello | minute |
| morning | nice | Hi | pleased | six | tea | two | |

Examples: *eight, six,* ....

      coffee, ..., ...

Choose the word with a different sound.

Example: *he she Hi meet* – *Hi* ....

1. eight   Hi   nice   fine   – ....   4. am   park   bad   thank   – ....

2. shop   so   not   on   – ....   5. great   day   eight   right   – ....

3. no   so   two   hello   – ....

REVIEW OF UNIT 1

1 How do you spell that?

Suggested steps

Before doing this exercise, revise the alphabet with the whole class. Ask a few: *How do you spell X?* questions. Learners now write five words of their own, then in pairs take turns to ask and answer questions.

2 Matching

This can be done as a whole class activity or by learners working individually or in pairs.

Answer key

1. Are you Hitomi?   Yes, I am.
2. What's your name?   Frederic Paris.
3. How are you?   Fine, thanks.
4. Is Julia in?   No, she isn't.
5. How's Renate?   She's OK.
6. How about a coffee? Yes, OK.

3 Words

Suggested steps

This first activity gives learners a chance to think about the spelling of words they know.
Possible answers: (all words from Unit 1)
• Words with double letters: *beer, class, coffee, greeting, letter, meeting, all, good, three, spell, goodbye, hello, sorry, really, correct*
• Words ending in *y*: *city, reply, they, sorry, really, my*

Before getting learners to do this exercise, check that they understand opposite. You could remind them of old and modern which were introduced earlier in Unit 2.

Answer key

1. Yes – *No*
2. question – *answer*
3. Hello – *Goodbye*
4. Hi – *Bye*   (more informal than *Hello* and *Goodbye*)
5. is – *isn't*.

Answer key

• *eight, six, two*   (numbers)
• *coffee, beer, tea*   (drinks)
• *Good morning, Hello, Hi* (greetings)
• *day, minute, morning*   (lengths of time)
• *fine, nice, pleased*   (adjectives/positive adjectives)

Get learners to read these sets of words aloud before deciding which words sound different from the others in their sets.

Answer key

1. **eight** (vowel sound is /eɪ/. The sound in the other words is /aɪ/).
2. **so** (vowel sound is /əʊ/. The sound in the other words is /ɒ/).
3. **two** (vowel sound is /uː/. The sound in the other words is /əʊ/).
4. **park** (vowel sound is /aː/. The sound in the other words is /æ/).
5. **right** (vowel sound is /aɪ/. The sound in the other words is /eɪ/).

Unit 2 Worksheet

Suggested steps

Make equal numbers of copies of the two maps and give them out to the class. Learners work in pairs, preferably sitting back-to-back to make sure that they do not see each other's information and to help them practise their listening skills.

Learners take turns to ask each other where people are from. Learner A has the answers to all Learner B's questions and vice versa.

They should ask and answer questions like this:
A: *Where's Peter from?*
B: *He's from Germany.*
When learners have the answers to their questions, they should write them in the spaces on their worksheet. When they have finished, they can check each other's answers.

Full answer key

2A
Peter: Germany Natalie: Britain Roman: Poland
Sophia: Italy Osman: Turkey Patty: USA
2B
Lucy: Australia Youssef: Egypt Sylvie: France
Noriko: Japan George: Greece Mikhail: Russia

PEOPLE AND THINGS IN MY LIFE

Introduction to the unit

Unit 3 takes as its central theme people and things that are important in our lives. In Lesson A students talk about people: husbands, wives, friends and colleagues and possessive adjectives and numbers 31–100 are presented. Lessons B and C focus on personal possessions and introduce *there is / there are*, adjectives, and the question *Where is something from?* Lesson C also presents and gives practice in the language of saying *thank you*.

A FRIENDS IN PHOTOGRAPHS

This lesson introduces some general vocabulary for different types of people, adjectives for describing people, and questions about age. Again the initial focus is on listening so that learners are not under too much pressure to speak.

1 Is your manager nice? ▭

Warm-up

You could bring in a few photos similar to ones in the Student's Book: perhaps of your wedding day, or you with a friend. Introduce vocabulary like *husband, wife, friend, colleague*.

Suggested steps

Practise pronunciation of the expressions in the box before asking your learners to complete 1, 2, 3, 4 and 5. Check the answers then ask your learners questions like: *Is your husband nice? Is your manager popular?* When the meaning of the adjectives is clear, let them answer *Yes* or *No*.

Clarify the listening task. Learners listen to the recording and write the responses to the questions. You can either let the learners try to write the answers as best they can and then check them, or, model: *Yes, he is/No, he isn't; Yes, they are/No, they aren't*, before listening.

Practise question and answer routines in small groups with each learner asking and then answering alternately. To help learners, give each group a sheet of paper with people and adjectives in two lists.

Tapescript

1. A: Is your wife busy?
   B Yes, she is.
2. A: Is your manager popular?
   B: No, she isn't.
3. A: Are your friends nice?
   B: Yes, they are.
4. A: Are your colleagues nice?
   B: No, they aren't.

Option

You might like to practise questions like: *Is your … nice?* and extend the variety of answers by recycling adjectives from Unit 1, e.g. *Yes, he's OK/ all right/not bad*.

Answer key

1. wife 2. husband 3. colleague 4. friend
5. manager
1. Yes, she is. 2. No, she isn't. 3. Yes, they are.
4. No, they aren't.

3

PEOPLE AND THINGS IN MY LIFE

Language focus:
possessive adjectives
Who is this/that?
Where ... from?
questions about age (*How old is ...?*)
questions (*to be*)
short answer forms
there is/are
saying thank you/responding

Vocabulary:
numbers 31–100
describing people
personal possessions

FRIENDS IN PHOTOGRAPHS

1 Is your manager nice? | *your; describing people; Yes, ... is/are; No, ... isn't/aren't* |

Write the words from the box in 1, 2, 3, 4 and 5.   friend   colleague   husband   manager   wife

1

4

Our teachers
Mr J Abbott, MA, CELTA
Mrs S Best, BA, DELTA
Mr A Clark, MA, MBA
Ms M Donovan, MA, DELTA

2

3

5

Listen to the questions. Write the answers.

Questions	Answers
1. Is your wife busy?	....
2. Is your manager popular?	....
3. Are your friends nice?	....
4. Are your colleagues nice?	....

HELP	In your language?
best friend	....

Ask two of the questions in groups.

2 Who's this?

How old is ...?; numbers 20–60; Who's this/that?; my, your, his, her, our, their

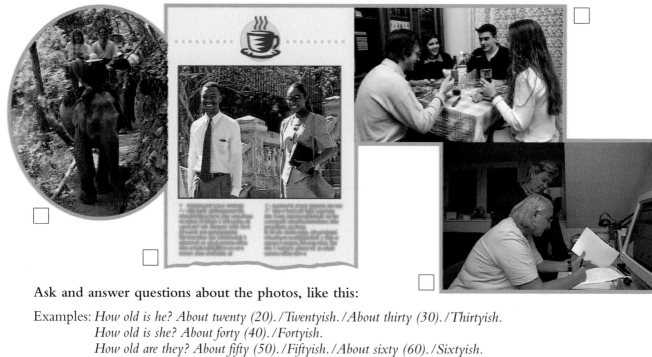

Ask and answer questions about the photos, like this:

Examples: *How old is he? About twenty (20)./Twentyish./About thirty (30)./Thirtyish.*
How old is she? About forty (40)./Fortyish.
How old are they? About fifty (50)./Fiftyish./About sixty (60)./Sixtyish.

Listen. Label the photos 1, 2, 3 or 4.

Read a–f. Listen again. Match a–f with photos 1–4.

a: *... and her husband Michael.*   Photo number ☐   d: *She's your manager?*   Photo number ☐
b: *They're our friends.*   Photo number ☐   e: *... that's their guide.*   Photo number ☐
c: *That's my manager – Maria.*   Photo number ☐   f: *That's his wife.*   Photo number ☐

Talk about pictures or photos, like this:

This is ...
Who's that? He's/She's ...
Who are they? They're ...

3 Money or books?

numbers 31–100

Listen to the numbers. Match the numbers and pictures.

Numbers										Which picture?
1. 31	32	33	34	35	36	37	38	39	40	....
2. 41	42	43	44	45	46	47	48	49	50	
51	52	53	54	55	56	57	58	59	60	....
3. 61	62	63	64	65	66	67	68	69	70	....
4. 71	72	73	74	75	76	77	78	79	80	
81	82	83	84	85	86	87	88	89	90	
91	92	93	94	95	96	97	98	99	100	....

A    B    C    D

Practise counting.

2 Who's this? 🔲

Suggested steps

Use the pictures of bank notes and stamps to establish *Who's this?* question and response. Use additional magazine pictures for pair practice if you can. Remember responses by native speakers often omit the *It's …* and just say *the Queen* or *George Washington* in answer to *Who's this?*

Write the numbers 20, 30, 40, 50, 60 on the board. Practise pronunciation and write the words for the numbers. Practise matching words and numbers. Use *What's this?* when pointing to numbers and contrast it with *Who's this?* for people.

Use the photos in the book to build questions and answers about age. Ask: *How old is he?* (point to a photo and then to the numbers on the board) *twenty? thirty?* Establish *about* and *–ish* as meaning approximately (as in *about thirty; thirtyish*). Build question forms: *How old is she/are they?*

Use the other photos in the book as a basis for learners to ask and answer *How old …?* questions, or, use magazine pictures of different people and put learners in pairs for the question and answer practice.

Prepare for listening by getting learners to identify other things in the photos (*drink, elephants, guide, coffee shop*).

Clarify the listening task. Learners listen to four short conversations and decide which photo is being talked about each time. Check answers by replaying the recording and trying to elicit key expressions.

A third listening will enable the final task to be completed. Again explain the task. Learners match phrases from the listening with particular photos.

Draw attention to the possessive adjectives, but wait until all the listening has been completed before demonstrating their meaning and use further.

Tapescript

Photo 1
A: Who's this, with the drink?
B: That's Sarah and her husband, Michael. They're our friends.
A: Is he old?
B: Erm, Michael's fifty-ish. She's about thirty.

Photo 2
A: Who's that with you?
B: That's my manager – Maria.
A: How old is she?
B: Oh, she's about thirty, I think.
A: You're sixty, she's about thirty, and she's your manager?
B: Mm, but she's a good manager.

Photo 3
A: Who's the man?
B: He's the manager of the coffee shop in the park.
A: And the woman?
B: That's his wife.
A: Oh, yes, I know.

Photo 4
A: Who are they?
B: My colleagues.
A: Aah. Where is it?
B: In Thailand.
A: Oh, yes. Nice elephants. Who's that man?
B: Mm, that's their guide.

> ### Language Point
>
> In natural speech *their* and *they're* sound the same but *they're* is often followed by little words like *in, on, at* to indicate location or by an adjective as complement, e.g. *They're nice/old*. The final practice will work better and be more realistic if learners bring in photos of friends, colleagues, husbands, wives.

Answer key

Photo 1: Four people at dinner table.
Photo 2: Two women in office.
Photo 3: Man and woman on coffee shop leaflet.
Photo 4: People on elephants.

a: Photo 1   b: Photo 2   c: Photo 2   d: Photo 2
e: Photo 4   f: Photo 3

3 Money or books? 🔲

This activity presents the pronunciation of the numbers 31 – 100. Revise the numbers 1 – 30 first, preferably using a guessing game or number bingo.

Suggested steps

Identify the pictures of the money, books, children and lift.

Explain the listening task. Learners listen to the numbers and identify which picture depicts the people or things being counted.

Establish the pronunciation of 31, 41, 61 and 71 as these are the first numbers of each part of the recording.

Practise counting in various ways, perhaps by pointing to particular numbers or by playing number bingo.

Tapescript

1. LIFT: 31, 32, 33, 34, 35, 36, 37, 38, 39, 40
   WOMAN: Wow! We're here!
2. MAN: 41, 42, 43, 44, 45, 46, 47, 48, 49, 50,
            51, 52, 53, 54, 55, 56, 57, 58, 59, 60
            That's it!
3. WOMAN: No John ssh … Listen 61, 62, 63, 64, 65,
            66, 67, 68, 69, and … er, yes, Jane? 70.
4. A: … 71, 72, 73, 74, 75, 76, 77, 78, 79, 80, 81,
            82, 83, 84, 85, 86, 87, 88, 89, 90 … 91, 92,
            93, 94, 95, 96, 97, 98, 99, 100. OK?
   B: Yes, thank you.

Answer key

1. D   2. B   3. C   4. A

Quick Check

Answer key

A 1. he's   2. she   3. they   4. you

B 1. Your house is very nice.   2. Their house is interesting.   3. Her husband is in his coffee shop. 4. You are his wife.   5. Who are they?   6. They are her friends.

C 1. Yes 2. No 3. No 4. Yes 5. No 6. No 7. No 8. Yes

D your;   He;   our;   their

E Man (husband);   woman (wife);   man or woman (friend, colleague, manager)

Personal Study Workbook

2: possessive adjectives; vocabulary
3: answers with the verb to be
4: pronunciation; question intonation

B RINGS AND ROOMS

1 This ring is 50 years old ◫

Warm-up

Use the photos to set up the context. Ask: *Is photo A a man or a woman?* Establish the vocabulary and plural forms: *ring/rings; earring/earrings; watch/watches*

Suggested steps

Clarify the listening task. Learners hear three conversations and choose the appropriate photo for each conversation.

Check answers by playing the recording again or letting learners play the recording themselves in groups checking their own answers and controlling the recording.

Answer key

1.C   2.A   3.B

Tapescript

1. A: Is your watch old?
   B: About 30 years old.
   A: Is it still OK?
   B: It's fine. Listen.

2. A: They're beautiful earrings!
   B: Thanks.
   A: Are they special?
   B: Mm, from my husband.
   A: They're really nice.

3. A: Is that a new ring?
   B: Mm, it is,
   A: Is it a bit small?
   B: Mm, it is a bit small, actually, but it's OK on this finger.
   A: It's nice.
   B: Thanks.

Use realia (e.g. shoes, watch, pen, ring) to contrast and demonstrate the meanings of: *old, new, small, big, special.*

Ask learners to write those same words in the appropriate places for the illustrations.

The final activity is a natural progression to talking about the learners' own possessions. Let learners sit in groups (or go for coffee together) and ask and answer questions about their watches, rings, earrings.

Option

You might like to record some of the learners' speaking practice for later review, as in multilingual groups especially, learners will have different difficulties with pronunciation, stress, rhythm and fluency.

Let learners listen to their recordings, compare them with the model recordings, and explain what they think are their weaknesses. Help them to build self-awareness of their language development in English.

A Write the missing pronouns.

1. Is he OK?
   Mm, ...'s fine!
2. Is .... all right?
   Yes, she's OK.
3. Are they busy?
   No, ... aren't.
4. Are .... OK?
   Mm, I'm fine, thanks.

B Correct the sentences.

1. You house is very nice.
2. They're house is interesting.
3. Her husband is in he's coffee shop.
4. Oh, you are her wife.
5. Who are their?
6. They are her friend.

C Tick Yes or No.

1. Who's = Who is   Yes ☐ No ☐
2. They're = Their   Yes ☐ No ☐
3. Your = You are   Yes ☐ No ☐
4. You're = You are   Yes ☐ No ☐
5. His = He's   Yes ☐ No ☐
6. His = He's 🤔?   Yes ☐ No ☐
7. About sixty = 50   Yes ☐ No ☐
8. Fortyish = 40 + or − 2 Yes ☐ No ☐

D Complete the table.

I	my	we	....
you	....	they	....
it	its		
she	her		
....	his		

E Write 1–5 under *man*, *woman* or *man* or *woman*.

1 friend   2 wife   3 manager
4 husband   5 colleague

---

1 This ring is 50 years old | personal possessions; pronoun *it*; adjectives |

Look at this photo. Is it a man or a woman?

📼 Listen. Match the speakers and the pictures.

A ☐    B ☐   C ☐

earrings

Write: *old, new, small, big, special.*

Ask and answer questions in your classroom.

Examples: *Is that a new ring? Yes, it is./No, it isn't.*
            Is that a special watch? Yes, it's very special.
            Are they old earrings? No, they're new, from my husband.

2 Where's it from?

Where ... from? questions; countries/nationalities; dual listening

Guess. Where's A from? Is it from Spain? (Is it Spanish?) And B, C?

Turkey – Turkish
Spain – Spanish
Japan – Japanese
China – Chinese
Ireland – Irish

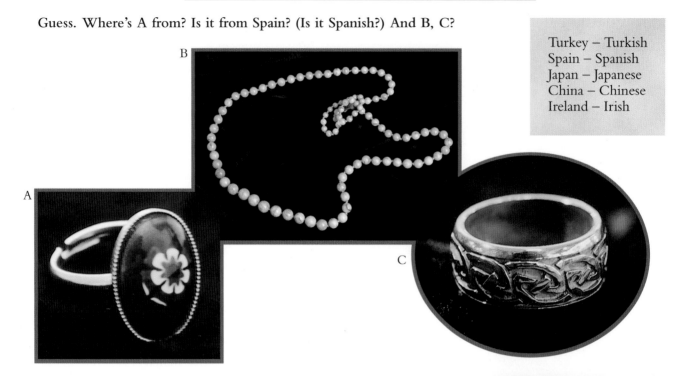

B

A

C

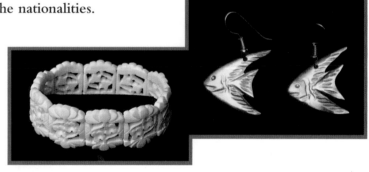

☐☐ ☐☐ Listen. Write the 3 countries or the nationalities.

Ask questions about these things, like this:

Where's the ring from?
Where are the earrings from?
Is the ring Indian?

The answers are on page 111.

3 Twenty rings and one mobile phone

vocabulary; plurals; there is/are

Guess the number of things in your group.

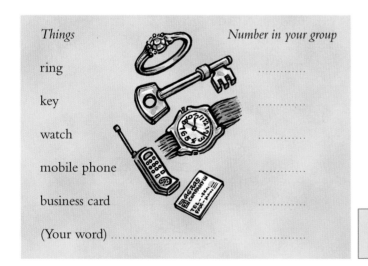

Things	Number in your group
ring	....
key	....
watch	....
mobile phone	....
business card	....
(Your word)	....

HELP   In your language?
There are no mobile phones. ....

Complete sentences like this:

*There's (There is) 1 mobile phone. There are **20** rings. There are **12** watches.*

2 Where's it from? ▢ ▢

Dual listening in this book

Dual listening is an innovative feature of the *True to Life* series. In the later books in this course series, the dual listening symbol means that two recordings are made of the same situation – one shorter (usually with less detail and less redundancy); the other longer (with more elaborate conversational style or additional information).

Teachers therefore have greater flexibility for listening tasks and exploitation. They can use the second recording as a basis for additional listening tasks, to explore discourse differences, and to cater for different ability levels.

In the Starter level the dual listening is used in an additional way for modelling and contrasting different language forms. For example, in this unit, Version 1 mentions countries and Version 2 mentions corresponding nationalities while also expanding the discourse marginally, e.g. *Is it Turkish?*; *really lovely* (Version 2); *lovely* (Version 1).

Suggested steps

Use an item of realia (if possible a ring or similar from one of the countries in the box). Establish the question form: *Where's it from?* and the response: *It's from (Turkey)*; *It's (Turkish)*.

Ask learners to look at the photos in the book and to guess from which country in the box each is from. Ask: *Where is A from?*

Clarify the listening task. Learners listen and write the 3 countries or nationalities. Let one half of the class listen to Version 1; the other, more confident half to Version 2. See if they can write the differences of spelling.

Check answers then move on to the next two photos. Tell learners to ask/answer the question *Where's the … from?* in pairs and then to check their answers.

Tapescript

Version 1

A: That ring's nice. Where's it from?
B: Er ... it's from Spain, I think.

A: Is this from Japan?
B: No, it's from China.
A: It's lovely.
B: Thanks.

A: Where's this from?
B: The ring?
A: Mmm.
B: It's from Ireland.

Version 2

A: That ring's nice. Where's it from? Is it Turkish?
B: No, it's Spanish, I think.

A: Is this Japanese?
B: No, it's Chinese.
A: It's really lovely.
B: Mm. Thanks very much; it is.

A: Where's this from?
B: The ring?
A: Mm.
B: It's Irish, from Dublin.

Answer key

A: Spanish (Spain)   B: Chinese (China)   C: Irish (Ireland)

3 Twenty rings and one mobile phone

Suggested steps

Check learners' understanding of the vocabulary and revise formation of plurals, especially *watches*.

Ask: *What's the total number of rings in this classroom? Guess. Is it 20, 10, 30?* Elicit a guess and write it down.

Put the class into groups and ask them to talk in English and guess the total number of the other things.

Nominate different learners to count the actual numbers of each item. Write a summary on the board, using *there are …* or *there is …* (or *there are no + (plural noun)'* from the Help box).

Ask learners to read out the guesses from their groups as a comparison, using: *there are … /there is … .* Extend the practice by asking about other things in your city or town. (Try to find out the number before the lesson.) Recycle the vocabulary from previous units, e.g. *parks, discos, swimming pools, gyms.* It may be natural to introduce *How many … are there?* for understanding rather than productive use.

4 Things on the floor

Suggested steps

Use the picture. Ask: *Where is this?* Elicit items on the floor by asking: *What is there on the floor?* Let learners answer: *There's an earring; there are books or just an earring; books.*

Before reading, teach the meaning of *under*. Ask learners to read the questions and then to read the text silently. Let learners complete True/False questions in pairs, then check answers.

Teach the difference between the use of the indefinite article *a* and *an*. Let learners try the indefinite article exercise without the text, then they can use the text to check answers.

Put learners into groups for the final discussion about things on their office, car or bedroom floors. Choose *office* if there is an issue of cultural appropriateness. Model possible questions and draw attention to the Help box. Tell learners in each group to write down two interesting things that are mentioned in their discussion.

Visit each group, monitoring use of language and giving encouragement.

Answer key
1. F   2. T   3. F   4. F

4 Things on the floor

reading; *there's/there are; there isn't a/an*

Look at the picture and read the text.

Things on the floor!

There are one or two things on the floor of our bedroom. There's a key, a letter (from my manager!) and there are two books, and, oh yes, under the bed there's an earring (so that's where it is!), an old business card (with the name Ms. Maria Suarez, Manager, Capital Disco) a magazine (called Ideal Homes), a phone book and a cat!!

But there isn't a cat in our flat!

phone book

cat

floor

magazine

Circle true or false. (T/F)

1. There's a key under the bed. T/F
2. There is an earring under the bed. T/F
3. The letter is to the manager. T/F
4. The cat isn't under the bed. T/F

HELP　　　　　In your language?

There's nothing on our floor. ....

Write *a* or *an*.

.... phone book .... key .... earring .... letter
.... bedroom .... business card .... cat

Talk about things on the floor of your office, car or bedroom. Use a dictionary.

A Match A and B.

A	B
an earring	he
a wife	they
colleagues	it
a husband	it
a key	she

And your teacher? …………

B Put these under *a thing, a place* or *a person*.

a mobile phone   a park
a friend   a ring   a woman
a room   a letter   a classroom
a business card   a husband

C Complete the questions.

1. A: ………………………………
    Italy?
   B: No, it's from France.
2. A: This is nice.
   B: Thanks.
   A: Is ……………… …………
    Greece?
   B: Yes, from Corfu.

C   IT'S OUR CAR, THANK YOU

1   Is that our car? | reading and speaking; practice with *we/our* |

A

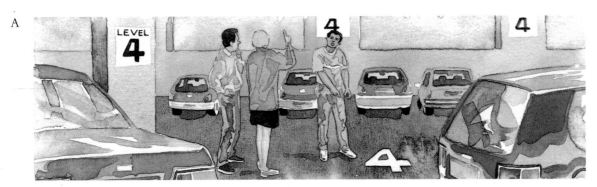

B

C

Read the conversations and put the correct numbers under the pictures.

1. A: Is that our car?   2. A: Are you lost?   3. A: This is the fourth level.
   B: I'm not sure.   B: Yes, I think we are.   B: Is it? Our car's on the fifth level.

🎧 Listen and check your answer. Practise the conversations.

A
an earring – it
a wife – she
colleagues – they
a husband – he
a key – it
B
Thing: a mobile phone; a ring; a letter; a business
        card
Place: a park; a room; a classroom
Person: a friend; a woman; a husband
C
1. **Is it from** Italy?   2. Is **it from** Greece?

Personal Study Workbook

1: practice with pronouns and ages
5: reading; writing; practice to be

C IT'S OUR CAR, THANK YOU

1 Is that our car?

Suggested steps

Use the pictures to establish context and problem.
Ask: *Where are they? Where is their car?* Establish task:
Which conversation goes with which picture?

Pre-teach *lost, car, I'm not sure*. Let learners read the
conversations. Ask them to match conversations with
appropriate pictures. They can then listen and check
their answers.

Use the conversations to practise question intonation.
You can change the floor levels to recycle first,
second, third, etc.

Tapescript

1. Picture C
A: Are you lost?
B: Yes, I think we are.
2. Picture A
A: This is the fourth level.
B: Is it? Our car's on the fifth level.
3. Picture B
A: Is that our car?
B: I'm not sure.

Answer key

Picture A:2   B:3   C:1

2 Cars

Suggested steps

This is basically structured conversation practice. Establish the meaning of the adjectives using magazine pictures of cars with people in the pictures to recycle possessive adjectives: *Is their/her/his car old/new/big/small/nice?*

Get learners to ask about your car. Elicit questions, e.g. *Is your car big/old?* or put prompt questions on the board.

Offer answers that practise response forms, e.g. *Yes, it is/No, it isn't/No, my car's … .* Draw attention to additional responses in the Help box.

Let learners talk in small groups about their cars. Monitor and encourage.

> ### Language Point
>
> Remember that the short response form *Yes, it is* cannot be shortened to *Yes, it's* but the response form *No, it isn't* is a shorter version of *No, it is not.*

3 In conversation 🔲

Suggested steps

Talk about pictures A, B and C. Elicit vocabulary (especially *information, drink*).

Clarify the listening task. Learners match conversations 1 – 3 with appropriate pictures A – C. Let learners try listening without reading the script to train them for unassisted listening.

Let learners discuss answers in pairs. Check answers. If they are having difficulty, replay the recording while they read the script.

Explain or revise the use of some of the new expressions in the conversations, e.g. *Don't mention it; here's; … a lot.* Use the pictures to model practice of simple thank you exchanges, e.g. *Thanks a lot for the book/coffee; You're welcome/Don't mention it.*

Ask learners to practise in pairs.

Tapescript

1. A: Are you OK now?
   B: Yeah, fine. Thanks for your help.
   A: Don't mention it. You're welcome any time.
2. A: Thank you very much for the information.
   B: You're very welcome.
3. A: Here's your drink.
   B: Thanks a lot.

Answer key

A:3   B:1   C:2

Option

Prepare cards with suitable vocabulary items written on them (or a mixture of words and pictures) from previous units to recycle vocabulary. Each learner in turn picks up a card and says thank you for the item shown on the card, e.g. *Thanks for the address*; the other learner responds, e.g. *You're welcome.* Examples of additional items to recycle: *beer, tea, taxi, address, telephone number.*

Unit 3 PEOPLE AND THINGS IN MY LIFE

2 Cars   `speaking practice with adjectives`

Ask and answer questions about your car or one of the photos. Use words in this box.

Old   NEW   **Big**   small   our   my   nice

Questions	Answers
Is your car ...?	No, it's ...
	No, our car's ...
	Yes, it is. / No, it isn't.

HELP
It's quite new/old.
We haven't got a car.

In your language?
....
....

3 In conversation   `saying thank you and responding`

Listen. Match the pictures with 1, 2 and 3.

1. A: Are you OK now?
   B: Yeah, fine. Thanks for your help.
   A: Don't mention it. You're welcome any time.

2. A: Thank you very much for the information.
   B: You're very welcome.

3. A: Here's your drink.
   B: Thanks a lot.

A

B

C

Partner A: Say *thanks* or *thank you* for one or two things.
Partner B: Respond.

4 Thank you very much for the ... writing 'thank you' notes

Write a 'thank you' note to a friend for one of the things.

flowers   earrings   book

Say: *They're/it's nice/beautiful/fantastic/great.*

> *Dear* _____
>
> *Thank you* _____
> _____ *for the*
> _____ . *It's/They're*
> _____ .
>
> *Best wishes*
>
> _____

✔ Quick Check

A Put a tick if 1 to 3 mean the same. Put a cross if they are different.

1. thank you very much = thanks a lot
2. small = big
3. our car's = our cars

B Match A and B.

A	B
I	our
she	their
it	his
you	my
he	its
they	her
we	your

C Are they places or things? Write the words in 2 lists.

car park   watch   office   bedroom
earring   car   key

Places   *Things*

PERSONAL STUDY WORKBOOK

- possessive adjective practice
- question intonation
- writing about a friend
- visual dictionary – personal things
- reading – episode 3 of *Lost in time*

4 Thank you very much for the ...

Suggested steps

This activity consolidates the work done orally. If you have a real person to write to, e.g. after a class excursion, or an English speaking visitor so much the better.

Establish the word *flowers* and the variety of adjectives learners can use in their 'thank you' notes (*nice/great/fantastic*). Explain that *fantastic* is a strong, positive description and shows great enthusiasm for a gift.

If possible, supply learners with simulated thank you notes for added realism.

Quick Check

A.
1. same   2. different   3. different

B
I – my
she – her
it – its
you – your
he – his
they – their
we – our

C
Places: car park; office; bedroom
Things: watch; earring; car; key

Personal Study Workbook

6: listening; vocabulary
7: writing sentences
8: writing numbers
9: visual dictionary

REVIEW OF UNIT 1

These activities all focus on pronunciation. Learners could do them as self-access in their own time.

1 Same or different? 🔲

Suggested steps

Clarify task. Ask individual learners to say a letter each for 1. Don't comment if pronunciation is incorrect. Ask learners to identify the letter that sounds different. Play the recording and check the pronunciation and answer. Repeat for 2 and 3.

Answer key

1. J   2. P   3. A

2 Same sounds? 🔲

Clarify the task. Procedure as for Exercise 1 above.

Answer key

1. day /deɪ/ The others have the vowel sound /aɪ/
2. am /æm/ The others have the vowel sound /eɪ/

3 What's good ...? How's she ...? 🔲

Suggested steps

This activity draws attention to sound differences that may be quite subtle to the ears of some learners, so it is important to be gentle with this activity.

Clarify task. Let learners practise in pairs and ask them to tell you whether the final 's' sounds the same. If the discrimination is hard to appreciate, you might show how the 't' sound in *What's* forces the 's' that follows further to the front of the mouth than the 's' in *How's*.

Let learners listen to the recording and practise again.

REVIEW OF UNIT 2

1 Quick quiz 🔲

Suggested steps

This activity practises rapid comprehension and response. It is best suited to individual work in a language lab. Clarify the task. Get them to write the numbers from 1 – 6 in a line down one side of a piece of paper and the answers *Yes, it is / No, it isn't* next to each number 1 – 6. Ask them to circle each answer as they say it. Start the recording. Time the quiz. Congratulate the learners on their speed. Ask learners for their answers: *Is number 1 Yes or No?* etc.

Tapescript

A
1. Is Athens in Greece?
2. Is London in France?
3. Is Rio in Brazil?

4. Is Paris in France?
5. Is New York in London?
6. Is Italy in Rome?

Play the second part of the recording (with the answers). Let learners listen and check.

Tapescript

B
1. A: Is Athens in Greece?
   B: Yes, it is.
2. A: Is London in France?
   B: No, it isn't, it's in England.
3. A: Is Rio in Brazil?
   B: Yes, it is.
4. A: Is Paris in France?
   B: Yes, it is.
5. A: Is New York in London?
   B: No, it isn't, it's in the USA.
6. A: Is Italy in Rome?
   B: No, it isn't. Rome is in Italy.

2 E-mail address 🔲

Suggested steps

Establish what an e-mail address is. Ask learners: *Who is on e-mail? What's your e-mail address?* Use the Help box to establish the meaning and pronunciation of '@' (*at*). Tell the learners that they will hear the two e-mail addresses and that there is one mistake in each recording compared with the addresses in the book.

Play the recording. Check the answers.

Tapescript

See page 129.
For the final task, learners have to write the complete e-mail address. Photocopy the business card if you don't want learners to write in the book.

Answer key

1. On the recording it's com (cum in the book)
2. On the recording it's Simex (Samex in the book)

Unit 3 Worksheet

Before being placed in pairs, each learner chooses one thing (from box 2) for one person (from box 1) and writes them down e.g. *a big cup of coffee for C.*

Then each learner must find out what the other has written down, by asking and answering questions like this

A: *Is it a watch?*   B: *No*
A: *Is it a cup of coffee?*   B: *Yes*
A: *Is it a big cup of coffee?*   B: *Yes*
A: *Is it for a woman?*   B: *No*
A: *For a man?*   B: *Yes*
A: *Is it for a young man?*   B: *No*
A: *A man in his sixties?*   B: *Yes*
A: *It's a big cup of coffee for C?*   B: *Yes*

REVIEW OF UNIT 1

1 Same or different? | alphabet pronunciation

Say the letters in 1, 2 and 3. Which letter sounds different?

1. B C E J T
2. J K P
3. I A Y

▭ Listen and check.

2 Same sounds? | vowel sounds in words

Say the words. Which vowel sound is different?

1. Hi   fine   nice   bye   day   I'm   nine
2. eight   day   name   am   great

▭ Listen and check.

3 What's good ...? How's she ...? | pronunciation final /s/, /z/

In pairs, say the questions and answers. Is the *s* in *How's* and the *s* in *What's* the same sound?

Question	*Answer*
How's he today?	He's fine.
How's she today?	She's fine.
What's nice at the coffee bar?	The coffee.
What's good at the restaurant?	The tea.

▭ Listen and check.

REVIEW OF UNIT 2

1 Quick quiz | *yes, it is/no, it isn't*; listening

A ▭ Listen and answer the six questions with *Yes, it is* or *No, it isn't* in 30 seconds!

B ▭ Listen to the answers.

2 E-mail address | writing

A ▭ Listen and correct the e-mail addresses.

1. maria.suarez@virtual.net.cum.br
2. angela.collins@Samex.demon.co.uk

B ▭ Listen and write the e-mail address on the business card.

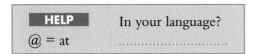

HELP	In your language?
@ = at	....

MAGRIC International ⓜ

John Smythe
International Marketing Manager

12 Linden Street
Burnside
South Australia 5027
Australia
Telephone (61) 88339 5812
Fax (61) 88339 57444
E-mail _____ @ _____

4

ABOUT TOWN

Language focus:
Is there ...? / Are there (any) ...?
uncertainty: *perhaps / I think*
showing interest: *Really? / Is it really? / That's interesting*
talking about age: *How old is it?*

Vocabulary:
numbers over 100
buildings in towns
north, south, east, west

A TOWNS

1 Public buildings | *perhaps/I think; vocabulary*

Match these town words with the symbols.

bank   cinema   library   nightclub   police station
post office   sports centre   theatre

Look at the picture of a Roman town. Where are these buildings?
You decide. Talk to your partner like this:

A: *What's this?*   B: *It's a library./Perhaps it's a bank./I think it's a theatre.*

HELP	In your language?
Perhaps	....
I think	....

2 Home towns | listening

CD CD Satoshi (Japan), Raymundo (Mexico) and Paloma (Spain) are answering
questions about their home towns. Listen and tick (✓) or cross (✗) the boxes.

	cinema	*nightclub*	*sports centre*	*theatre*
Satoshi	☐	☐	☐	☐
Raymundo	☐	☐	☐	☐
Paloma	☐	☐	☐	☐

ABOUT TOWN

This unit continues the Unit 2 focus on places, by looking more closely at cities and towns. In Lesson A learners are introduced to the vocabulary of typical town buildings and other facilities and practise *There is/are* and related forms. Lesson B introduces large numbers in the context of the age of famous buildings. In Lesson C learners practise the language of simple street directions.

Warm-up

Before learners open their books, revise briefly some of the place language introduced in Unit 2.

Ask questions like this:
1. *What are Paris and New York?* (*They're cities.*)
2. *What's Brazil?* (*It's a country.*)
3. *Where's Athens?* (*It's in Greece.*)
4. *What's the capital of Italy?* (*Rome. / Rome's the capital of Italy.*)
5. *Where are you from?* (*I'm from … .*)

A TOWNS

1 Public buildings

Suggested steps

Ask learners to look at the symbols and match each one with a 'town word'. Elicit as many as possible, by pointing to a symbol and asking: *What's this?* (*It's a bank.*) If any of the words are unknown, get the class to repeat *It's a* + noun.

> ### Language Point: pronunciation
> Learners should say these compound nouns naturally at normal speed – this means getting them to say:
> | *nightclub* | /ˈnaɪtklʌb/ |
> | *police station* | /pəˈliːs ˈsteɪʃn/ |
> | *sports centre* | /spɔːts ˈsentə/ |

Next learners look at the illustration of a Roman town and *imagine* what the various buildings are. There are none of the clues that there would be if this illustration was a photo of a real town. This is to enable learners to practise using uncertainty expressions: *Perhaps / I think it's a … .*

2 Home towns

There are two versions of this recording.

Suggested steps

Clarify the activity and play the recording for the first time. Learners tick and cross the boxes individually, then compare answers with a partner.
Play the recording a second time, then elicit answers.

Tapescript
See page 129.

Answer key

	cinema	nightclub	sports centre	theatre
Satoshi	✓	✗	✓	✓
Raymundo	✓	✓	✓	✗
Paloma	✓	✓	✓	✗

Options

1   In addition to putting ticks in the boxes, learners could write how many of each building there are.

Answer key

Satoshi: 3 cinemas;   no nightclub;
              1 sports centre;   1 theatre
Raymundo: 1 cinema;   4 nightclubs;
              1 sports centre;   no theatres
Paloma: 1 cinema;   1 nightclub;
              1 sports centre;   no theatres

2   Ask learners to listen for anything else that the speakers say about the places. Try to elicit the words listed below, with questions like these:
Here's Satoshi. Is there a theatre in his town? (*Yes, there is.*)
Is it old or modern?   (*It's very old.*)

Answer key

Satoshi: *big/really big* sports centre; *very old /beautiful old* theatre
Raymundo: *two good* nightclubs; *small/not very big* sports centre
Paloma: *very good/good, very expensive* nightclub; *new, fantastic/great* sports centre

Note: Option 1 is for the first version of the recording and Option 2 is for the second.

3 Another town

Suggested steps

Learners fill in this table with details of a town they know well (probably the town they live in) or of an imaginary town.

Get the class to practise the conversations by repeating the examples in their books. (Half the class could be A and the other half B.)

Learners then ask each other about their towns, filling in the details in the table.

Monitor conversations, correcting any mistakes of grammar or pronunciation you hear.

Finally get learners to talk about other facilities in their towns. This could be done as a freer pair or group activity or as a whole class question and answer activity.

> ### Language Point
>
> This exercise presents *any* as the plural of *a/an* in the question form: ·
> *Are there **any** cinemas in your town?*
> The standard answers in this exercise are the short forms:
> *Yes, there are.* or *No, there aren't.*
> If you wish, you can teach this use of *any* in negative statements, like *There aren't **any** cinemas.*
> This form is used in the reading text in Exercise 4.

4 Your dream town

This is a chance for learners to consolidate in writing some of the language they have been practising orally.

Suggested steps

Read through the short example text with the class. Ask a few simple comprehension questions.
Example:
> *Is the town big or small?*
> *Are there any banks in this town?* etc.

Get learners to write about the towns they talked about in Exercise 3. Allow about five minutes for this.

Now get learners to exchange work and read each other's writing.

Option

For homework, learners could write about a nightmare town, following the same pattern.

Quick Check

Set this either as classwork or for homework.

Answer key

A
1. b & d   2. a & e   3. f   4. c
B
1. are 2. A: Is; B: No; 3. A: any; B: are 4. but
5. there is
C
1. four banks   2. a nightclub   3. two libraries
4. fifteen offices   5. a city

Personal Study Workbook

1: singular or plural; *is/are*; *a(n)/any*
2: *is there/are there? numbers*

3 Another town | is there?/are there?; speaking |

Think about a town you know well. Write numbers in the table.

	sports centre	cinema	nightclub	theatre
Example:	0	3	1	1
You	....	....	....	....
1.	....	....	....	....
2.	....	....	....	....

Ask two people about their towns. Make conversations like this:

A: *Is there a sports centre in your town?*   B: *Yes, there is./No, there isn't.*
A: *Are there any cinemas?*   B: *Yes, there are./No, there aren't.*

Now talk about other places. For example, banks, libraries or discos.

Statement:	Question:	Short answer:
There is/There's a cinema in my town.	**Is there a** cinema in your town?	Yes, **there is.**/No, **there isn't.**
There are six banks in my town.	**Are there any** banks in your town?	Yes, **there are.**/No, **there aren't.**

4 Your dream town | reading; writing |

Read about a real town.

My town is small.
There are two banks,
a police station and a
cinema, but there isn't
a sports centre. There's
a hotel and six or seven
shops, but there aren't
any nightclubs.

Write about your dream town.

✓ Quick Check

A Match the questions and the answers. Sometimes there are two answers.

Questions
1. Is there a cinema in your town?
2. Are there any nightclubs in your town?
3. Can I ask you about your town?
4. What about a cinema?

Answers
a. No, there aren't.   d. No, there isn't.
b. Yes, there is.   e. Yes, there are.
c. There are two.   f. Yes, OK.

B Fill in the missing words.

1. There .... three nightclubs in my town.
2. A: .... there a library?
   B: ...., there isn't.

3. A: Are there .... hotels in your town?
   B: Yes, there .... about three or four.
4. There's a theatre, ... there isn't a cinema.
5. A: Is there a police station?
   B: Yes, ...

C Fill in the gaps with a singular or a plural word.

Example: *a cinema* two *cinemas* ....

1. a bank   four ....
2. a ....   five nightclubs
3. a library   two ....
4. an office   fifteen ....
5. a ....   four cities

---

1 Hundreds and thousands [numbers 100–10,000]

Listen and match the numbers on the recording with the pictures.

	Recording	Picture
Example:	1	*B*
	2	....
	3	....
	4	....
	5	....
	6	....
	7	....
	8	....

Listen again and repeat the numbers.

Write your own large numbers and say them with another learner.

2 How old is it? [*How old?* speaking]

Match the buildings with the captions.

The Sydney Opera House	☐
The theatre at Epidaurus	☐
The Bank of England	☐
The Great Wall of China	☐
Chartres Cathedral	☐
Topkapı Palace	☐

A   B   D   F

How old are the buildings? Make guesses like this.

A: *How old is the Great Wall of China?*
B: *I think it's about three thousand years old.*

HELP	
over 800 years old	In your language? ....

Listen and check your guesses. Write the missing numbers.

1. Topkapı Palace is over .... years old.
2. The theatre at Epidaurus in Greece is over .... years old.
3. The Sydney Opera House is about .... years old.
4. Chartres Cathedral in France is over .... years old.
5. The Bank of England is about .... years old.
6. The Great Wall of China is over .... years old.

B LARGE NUMBERS

1 Hundreds and thousands ▭ ▭

Suggested steps

Note: There are two versions of the recording for this exercise. The first version is simply the numbers; the second version contextualises the numbers and links them with the illustrations on page 30 of the Class Book. For this reason, the second version of the listening might actually be easier for some learners.

Before playing the recording, ask learners to say what they can see in the illustration. Ask: *What's this?* questions to elicit the nouns illustrated; *book, computer, cheque,* etc. (It is particularly important to do this if you are intending to play the second version of the recording.)

Check that learners remember *a hundred*, then introduce them to *two hundred* (no -*s*) and *thousand* (*a thousand / four thousand*).

Clarify the activity and play the recording for the first time. Allow learners to compare ideas.

Play the recording once or twice more, as necessary, then elicit answers.

Tapescript

Version 1
1. a hundred and eleven
2. two hundred and ninety-four
3. ten thousand and ten
4. three thousand four hundred and fifty-six
5. a hundred and seventy-six
6. three hundred and thirty-seven
7. one thousand and one
8. seven hundred and twenty-one

Version 2
1. This is my address, a hundred and eleven Oxford Street.
2. That's two hundred and ninety-four pounds, please.
3. My computer is a ten thousand and ten model.
4. It's three thousand four hundred and fifty-six kilometres to Moscow.
5. It's on page a hundred and seventy-six.
6. Is your address three hundred and thirty-seven Station Road?
7. It's only one thousand and one dollars.
8. Six hundred and twenty and one hundred and one is seven hundred and twenty-one.

Answer key

1. B   2. F   3. A   4. H   5. G   6. D   7. E   8. C

Play the recording again and get the class to repeat. If you play the second version of the recording, pause from time to time in the longer sentences, but do not stop the recording in the middle of large numbers.

At this stage, refer the class to the first page of the Grammar Reference section at the back of the Class Book and work through large numbers with them, pointing out any difficult points.

Learners now write four or five large numbers of their own and practise them with partners. Monitor this exercise, correcting as necessary.

2 How old is it? ▭

Suggested steps

To help learners with the listening exercise which follows, work through the names of the buildings, getting them to repeat each one after you. You could also ask *Where?* questions.
Example: *Where's the Sydney Opera House?* (*In Australia.*)

Elicit ideas from the class about how old they think each of the places is, then list some suggestions on the board. Remind learners to use *about* and *over* when they are not sure about the exact ages. Correct any number mistakes you hear.

Get learners to choose an age for each place, then play the recording so that they can check their ideas. They can write the correct answers in the gaps in sentences 1 – 6.

Tapescript

A: Great! Postcards!
B: Yeah, they're from my friends.
A: What's this?
B: It's the Topkapı Palace.
A: How old is it?
B: It's over 500 years old.
A: This theatre is fantastic! How old is it?
B: It's the theatre at Epidaurus in Greece. It's over two thousand years old.
A: And is this in Australia?
B: Yes, it is – it's the Sydney Opera House. That's about 30 years old, I think.
A: And what's this?
B: That's Chartres Cathedral in France.
A: Is it very old?
B: It's over 800 years old.
A: Is this Buckingham Palace?
B: No, it isn't. It's the Bank of England.
A: How old is it?
B: It's only about 300 years old.
A: And of course this is the Great Wall of China.
B: That's right. That's over 3,000 years old.
A: Fantastic!

Answer key

1. five hundred   2. two thousand   3. thirty
4. eight hundred   5. three hundred
6. three thousand

Round off this exercise by asking learners to read the completed sentences to each other.

3 Your town

This is a freer practice activity which gives the class the chance to talk about the ages of places they know well.

Suggested steps

Elicit a few examples from the whole class, then let learners continue talking in pairs or groups.

Clarify the activity. Learners fill the gaps in the postcard with words from lists 1 – 5. Point out that the answers to gaps 6, 7 and 8 will depend on each learner's choice of place.

Work through the vocabulary items illustrated, getting the class to practise pronouncing the four words correctly. Go round the class helping learners.

Possible completed postcard:

Dear Paulo,
This is my **town**. It's very **big**. There are some beautiful **old** buildings. The **cathedral is over 500** years old and the **bridge** is about **250** years old.
Best wishes
(Sender's name)

Option

For homework the class could write another postcard from a real or an imaginary holiday town.

Quick Check

Answer key

A
1. a/one hundred and one
2. three hundred and sixty-five
3. nine hundred and ninety-nine
4. one thousand, one hundred and four
5. one thousand five hundred (This can also be *fifteen hundred* as in the *fifteen hundred metres race*.)

B
1. 9876   2. 4627   3. 1111   4. 713   5. 202

C
A: How old **is** your town?
B: The theatre is over **a/one/two** hundred years old.
A: Is that **your** (not a) house?
B: No, **it** isn't.
A: How old **is it**?
B: **It's** about 30 years.
A: **It's** very big.

D
1. c 2. d 3. a 4. e 5. b

Personal Study Workbook

3: talking about age; *How old?*
6: vocabulary

3 Your town   speaking and writing

Talk about the ages of places in your town. For example, an old theatre, a modern cinema, a new sports centre.

Write a postcard to a friend. Tell your friend about your town. Use these words or your own words.

1. town/city
2. big/small/old/modern
3. old/new
4. theatre/cathedral/city walls
5. about/over
6., 7., 8.?

Dear Paulo,
This is my (1) ....
It's very (2) ....
There are some beautiful
(3) .... buildings.
The (4) .... is/are
(5) .... (6)
.... years old and
the (7) .... is about
(8) .... years old.

Best wishes

....

mosque

bridge

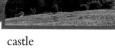

castle

church

✔ Quick Check

A Write the words.

1. 101 ....
2. 365 ....
3. 999 ....
4. 1,104 ....
5. 1,500 ....

B Write the numbers.

1. nine thousand eight hundred and seventy-six
2. four thousand six hundred and twenty-seven
3. one thousand one hundred and eleven
4. seven hundred and thirteen
5. two hundred and two

C Find 7 mistakes in the conversation.

A: How old are your town?
B: The theatre is over hundred years old.
A: Is that your a house?
B: No, she isn't.
A: How old it is?
B: Is about 30 years.
A: It very big.

D Match the questions and answers.

1. What's this?   a. No, it's in England.
2. How old is it?   b. No, it's only about 30
3. Is it in Turkey?   years old.
4. Is this a cinema?   c. It's a library.
5. Is it very old?   d. It's over 800 years old.
                         e. Yes, it is.

1   Geography | vocabulary |

Look at this map and make sentences about Edinburgh, London, Cardiff and Belfast.

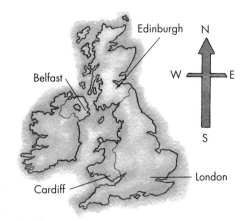

Edinburgh		in	the south		England
London	is		the north	of	Scotland
Cardiff			the east		Britain
Belfast			the west		Northern Ireland
		the	capital		Wales

What do you know about Edinburgh? Talk to a partner.
Read about Edinburgh and check your ideas.

EDINBURGH is the capital of Scotland. It is a big city in the south of the country with about 450,000 people. There is a famous castle and a very old university. Every year there is an important theatre and music festival in Edinburgh.

Edinburgh Castle

2   Where's the castle? | listening; speaking |

Edinburgh Festival

Listen to the conversations. Find the places on the map.

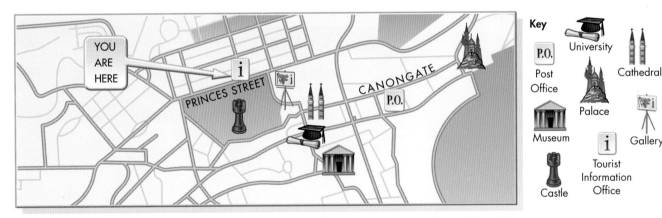

Key

P.O. Post Office

University

Cathedral

Museum

Palace

i Tourist Information Office

i Gallery

Castle

Work in pairs. Ask about more places in Edinburgh. Make conversations, like this:

A: *Excuse me, where's the castle?*
B: *It's near the cathedral.*
A: *Thanks very much.*
B: *You're welcome.*

Ask your partner about places in one of these:

– his or her home town or city;
– the capital city of her or his country;
– another town or city she or he knows well;
– a famous old town or city in her or his country.

Warm-up

This first set of activities starts by looking at the British Isles, then focuses on Edinburgh. Before the class looks at the book, find out how much they know about Britain. Here are a few questions you could ask, in the learners' own language if appropriate.

What countries are there in the United Kingdom?
[England, Scotland, Wales, Northern Ireland]
What are the capitals of these countries?
[London, Edinburgh, Cardiff, Belfast]

Draw a quick sketch map of the British Isles on the board and ask individuals to mark where they think the four countries and their capitals are.

1 Geography

Suggested steps

Learners open their books and look at the map. Check that they understand and can say *north, south, east, west*, then elicit sentences from the box.

Possible answers:

Edinburgh is	*in the north of Britain / in the south of Scotland.*
	the capital of Scotland.
London is	*in the south of England/Britain.*
	the capital of England.
Cardiff is	*in the south of Wales / in the west of Britain.*
	the capital of Wales.
Belfast is	*in the west of Northern Ireland.*
	the capital of Northern Ireland.

> ### Language Points
>
> 1. Don't confuse **in** *the north/south of*, etc. with **to** *the north/south of* or *north/south of*.
>   **in** *the south of Scotland* = in the southern part of Scotland
>   **to** *the south of Scotland and south of Scotland* = outside Scotland in a southerly direction
> 2. Point out, if you wish, that it is possible to say *in the south-east, north-west*, etc.

Elicit from the class everything they know about Edinburgh and note ideas on the board. Start by asking about the photographs of the castle and the Edinburgh Festival.

Learners now read the short text to check whether it includes any of their suggestions. Ask questions based on the text.

Examples:

> *Is Edinburgh the capital of Britain?*
> *Is it in the north of Scotland?*
> *Is there an old university in Edinburgh?*
> *Are there a million people in Edinburgh?* etc.

2 Where's the castle? ▭

Suggested steps

Before learners listen to the recording, give them time to look at the plan of Edinburgh and get them to say some of the names on it, especially *Princes Street* and *Canongate*.

Play the recording, once or twice, as necessary. Learners find the places on the plan as they hear them.

Tapescript

1. A: Where's the castle?
   B: Here's a map of the city centre. We're here ... in Princes Street ... and there's the castle.
   A: Oh, yes. And there's the cathedral.
   B: They're very near.
   A: Great!
2. A: Excuse me. Where's the university?
   B: It's near the museum. Here.
   A: Thanks very much.
   B: You're welcome.
3. A: How can I help you?
   B: Is there a post office near here?
   A: Yes, there's one in Canongate.
   B: Thanks.

Before learners make their own conversations, give the class the chance to practise by getting them to repeat after you the conversation in their books.

First of all, they should ask each other about more places in Edinburgh, then move on to talking about their own town/s.

Option

Other town plans could be used for more authentic conversations.

3 In conversation 🔲

The focus now moves from Edinburgh to Dublin, as learners hear someone talking about their holiday photographs.

Suggested steps

Before playing the recording, ask: *What's this?* questions about the three photos. Don't give the answers yet. Explain the matching task and play the recording for the first time. Play again if necessary. Check answers.

Answer key

Conversation 1 = Picture B
Conversation 2 = Picture C
Conversation 3 = Picture A

Point out that Dublin is the capital of the Republic of Ireland (Eire / Southern Ireland).

The class listens to another version of the recording which has gaps instead of B's words. They read B's words from the complete conversations in their books. Insist that learners sound interested when they say these expressions: *Really? / Is it really? / That's interesting.*

Repeat this task until learners' language sounds natural. Learners now work in pairs. They take it in turns to tell each other about places in their towns. The partner being told should show interest.

Quick Check
Answer key

A
1. A: Where's
   B: It's
   A: very
   B: You're
2. A: help
   B: Is; here
   A: there's
3. B: old
   A: years
   B: it

B
1. in; of   2. near   3. in   4. of   5. in; of

C
1. castle   *cathedral, theatre*
2. city   *country, town*
3. east   *south, north*
4. famous   *important, interesting*
5. hundred   *thousand, million*

Personal Study Workbook

4: showing interest
7: reading; vocabulary
8: questionnaire
9: listening and speaking
10: pronunciation
11: visual dictionary

3 In conversation | showing interest |

A 📼 Listen and read. Match the right photograph.

1. A: Here are my holiday photos.
   B: Thanks. Where's this?
   A: It's Dublin.
   B: Is it a big city?
   A: Yes, it is, there are over a million people.
   B: Really? That's very big.

2. A: And that's St Patrick's Cathedral.
   B: How old is it?
   A: It's about eight hundred years old.
   B: Is it really?

3. A: This is a good photo.
   B: Is it a castle?
   A: Yes, it's Dublin Castle.
   B: Is it very old?
   A: No, it's only about two hundred years old.
   B: That's interesting.

A

B

C

B 📼 Listen again. A is on the cassette. You are B. Say B's words.

Do this role play.

Partner A: Tell another person about a place in your town.

Partner B: Answer with *Really?/Is it really?/That's interesting*.

Change roles.

✔ Quick Check

A   Fill in the missing words.

1. A: .... the cathedral?
   B: .... in Queen Street.
   A: Thanks .... much.
   B: .... welcome.

2. A: Can I .... you?
   B: Yes. .... there a bank near .... ?
   A: Yes, ... one near the tourist office.

3. A: Here's a photo of my university.
   B: How .... is it?
   A: It's about 600 .... old.
   B: Is .... really?

B Write one of these words in the gaps.

in   near   of

1. Milan is .... the north .... Italy.
2. The castle is .... the cathedral.
3. There's a bank .... Oxford Street.
4. This is a photograph .... my house.
5. London is .... the south .... England.

C Put these words into five groups of three.

castle cathedral city country east famous
hundred important interesting million
north   south   theatre   thousand   town

Here are the first words in each group:

1. castle   2. city   3. east   4. famous   5. hundred

PERSONAL STUDY WORKBOOK

- vocabulary of towns and public buildings
- a listening exercise about how old places are
- a reading text about Edinburgh
- asking and saying where places in a town are
- pronunciation work
- visual dictionary – the city
- reading – episode 4 of *Lost in time*

REVIEW OF UNIT 2

1 Postcards ⏐ reading; writing ⏐

This is a holiday postcard to a good friend.
Fill in the gaps.

Now write the address of your friend on
the postcard.

Hi ....,
How .... you? I'm ....
France. My hotel .... in
the centre .... Paris. It's
.... beautiful city.
My room is .... the second
floor.
......'.. small but it's .... nice.

See you soon.
Bye.

2 Offices ⏐ numbers; speaking ⏐

Where are these places in the office? Write the floors and
the room numbers in the gaps. Don't show other people!

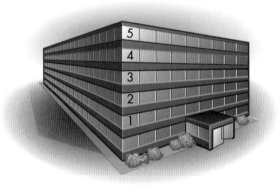

Restaurant	.... floor	Room	....
Conference room	.... floor	Room	....
Computer room	.... floor	Room	....
Manager's office	.... floor	Room	....
Coffee bar	.... floor	Room	....

Ask your partner questions about his or her office.

Example: A: *Is the conference room on the first floor?* B: *No, it isn't. It's on the second floor.*
            A: *What number is it?* B: *It's number 207.*
Now write about a building you know well. For example:

– an office; – a big shop; – a school or college.

REVIEW OF UNIT 3

1 My wife is Japanese ⏐ *my, his, her, its, our, their* ⏐

Write *my*, *her*, *his*, *its*, *our*, *your* or *their* in the spaces.

1. They are American and .... car is American.
2. We are Spanish, and .... colleagues are Spanish.
3. Our cat is nice, and .... name is Tiddles.
4. Maria is twentyish and .... husband is sixty.
5. I'm married and .... wife is Japanese.
6. Juan is nice and .... wife, Almudena, is great.

2 Friends and colleagues ⏐ *his, her, my, their*; speaking ⏐

Write the names:

1. a colleague   ....
   his/her wife/husband ....
   Their flat/house is in .... (place)

2. a friend   ....
   his/her wife/husband ....
   Their flat/house is in .... (place)

Talk in groups, like this:
A: *My friend, Jacques, is nice. His wife, Alice, is English. Their flat is in* ....
      What about your friend?
B: *My friend, Britte, is great. Her husband, Jurgen, is an interesting man. Their house is in*

....

REVIEW OF UNIT 2

1 Postcards

Suggested steps

Check that learners understand the task and give them about five minutes to complete the postcard.

Now get pairs to exchange work and read each other's postcards. Partners could suggest corrections.

Answer key

Completed postcard:
  Hi **Pete**,
  How **are** you? I'm **in** France. My
  hotel **is** in the centre **of** Paris.
  It's **a** beautiful city.
  My room is **on** the second floor.
  It's small but it's **very** nice.
  See you soon.
  Bye.

2 Offices

Suggested steps

Explain the first part of the task: learners make their own choices about where these places are in the office. They should not tell or show each other yet – this is to ensure that there is a genuine information gap in the conversations which follow.

In pairs, learners make conversations following the example in their books. They should make a written note of where the places are in their partner's office block.

Finally partners should compare facts.
This final part of the exercise could be done for homework: learners write about another multi-storey building they know.

REVIEW OF UNIT 3

1 My wife is Japanese

Answer key

1. *their* 2. *our* 3. *its* 4. *her* 5. *my* 6. *his*

2 Friends and colleagues

Point out that learners should fill the gaps with information about people they know.

Once the information has been filled in, they can tell each other in groups about colleagues and friends.

Monitor conversations and round off the activity by asking a few individuals to tell the class about colleagues and friends.

Unit 4 Worksheet

Suggested steps

Make equal numbers of the two Worksheets and give them out to the class. Each learner decides the function of the different unmarked buildings on their maps; e.g. *bank, restaurant* etc. Make it clear that they can only use ten of the words in the list. This is intended to ensure that, when they are asked questions about the buildings in their towns, learners will have practice in three different answer forms:
• *There aren't any* + plural noun
• *There's one* + singular noun
• *There are two/three* + plural noun.

Learners then work in pairs and ask each other questions about their towns. They note their answers in the table.

If you wish, you could round off this activity with the whole class by asking learners questions about their partner's towns.

Example:
Teacher: *Are there any cinemas in Maria's town?*
Paloma: *Yes, there are two cinemas in her town.*

2 How big is their family?

listening; *hasn't/haven't got*

📖 Listen and write the numbers of brothers and sisters.

	brothers	*sisters*
David's got ...	....	....
His mother's got ...	....	....
His father's got ...	....	....
Ruiko's got ...	....	....
Her mother's got ...	....	....
Her father's got ...	....	....

3 Have you got a big family?

How many? Have you got ...? writing; speaking

Write numbers for your family or a family you know.

I've got .... brothers and .... sisters.

My mother's got .... sisters and .... brothers.

My father's got .... sisters and .... brothers.

Find out about families in your class.

Ask two people about their families, like this:

Have you got a big family?
How many brothers and sisters have you got?
How many brothers and sisters have your parents got?

Tell the class about the two people, like this:

Silvia's got a big family. She's got one brother and three sisters. Her mother's got ... and ..., and her father's got ... and ....

Mario hasn't got a big family. He's got no brothers or sisters. His mother's got a sister and his father's got a brother.

HELP	In your language?
My friend's got ...	....
twin brother/sister	....
an only child	....

✔ Quick Check

A Circle *yes* or *no*.

1. she's got = she is got — Y/N
2. I have got = I've got — Y/N
3. twenty-one = three × seven — Y/N
4. the son of your mother = your brother — Y/N
5. your father = the husband of your sister — Y/N

B Complete the answers.

1. Have you got any brothers? Yes, I ....
2. Has she got a sister? No, ... hasn't.
3. Have they got a father? Yes, ...

   ....

4. Has it got a window? No, it ....

C Write the family members under *Women* or *Men*.

sister   father   brother   wife   mother
husband   son   daughter

---

2 How big is their family?

Suggested steps

Establish the listening task. The learners will hear two people talking about their families. They have to write the number of brothers and sisters each has.

If your class is still finding it difficult to listen with confidence, play each part of the recording separately and check answers each time by asking: *How many brothers has David got / his mother got / his father got?*

Tapescript

RUIKO: Where are you from, David?

DAVID: I'm from New Zealand.

RUIKO: Is your family a big one?

DAVID: Mmm ... quite big.

RUIKO: Have you got any brothers and sisters?

DAVID: I've got two brothers and three sisters.

RUIKO: What about your mother and father? Have they got brothers and sisters?

DAVID: Mmm. My mother's got two brothers, but she hasn't got any sisters, and my father's got three sisters and a brother.

RUIKO: That's quite a lot.

DAVID: Mm. What about you, Ruiko?

RUIKO: I'm Japanese. I've got one brother.

DAVID: Have you got any sisters?

RUIKO: No, I haven't. My father's got a sister.

DAVID: What about your mother?

RUIKO: My mother hasn't got any sisters, but she's got a brother.

DAVID: That's a small family.

RUIKO: Mmm, it is.

> ### Language Point
> There will probably be confusion with the form ...'s got. Some learners will think that *He's got* (*He has got*) is short for *He is got*. It might be worth putting up a chart on a wall to show contracted forms and the distinction between *is* and *has* forms when contracted to *'s*.

Answer key

David's got ...	2 brothers and 3 sisters
His mother's got ...	2 brothers and no sisters
His father's got ...	3 sisters and 1 brother
Ruiko's got ...	1 brother
Her father's got ...	1 sister
Her mother's got ...	1 brother

3 Have you got a big family?

Suggested steps

This is a natural personalised progression from the previous input, giving learners the chance to talk about their own families. Ask learners to write in numbers as words for their own family members using the gapped sentences.

The finding-out task could be done by getting learners to walk around the class if that is practical, otherwise put learners in groups of four or five. Model the question forms so that learners can ask them fluently and with appropriate intonation. Model possible responses. Draw attention to the Help box for any learners who are either twins or only children. Monitor the groups and give encouragement.

Ask members of each group to report on the two people they questioned. Note that the form *any* as in: *Maria hasn't got any brothers* is in the listening in Exercise 2 but has not yet been presented in written form. You might model it at this stage if that is manageable for your learners.

Quick Check
Answer key

A

1. No 2. Yes 3. Yes 4. Yes 5. No

B

1. Yes, I have. 2. No, she hasn't. 3. Yes, they have.

4. No, it hasn't.

C

Women: sister; wife; mother; daughter

Men: father; brother; husband; son

Personal Study Workbook

1: *have got*

8: questions with *have / has got*

1 In conversation – headaches and envelopes ⊂⊃

Suggested steps

Use the picture to establish the context. *Ask: Is the man OK? Where are they? What's in her bag?*

Clarify the listening task. Play the recording and check the underlining.

Elicit learners' preliminary thoughts on how *some/any* are used and their meaning.

Put learners into pairs for the *some/any* exercise and rule completion.

Play the recording for learners to check answers to Conversation 2.

In the same pairs ask learners to practise one of the conversations. Model additional vocabulary items, e.g. *water, vitamin tablets, magazines and maps.*

Tapescript

B
Conversation 2
A: Have you got any envelopes?
B: There are some in your room.
A: What about postcards?
B: Sorry, we haven't got any postcards.

Answer key

No, *some* and *any* are not strong sounds.

Have you got **any** envelopes?
There are **some** in your room.
Sorry we haven't got **any** postcards.

Any is for answers with *not* and for questions.
Some is for other answers.

1   In conversation – headaches and envelopes   `some, any`

A 〔CD〕 Listen to Conversation 1 and underline *some* and *any*. Are they strong sounds?

Conversation 1

MAN: I've got a terrible headache, have you got any tablets?
WOMAN: I've got some in my bag ... Here you are.
MAN: Thanks.
WOMAN: Keep the bottle.
MAN: No, really, it's OK.
WOMAN: Go on, I've got some at home.
MAN: But I haven't got any money.
WOMAN: That's OK.

B Put *some* or *any* in the spaces in Conversation 2.

Conversation 2

A: Have you got .... envelopes?

B: There are .... in your room.

A: What about postcards?

B: Sorry, we haven't got .... postcards.

〔CD〕 Listen and check.

Write *some* or *any* in this rule.

> *Some/any* rule
>
> .... is for answers with *not*, and for questions.
>
> .... is for other answers.

Have you got words for *some* and *any* in your language?

Have Conversation 1 or 2 about:

– water

– vitamin C, B or E tablets

– magazines

– maps

2 In conversation with friends

adjectives and *see you* expressions

A Read the conversations and match pictures A, B and C with the conversations.

1. A: I'm off to bed now. I'm really tired.
   B: OK. Goodnight, sleep well.
   A: Goodnight. See you in the morning.
   (Write your line) ....

A

B

2. A: See you later, then.
   B: What time?
   A: Oh, about seven.
   Write your line) ....
   ....

3. A: Are you happy here?
   B: Mmm, it's a really good flat.
   A: Is that one of your pictures?
   B: Mmm.
   A: The colours are lovely.
   (Write your line) ....

C

📼 Choose one of the conversations and listen to it. With a partner, write one final line of conversation, then practise the conversation.

B 📼 Listen to the final lines on the recording.

✔ Quick Check

A Write *some* or *any*.

1. Have you got .... tablets?

   No, sorry I haven't got ....

   Karin's got ....

2. I've got .... friends in Turkey.

3. Have they got .... pictures on the wall?

   Yes, they've got .... in the living room.

B Write different expressions after *See you*.

1. Bye. See you ....

2. Goodnight See you in the ....

C Write the words under the correct face.

happy   headache   tired   good
terrible   lovely

....

....

....

PERSONAL STUDY WORKBOOK

- *have got*; *some/any* practice
- reading and writing accommodation ads
- colour vocabulary
- visual dictionary – rooms and family
- reading – episode 5 of *Lost in time*

---

2 In conversation with friends

Suggested steps

Put learners into pairs and ask them to read the three conversations quietly, and match each with a picture A, B, C.

Check the answers and then allocate one of the conversations to each pair.

Tell each pair to listen to their conversation and then to think of a final line.

Play all three conversations. Circulate and help pairs.

Play the recording with the final lines.

Tapescript

B
1. A: I'm off to bed now ... I'm really tired.
   B: OK. Good night, sleep well.
   A: Good night. See you in the morning.
   B: Yeah see you tomorrow.
2. A: See you later, then.
   B: What time?
   A: Oh about seven.
   B: OK ... See you.
3. A: Are you happy here?
   B: Mmm it's a really good flat.
   A: Is that one of your pictures?
   B: Mmm.
   A: The colours are lovely.
   B: Yes, I'm really pleased with it.

Answer key

Conversation 1: C
Conversation 2: B
Conversation 3: A

Quick Check

Answer key

A
1. any; any; some   2. some   3 any; some
B
later; morning
C
happy; good; lovely
headache; tired; terrible

Personal Study Workbook

4: vocabulary
9: visual dictionary

DON'T FORGET YOUR SUNGLASSES

Language focus:	Vocabulary:
imperative forms	holidays and travel
prepositions (*to, for, in, on, under, by*)	countries and places
	days of the week

A HAVE A HOLIDAY

1 Holiday ads   `vocabulary: nationalities`

Look quickly at the ads for holidays and write the countries next to the nationalities.

BRAZIL
Holidays in Brazil
for less than you think!
**Call us now and get your
ticket to paradise**

Special Offer
A WEEK IN HUNGARY
*Includes air
travel, hotels* **£220**

SCANDITOURS
Travel to Norway and have
the holiday of a lifetime!
Departures
August 4, 11, 18, 25   £295
September 1, 18, 15   £240

BEAUTIFUL TURKEY
Seven nights from £350
*Come to Turkey
this summer*
GO travel

USA
Visit the USA this year.
✗ Coach tours around the States
✗ Visit fabulous San Francisco and
see the beautiful scenery of
Yosemite National Park.
✗ Take a helicopter flight over the
Grand Canyon.

Call Windward Travel on 0171 360 1111

**Come to Greece,
home of the sun**
Return flights from London and Manchester
CALL NOW ON 0161 474 7555

FRANCE
*Self-catering holidays in
the beautiful Loire Valley*
**Call us now on
0181 5437 6000.**

EGYPT
Fly to Egypt this autumn and
visit the land of the pharaohs!
From £186 return

MEDICI TRAVEL
Holidays in Italy from £350
Call 0171 636 1551

Country	*Nationality*
....	Norwegian
....	American
....	Turkish
....	Brazilian
....	Greek
....	French
....	Hungarian
....	Italian
....	Egyptian

DON'T FORGET YOUR SUNGLASSES

This unit gives learners exposure to imperative forms around the theme of travel and holidays. In Lesson A advertisements are used as a realistic context for the introduction of imperatives. Lesson B takes cities, countries and nationalities as its themes and has a special focus on listening skills. Lesson C introduces prepositions of place in the context of furniture in hotel rooms.

This unit is an active one with plenty of opportunity for manageable speaking, listening and writing tasks.

A HAVE A HOLIDAY

1 Holiday ads

Warm-up

Use magazine pictures of famous people or people in national costume to elicit the nationalities that are mentioned in this activity. Write the nationalities on pieces of card, hand out the magazine pictures and ask learners to match them. Real objects associated with the different nationalities could be used, if available, instead of pictures.

Suggested steps

Let learners work in pairs if this is convenient; one learner writes the countries.

Practise pronunciation of the countries and nationalities by asking: *What nationality is a person from* Norway? etc. Monitor word stress and elicit appropriate stress by silent correction, perhaps using a different finger for each syllable and pointing to the finger (syllable) with the main stress.

Option

To make it more interesting you can try naming key cities in the countries, e.g. *What nationality is a person from Oslo? (Ankara, New York,* etc.)

Answer key

Norway; USA; Turkey; Brazil; Greece; France; Hungary; Italy; Egypt

2 Radio ad 📼

Suggested steps

Explain the meaning of *ad* (short for *advertisement* and *advert*). Ask for examples of simple adverts or jingles in their own language (preferably ones with imperative forms).

Use the illustrated part of the gapped advert to elicit answers about Brazil: *Is Brazil nice? big? good for holidays?*

Let learners look at lists A and B. They can use a dictionary to clarify the meanings. Explain that the imperative in advertising is like a direct form of persuasion to do something.

Encourage learners to guess the possible matches and to call out their guesses.

Clarify the listening task and play the recording. Check the answers; play the recording again with no task.

Tapescript

A
DJ: OK, OK we've got some great holidays for you. Come to Italy, yes, beautiful Italy, and have a great, great time. Fly Qantas, a top airline, and stay at the Sheraton Hotel in wonderful Rome. 500 dollars, yes, 500 dollars. Tell your friends, tell your manager, tell the cat!
Or go to Greece, mmmmmm, lovely Athens. Call International Tours today on 0182 55683. See you later!

B
DJ: Come to Brazil for 10 days for 2,000 dollars. Fly Air New Zealand. Stay at the Excelsior Hotel in beautiful Bahia. Call Cheap Travel on 303 67819 today!

Ask the learners, perhaps in pairs to complete the advert in the book. This will act as a check on their understanding of the meaning of some of the imperatives.

Check the answers by playing the recording and clarify any vocabulary, e.g. *cheap, today*.

Note: there are alternative answers for parts of the advert, e.g. *Come/Fly/Go to Brazil ... .*

Answer key

Come to Italy
Go to Greece
Stay at the Sheraton Hotel
Call International Tours
Tell your friends
Have a great time
Fly Qantas

3 Your holiday advert

Suggested steps

This activity is a natural development of the previous two.

Check understanding of the adjectives in the box by asking and eliciting questions: *Is Paris nice? dirty? Is Brazil wonderful? Is 'wonderful' a nice word or not very nice?*

Practise pronunciation by asking learners to say: *It's beautiful; it's wonderful/awful*, etc. Demonstrate the main stressed syllable. Build a chant, like this: *Is Norway nice? It's wonderful. What about Greece? It's beautiful. And Brazil? It's lovely.*

Model an advert for a place in your country. You might prepare one on a transparency before class and use an OHP (overhead projector) to let learners guess the advert as you reveal it bit by bit.

Let the learners write their own adverts; circulate and encourage.

Option

Divide the class into two halves; one half writes a positive advert, the other writes a negative advert for the same place. Make sure that the negative imperative is clear to the half writing the negative advert, e.g. *Don't go to ...; don't stay at ... .* Put learners in pairs to read their adverts to each other. Ask for one or two to be read aloud to the whole class.

Answer key

+ beautiful; wonderful; lovely − awful; terrible; dirty

Quick Check
Answer key

A 1. first picture   2. second picture   3. second picture
B 1. at   2 to   3. to   4. 's (is)   5. a

Personal Study Workbook

1: vocabulary: adjectives
2: imperatives

2 Radio ad | speaking; listening for imperative forms

A Listen to the ads and match *A* and *B*.

A	*B*
Come	at the Sheraton Hotel
Go	International Tours
Stay	a great time
Call	Qantas
Tell	to Italy
Have	your friends
Fly	to Greece

B Choose verbs from *A* to complete this ad.

 Listen and check.

TO ~~BRAZIL~~ FOR 10 DAYS FOR 2,000 DOLLARS.

.... **Air New Zealand.**

.... **at the Excelsior Hotel in beautiful Bahia.**

.... **Cheap Travel on**
303 67819 today!

3 Your holiday advert | adjectives; writing and speaking

Put the words in the box into two lists.

beautiful   wonderful   awful   lovely   terrible   dirty

+ (nice)   − (not very nice)

....

....

....

Say the words in the lists in this sentence: *It's (wonderful)!*

Write a simple advert for a holiday in your country.
Write a nice advert or a not very nice advert.
Read your advert to a partner.

 **Quick Check**

A Tick the right picture.

1. Call Cheap Travel today.   2. Fly Air Lanka.   3. Tell your friends.

B Put in the missing word.

1. Stay ____ the Sheraton hotel.   3. Go ____ New Zealand.   5. Have ____ great time.
2. Come ____ beautiful France.   4. It ____ wonderful!

1 Favourite cities | listening and discussion |

⚏ Listen. Which two cities in the box are not in the conversation?

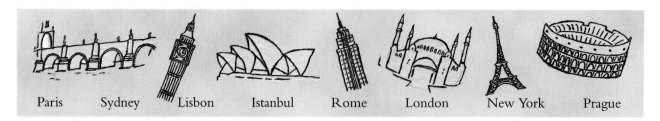

Paris   Sydney   Lisbon   Istanbul   Rome   London   New York   Prague

Write three of your favourite cities.

1 ....   2 ....   3 ....

Talk about your favourite cities with expressions from boxes A(djectives) and N(ouns).

A

| beautiful   busy   popular modern   famous   interesting old   fantastic   lovely   great |

N

| restaurants   buildings   beer shops   parks   museums universities |

Example: *My favourite city is Rome. It's a beautiful old city with lovely buildings and interesting museums. Copenhagen is also a favourite. It's got some interesting, modern buildings, great beer and some nice shops.*

2 Go to Oslo in November? | dual listening; *don't go* |

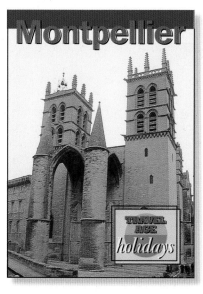

Where are the two cities on the brochures?

⚏ ⚏ Listen to two people – one is a travel agent. Write the names of the four countries in their conversation.

COUNTRIES: Brazil   Spain (Catalonia)   Slovakia   Greece   Turkey
France   Norway

1. ....   2. ....   3. ....   4. ....

B TOURS TO CITIES AND COUNTRIES

1 Favourite cities 〇〇

Suggested steps

Use the pictures in the box to elicit the names of the cities. *Where's this?* (pointing to Big Ben) *Yes, London, good.*

Clarify the listening task; two cities in the box are not on the recording.

Pre-teach *favourite* if necessary (your 'number 1' place, or top three *places*).

Play the recording right through. Check the names of the missing cities.

Tapescript

A: My favourite cities are Rome, er, Paris and Prague.
B: Why Prague?
A: Prague is very beautiful – it's got lots of old buildings.
B: Mm, you're right.
A: What about you? What are your favourite cities?
B: Er, New York ... er ... Istanbul and Sydney.
A: Why Sydney? Is it nice there?
B: Yes, it's a beautiful city and there are lots of good restaurants.

Ask learners to write their three favourite cities; give your own examples first, if necessary.

Talk about your favourite cities using words from the boxes. Write up some of the things you said to clarify forms. Check understanding and pronunciation of other words in the adjective and noun boxes.

Put learners into groups of three to talk about their favourite cities.

Circulate, monitor and encourage learners.

Answer key

Lisbon; London

2 Go to Oslo in November? 〇〇 〇〇

Suggested steps

Identify the cities in the brochures, using the pictures. Extend the questioning to recycle vocabulary: *Is it in France? Is it nice? Is it busy?* etc.

Clarify the first listening task. Learners listen for four of the countries from the seven in the book.

Let learners check their answers in pairs.

Clarify the second listening task. Learners listen for the imperative forms and choose a or b.

Again, let the same pairs compare answers.

Use the second recording as a reinforcement: learners listen and try to find additional information, e.g. La Sagrada Familia.

Tapescript

Version 1

CUSTOMER: Hello.
TRAVEL AGENT: Morning. Can I help you?
CUSTOMER: I'm not sure. Have you got any information on holidays in France?
TRAVEL AGENT: France, erm, hang on, yes ... how about Montpellier?
CUSTOMER: Mmm, Where is it?
TRAVEL AGENT: In the south of France. It's nice.
CUSTOMER: Is it? Mm, er, I'm not sure.
TRAVEL AGENT: OK. Er, how about Greece? Have a look at this brochure of Athens.
CUSTOMER: OK. Thanks. Mm, interesting. What about Oslo?
TRAVEL AGENT: Oh, don't go to Oslo this month – Norway's so cold.
CUSTOMER: Oh, is it? OK. What about Barcelona?
TRAVEL AGENT: One minute, please. John?
JOHN: Yes?
TRAVEL AGENT: Get me that new brochure on Spain and Catalonia, please.
JOHN: OK.
TRAVEL AGENT: Thanks. Here you are ... .
CUSTOMER: Thanks. Mmm ... interesting buildings ... mm nice shops and restaurants.
TRAVEL AGENT: Yes, it's a great city. Take the brochure and read it at home.
CUSTOMER: OK, thanks. Er, what about ... .

Version 2

TRAVEL AGENT: Hi, can I help you?
CUSTOMER: Hello. Yes, I'm interested in holidays in Europe.
TRAVEL AGENT: Which countries are you interested in?
CUSTOMER: I'm not sure ... France, I think.
TRAVEL AGENT: What about a short holiday in Montpellier?
CUSTOMER: Mmm, where is it?
TRAVEL AGENT: In the south of France. It's nice.
CUSTOMER: Have you got a brochure?
TRAVEL AGENT: Montpellier, erm, hang on a minute, erm, yes, here we are. Look at the pictures in this brochure of the South of France.
CUSTOMER: Mm, lots of old buildings, and near the sea.
TRAVEL AGENT: How about Greece? Have a look at this brochure of Athens.
CUSTOMER: Mmm, lovely. Is that the Parthenon?
TRAVEL AGENT: Yeah that's it.
CUSTOMER: Er, what about Oslo?
TRAVEL AGENT: Oh don't go to Oslo this month – it's so cold in Norway in November.
CUSTOMER: Oh, is it? OK. What about Barcelona, then?
TRAVEL AGENT: Wait a minute, please. John?
JOHN: Uh huh.
TRAVEL AGENT: Get me that new brochure on Spain and Catalonia, please, it's on Jill's table.
JOHN: Yeah, OK.
TRAVEL AGENT: Thanks. Here you are.

CUSTOMER:	Mmm, interesting buildings. Look at this cathedral.
TRAVEL AGENT:	Yes, it's Gaudi's La Sagrada Familia. Take the brochure and read it at home.
CUSTOMER:	That's great. Thanks a lot ... .

Option

Divide the class into two halves. One half listens to one recording; the other half listens to the other recording. Then learners form pairs, one member from each half. They have to find two differences between the information in the recordings.

Answer key

Montpellier; Oslo
France; Greece; Norway; Spain (Catalonia)
1. a   2. b   3. b

3 Plan a tour 🔲

Suggested steps

Warm-up

Ask learners to write down three cities that are interesting and new to them. Let them walk around the room and find out which cities are the top three in the class.

Use the tour planner to establish the context for the task. Elicit the following language: *What is a tour? Is the tour long? What is a guest?*

Ask them to think of one new thing for the *Don't forget* list. Use the recorded example to model the task. Ask learners to listen with their books closed and to remember the guest, the three cities, and the new *Don't forget* item.

Let learners check answers in pairs.

You might spend a little time looking at the use of the prepositions *to, for* and *in*, as the learners will need to use these when they talk about their tour.

It might be good to let them plan their tour in pairs. When pairs are ready, form groups of four (two pairs) for exchange of tour information.

Circulate, monitor and encourage the learners.

Quick Check
Answer key

A 1. to; for   2. for   3. to; for; for
B Turkish;   Irish;   American;   Greek;   English

Personal Study Workbook

3: reading
4: writing

📼 Listen again. Is it a or b? Tick the correct boxes.

1. a. Have a look at this brochure of Athens. ☐
   b. Don't have a look at this brochure of Athens. ☐
2. a. Go to Oslo. ☐
   b. Don't go to Oslo. ☐
3. a. Don't take the brochure and read it at home. ☐
   b. Take the brochure and read it at home. ☐

3 Plan a tour | speaking: imperative forms; prepositions *to* and *for* |

Read the example. Write in three cities for a one-week tour. Add things to the *Don't forget* list.

📼 Listen to the example.

Example: A: *This is my tour. My guest is Mel Gibson. Day 1, fly to Dublin in Ireland and stay for two nights. Day 3, fly to Edinburgh in Scotland; stay for one night. Day 4, fly to Florence in Italy for three nights and fly home Day 7. What about you?*
B: *What about your 'Don't forget' list?*
A: *Oh, yes, don't forget your money and your camera … and your husband!*

Talk about your tour.

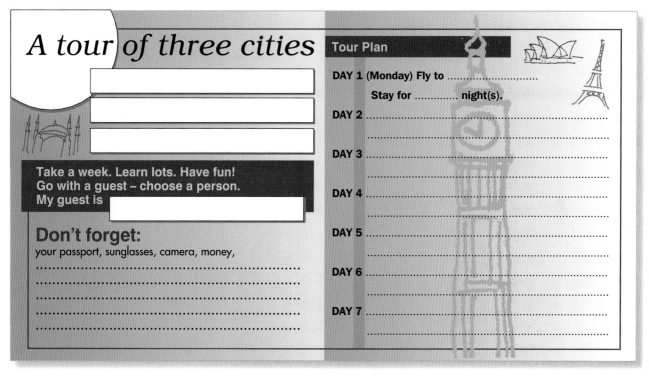

A tour of three cities

Take a week. Learn lots. Have fun!
Go with a guest – choose a person.
My guest is

Don't forget:
your passport, sunglasses, camera, money,
....
....
....

Tour Plan

DAY 1 (Monday) Fly to ....
          Stay for .... night(s).
DAY 2 ....
          ....
DAY 3 ....
          ....
DAY 4 ....
          ....
DAY 5 ....
          ....
DAY 6 ....
          ....
DAY 7 ....
          ....

✔ Quick Check

A Write *to* or *for* in the spaces.

1. Go .... London .... two nights.
2. Stay .... one night in Singapore.
3. Don't go .... London .... three nights.
   Go .... a week!

B Complete the nationalities.

Countries	Nationalities
Turkey	....
Ireland	....
USA	....
Greece	....
England	....

1 Today's Monday   vocabulary: days of the week

A Look at the days in this month. Say the days after Sunday.

Thursday   Saturday   Friday   Monday   Tuesday
Sunday   Wednesday

S	M	Tu	W	T	F	Sa
	1	2	3	4	5	6
7	8	9	10	11	12	13
14	15	16	17	18	19	20
21	22	23	24	25	26	27
28	29	30				

Listen and check.

B Listen to the examples.

Examples:
1. A: *What day is it today?*
   B: *Thursday.*
2. A: *What day is it tomorrow?*
   B: *Friday.*
3. A: *What day is the 8th?*
   B: *Monday.*

Ask and answer two questions.

HELP	In your language?
weekend	....

2 Don't forget the tickets   vocabulary; writing notes

Match a picture with a day of the week in the note.

B: ....

A: ....

NOTE
Don't forget!
Monday   Get tickets for the holiday
Tuesday
Wednesday   Buy a film for the camera
Thursday
Friday   Go to the bank
Saturday   Phone Mum and Dad
Sunday   Restaurant 6 pm

C: ....

E: ....   D: ....

Read the note. Write a note for one or two days of *your* week.

1 Today's Monday ▭

Suggested steps

Put learners in pairs. Tell them to look at the calendar for a month and to say the days in the right order using the vocabulary box for help if necessary.

Listen to the recording. Ask learners to change their pronunciation if necessary.

Tapescript

A
Monday
Tuesday
Wednesday
Thursday
Friday
Saturday
Sunday

Elicit any changes in pronunciation of the days. Remember that the main stress is usually on the first syllable of the days, and that Wednesday is often pronounced 'Wensday'.

Play the next recording with books closed having asked learners to listen for the questions.

Elicit and write the questions on the board, drawing out the items *today* and *tomorrow*.

Model the questions again in quick practice sequences, using the calendar in the book: *What day is the fourth? What day is the tenth?* until most days have been elicited.

Let learners ask each other two questions in pairs.

Option

Divide the class into two groups.

Group 1: stick a card with one day of the week to the back of each of a maximum of seven learners.

Group 2: stick the numbers corresponding to the dates for that week, e.g. 8th, 9th, 10th, etc. on their backs. Ask learners to walk around trying to find out what is the day or number on their back by asking: *Is it Monday/Tuesday? Is it the 10th/8th?* until they have found out their day or number. Bring the groups together and ask learners to find their calendar pair.

2 Don't forget the tickets

Suggested steps

Let learners do the matching activity in pairs. Check the answers *What day is A/B?* etc.

On the board, model a note for your week, preferably recycling vocabulary.

Ask learners to write their notes on blank pieces of paper. Dictionaries might be useful if learners want to be realistic about their plans for the week.

Monitor, encourage and offer help. If notes are varied and interesting, collect them and read one or two out to see if learners can guess who wrote them.

Answer key

A Saturday; B Monday; C Friday; D Wednesday; E Sunday

3 In hotel room 512 📼

Suggested steps

It is probably a good idea to teach the four prepositions of place first. Use a real key or a drawing and position it *by, on, under* and *in* various things asking and answering: *Where's the key? It's ...* Try to elicit the correct prepositions gradually.

Open the book and practise pronunciation of the labelled items. Use flash cards to consolidate.

Put learners in pairs to practise the questions/answers with the four illustrations of the hotel room.

> **Language Point**
>
> Remember it is more natural to respond to questions like *Where's the key?* with just *By the phone* rather than *The key is by the phone.* For this reason do not always insist on the full sentence response even though it does practise more words and subject–verb order.

Use the next picture of the hotel room to teach additional vocabulary *safe, wardrobe* and to recycle other items. Ask: *What's in the room?*

In the same pairs, learners can ask and answer the five questions, alternating as questioner and responder. Monitor and assist.

Clarify the listening task. There are some things in the room mentioned on the recording that are different from what is shown in the picture.

Let learners listen and then check with their partner.

Tapescript

A: What room are you in?

B: 512.

A: Is it nice?

B: It's OK. The bed's pretty big and there's a telephone on a little old table by the door and a ... er there's a little safe in the wardrobe. There's a lamp by the window and a big old chair under the window. There's an interesting picture by the door, I think. It's a big photo of a king and queen. It's pretty old.

Put learners in groups for the final personalised question and answer practice if this is practicable. Practise the expressions in the Help box before they talk in groups.

Monitor and encourage the learners. Make a note of any points that need further practice.

Answer key

Where's the phone?	It's **on** the table **by** the door.
Where's the lamp?	It's **by** the bed.
Where's the book?	It's **on** the chair.
Where's the bin?	It's **under** the window.
Where's the safe?	It's **in** the wardrobe.

The lamp is not by the window, it's by the bed.
The picture is not by the door, it's by the bed.
The picture is not a photo of a king and queen.
The chair is not old.
The table is not old.

3 In hotel room number 512
prepositions of place; vocabulary: furniture

Look at these things.

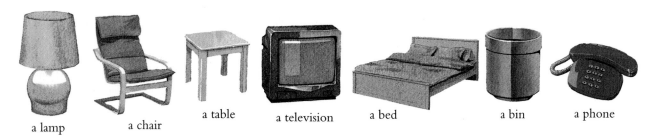

a lamp   a chair   a table   a television   a bed   a bin   a phone

Look at these pictures and answer the question *Where's the room key?*

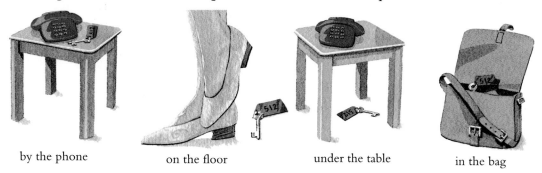

by the phone   on the floor   under the table   in the bag

Example: *Where's the room key?*
By the phone. (The key is by the phone.)

What's in the hotel room? Ask and answer the questions.

safe

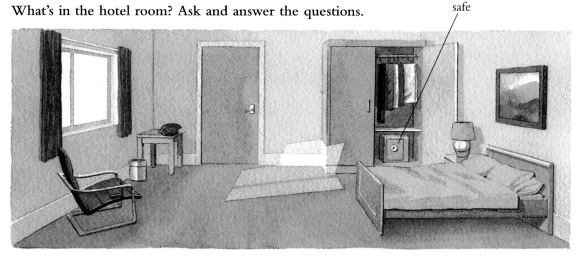

Where's the phone?
.... the table, ... the door.

Where's the lamp?
.... the bed.

Where's the book?
.... the chair.

Where's the bin?
.... the window.

Where's the safe?
.... the wardrobe.

Listen to a conversation about room 512. Some things are different. What are two different things?

1. ....   2. ....

Where are these things in your bedroom? Ask and answer the questions.

1. Where's the bin?
2. Where's the lamp?
3. Where's the chair?
4. Where are your books?

HELP	In your language?
There aren't any books in my bedroom.	....
There isn't a bin.	....
bedside table	....

4 In conversation

conversation practice

🎧 **Listen and read.**

ARNE: Come on Sunday, about nine. Is that OK?
ERICA: Yeah, that's fine.
ARNE: Don't forget your CDs.
ERICA: No, OK.
ARNE: See you on Sunday evening then.
ERICA: Yeah, see you. Bye.
ARNE: Bye.

1. Are there strong sounds on these words in the conversation?

Sunday	Y/N	on	Y/N
nine	Y/N	your	Y/N
CDs	Y/N	then	Y/N

2. Say *Yeah, that's fine* and *Yeah, see you. Bye* in your language.

Practise the same conversation in English. Change these things:

the day (not Sunday: *Thursday, Friday, Saturday*)
the time (not nine: *seven, eight, ten*)
the thing (not CDs: *photos, videos*)

✔ Quick Check

A Is it a or b? In spoken English, are strong sounds often on:

a. little words like *are*, *in*, *at* and *the*?
or
b. words for things, times, days and other information words?

B Write the words in these sentences in the right order.

1. bin under table is The the.
2. The by is door lamp the.
3. book your on Put table the.
4. bag my sunglasses in are Your.
5. put door Don't by bag your the.

C Answer the questions.

1. How many days are there in a week?

....

2. Which days start with T?

Thursday and ....

3. Which days start with S?

Saturday and ....

4. What are the three other days?

Monday, ... and ....

PERSONAL STUDY WORKBOOK

- vocabulary – adjectives; days of the week
- reading – travelling in London
- prepositions
- visual dictionary – hotel room and furniture and travel items
- reading – episode 6 of *Lost in time*

4 In conversation ⊡

Suggested steps

Ask learners to read the conversation and to answer the question: *Are they friends?* This will establish the relationship between the speakers. Ask them also to guess what the conversation is about generally (a party perhaps, a dinner at Arne's house).

Play the recording with a task to check the presence or absence of strong sounds on the listed words.

Check answers in pairs.

In the same pairs ask learners to practise the conversation. Model the changed elements (day, time, thing) using another learner to be the voice of Erica.

Monitor and encourage learners.

Answer key

Sunday – yes;   Nine – yes;   CDs – yes;   on – No; your – No;   then – No

Quick Check

Answer key

A
b
B
1. The bin is under the table.
2. The lamp is by the door.
3. Put your book on the table.
4. Your sunglasses are in my bag.
5. Don't put your bag by the door.
C
1. Seven   2. Tuesday; Thursday   3. Saturday; Sunday
4. Monday; Wednesday; Friday

Personal Study Workbook

4: writing
5: prepositions
6: listening and pronunciation
7: visual dictionary

REVIEW OF UNIT 4

1 Auction 🔲

Suggested steps

Use the picture to elicit descriptions of item 1.

Establish the context (an auction) and the listening task. Learners will hear an auctioneer auctioning item 1; they have to answer the four questions.

Play the recording; let learners talk about their answers in pairs.

Play the recording again as it is quite challenging.

Tapescript

AUCTIONEER: OK. What am I bid for this beautiful French chair? About 1899, about 100 years old. Do I hear 200 dollars? 200 dollars. Thank you. 300 dollars? Yes, 300 dollars, thank you, madam.
400? Do I hear 400? It's a beautiful chair from a home in the South of France.
400, thank you, sir. At 400 ... do I hear 500? 500? Thank you, the woman in red.
600? 600? please? 600 dollars? Yes? Thank you, sir.
700, come on, it's a lovely little chair for a bedroom or living room. 700? Is that a yes? OK, thank you, madam.
OK 800? 800, yes, 800, from the floor, nine hu? ... and 900. Thank you, madam.
1,000 ... do I hear 1,000? a thousand? No? OK at 900 then, 900 it is.
900, once, twice ... sold. Item number 23, a lovely ...

If the class is not ready to take too many risks, you could be the auctioneer and invite bids for the other items.

Encourage one or two class members to be auctioneers in groups.

Monitor and encourage the learners.

Answer key

1. France   2. about 100 years old   3. a woman
4. 900 dollars

2 Where are my keys? 🔲

Suggested steps

The cards are flash cards to prompt statements of probability. The mini conversations establish the use of the picture cards and probability cards for pair practice.

Practise the weak form for *Where are ...?* to get learners used to using the schwa (ə) for pronouncing *are* in normal speed questions with *Where ...?*

Check use of prepositions *in, on*. If you have made the cards, distribute them to pairs for pair practice.

Make sure that pairs practise both answering and asking questions. (This is more interesting if you have an additional set of illustrations to recycle other vocabulary items from previous units.)

D   **REVIEW AND DEVELOPMENT**

REVIEW OF UNIT 4

1 Auction | *How old ...? numbers 100–1000; speaking; listening* |

1

2

3

Look at Number 1. Where is it from? How old is it?

Talk about Number 1 like this:

Number 1 is a beautiful/nice/lovely .... from ....
It's about .... years old.

 Listen and answer the questions.

1. Where is it from? ....
2. How old is it? ....
3. Who buys the chair?   a man? (Listen for *sir.*) ....
                          a woman? (Listen for *madam.*) ....
4. What is the final price? ....

In groups, auction numbers 2, 3 and 4.

2 Where are my keys? | *Where are ...? (weak form); perhaps; I think; speaking* |

Make three cards like this.

| *Perhaps it's/they're = 30%* | | *I think it's/they're =50%* | | *It's/they're = 100%* |

Now make cards like this.

 Listen and read. Ask and answer questions with a partner.

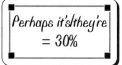 *Where are my keys?*

1. A: Where are my keys?
   B: Perhaps they're on the table.
   A: OK, thanks.

2. A: Where is my book?
   B: It's in my bag.
   A: Thanks.

3. A: Where are my tablets?
   B: I think they're on the bed.
   A: OK.

REVIEW OF UNIT 5

1 Survey   `have got; vocabulary`

Write questions about people's homes.

Write three questions about rooms: kitchen, bathroom, living room, bedroom, toilet.

Write three questions about other things: telephone, radio, television, mobile phone, computer.

Examples: *Have you got a living room?*
           How many bedrooms have you got?
           Have you got a computer in your living room?

Ask two other learners these questions. Then ask about colours.

Example: What colour is your kitchen?

Write their answers like this:

Marcia has got two bedrooms, a green bedroom and a white bedroom.

2 Who's who?   `vocabulary`

Look at this family. Fill the gaps in these sentences with family words from the box.

father	mother	brother	sister	son	daughter	wife	husband

1. Hi, my name's John. This is Jackie. She's my ....

2. I'm Helga. I've got two .... – Peter and Paul.

3. I'm Peter. I've got one ...., Paul, and three ....

4. We're Jackie and John. We've got three ....

5. I'm Paul. My .... is John and my .... is Jackie.

6. My name is Jackie. This is John. He's my ....

7. I'm John. Peter and Paul are my two ....

Write five sentences about a famous family in your country.

REVIEW OF UNIT 5

1 Survey

Suggested steps

Talk about your own home to elicit vocabulary and build model questions.

With the learners' help, build a text to summarise the answers to the questions about your home.
Put learners into pairs. Each one asks the other their questions and makes notes, then one of the pair moves on to another learner and the process is repeated. Learners write their summaries.

Option

Learners read out a summary text without the name of the learner; others have to guess whose house is being described.

2 Who's who?

Suggested steps

This activity could be done as an individual task initially after some discussion about the photo and the aim of activity.

Put learners in pairs to compare and check their answers.

Write up suggestions for the famous families as this saves time. If you have magazine pictures, so much the better.

Give the magazine pictures to pairs of learners. Pairs jointly write five sentences without mentioning the family name.

One of the pair reads their sentences out; the others try to guess the identity of the family.

Answer key

1. wife
2. brothers
3. brother; sisters
4. daughters
5. father; mother
6. husband
7. sons

Unit 6 Worksheet

Suggested steps

Learners work in pairs. Each learner reads out the diary. The partner writes the diary down as they listen (Each learner can ask for any word to be spelled out one letter at a time). Example: *Sunday, fly to Italy*

When both dictations are finished, learners give the dictation to their partner for checking. They discuss problems with each other and/or with their teacher.

7

TIME FOR WORK

The most important feature of this unit is the introduction of the present simple tense. From the topic point of view, Lesson A presents and practises the time and a few very basic daily routines. Lesson B focuses on jobs and workplaces, again practising present simple verbs in the *I/you* forms. Lesson C introduces the *he/she* form of the present simple and looks at the particular activities involved in the different kinds of work people do.

Warm-up

Before the class look at their books, introduce the topic of time. Write these numbers in a list on the board: 3; 6; 8; 10, point to each number in turn and ask the class: *What's this?* to elicit simple numbers three, six, eight, ten.

Now change the list like this: 3.00; 6.15; 8.30; 10.45, again point to all the numbers and ask: *What are these?* If the class doesn't answer, look at your watch or point to a clock. Do not take this activity any further even if it turns out that some learners do know how to say the time and are keen to show off their knowledge to others. Instead, ask the class to open their books at the beginning of Unit 7.

A WHAT'S THE TIME?

1 Clocks and watches ⫐

Suggested steps

This first part of Exercise 1 is simply to establish that there are different kinds of clocks and watches. Get learners to match the sentences with the illustrations. Elicit answers.

Answer key

1. It's in London.	C Big Ben (This is the famous clock tower near the Houses of Parliament.)
2. It's in her hand.	A This is a woman's wrist watch.
3. That's in your car.	B A car clock.
4. It's in our office.	D This is a wall clock.

Teach the words *clock* and *watch*. Ask the class: *What's this?* questions, about the illustrations in the book or about clocks and watches in the classroom.

Now get learners to look at the pictures of the two clocks in the book, explain the activity and play the recording. Three different *time* questions are used in the recording. Get the class to repeat the times in sets of three, pausing and checking pronunciation after each set. The times in this first recordings and illustrations are sequenced logically to aid understanding: *six o'clock / five past seven / ten past eight, etc.*

You may well want to give more intensive practice of the time at this stage before moving on to the next activity. You can refer learners to the first page of the Grammar Reference section at the back of their books for a complete written summary of time expressions. Pay particular attention to: *past/to* and *a quarter / half.*

Tapescript
Clock 1
A: What's the time?
B: It's six o'clock.
C: It's five past seven.
D: It's ten past eight.

A: What time is it?
B: It's a quarter past nine.
C: It's twenty past ten.
D: It's twenty-five past eleven.

Clock 2
A: Have you got the time?
B: It's half past twelve.
C: It's twenty-five to one.
D: It's twenty to two.

A: What's the time?
B: It's a quarter to three.
C: It's ten to four.
D: It's five to five.

Use a large clock with movable hands if one is available. In the second recording the times are not in any sequence. Clarify the task, pointing out that the class will only hear eight of the times illustrated. Play the recording and get learners to match the time they hear with the appropriate illustrations. Play two or three times as necessary, then elicit answers.

Tapescript

See page 130.

Answer key
1. g – 7.30   2. l – 12.55   3. a – 1.00   4. d – 4.15
5. j – 10.45   6. e – 5.20   7. b – 2.05   8. i – 9.40

7

TIME FOR WORK

Language focus:
present simple: statements, questions, short answers
asking for and giving the time: *What's the time?/It's 6 o'clock.*
showing enthusiasm: *It's fantastic!*

Vocabulary:
jobs
workplaces

A WHAT'S THE TIME?

1 Clocks and watches saying the time

A Here are four pictures of clocks and watches. Match the pictures with the right sentences.

1. It's in London.

2. It's in her hand.

3. That's in your car.

4. It's in our office.

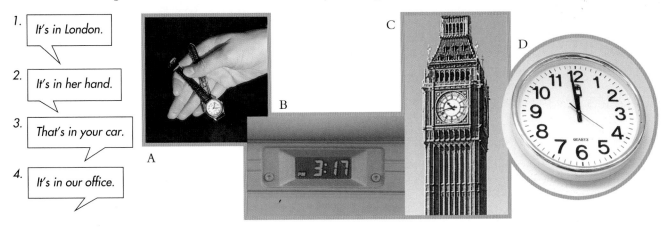

B 🔲 Look at the clocks, listen to the recording and repeat the times.

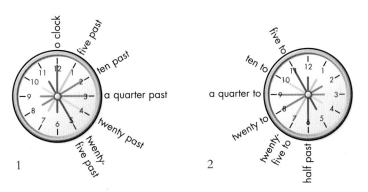

C 🔲 Listen and match the conversations with the clocks.

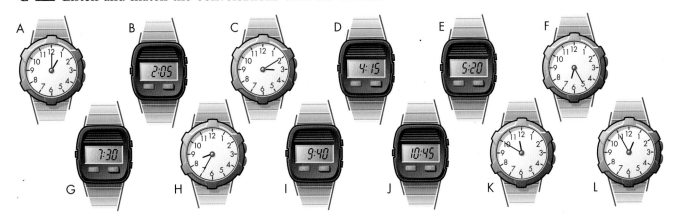

Listen again and fill in the numbers you hear.

1. Yes, it's half past ....
2. It's .... to one.
3. It's .... o'clock.
4. A quarter past .... !
5. Erm, yes, it's a quarter to ....
6. It's .... past five.
7. Yes, five past ....
8. It's .... to ten.

Ask and say the time in pairs, like this:

A: *What's the time?/What time is it?/Have you got the time?*
B: *It's ten past three.*
A: *Thanks a lot.*

2 Times of day | present simple; listening and speaking |

I get up early. I get up late. I have breakfast. I go to work. I get home.

 Listen to the conversation. Fill in the times you hear for the man and the woman.

	man	woman	you	friend
1. get up	....	....	....	....
2. have breakfast	....	....	....	....
3. go to work	....	....	....	....
4. get home	....	....	....	....

Write your times under *you*. Then make conversations in pairs, like this:

A: *I get up at half past six.*
B: *That's very early!*
A: *What about you?*
B: *I get up at eight o'clock.*
A: *That's late.*

Write the other person's times under *friend*.

Talk to other learners about your times for:

– breakfast/lunch/dinner (with *have*)   – English classes/bed (with *go to*)

✔ Quick Check

A Write these times in words.
Example: *2.05*
five past two

1. 2.35 ....
2. 10.15 ....
3. 6.00 ....
4. 11.45 ....
5. 12.55 ....
6. 1.30 ....

B Write the numbers.
Example: *twenty to nine*
8.40

1. five to three ....
2. five past twelve ....
3. a quarter past eight ....
4. half past three ....
5. ten to four ....

C Write these sentences in the right order.

1. up eight at get o'clock I.
2. the What's time?
3. past It's six half.
4. five It's to a quarter.
5. you got Have the time?
6. seven have at breakfast I past a quarter.

Language Point

In this second recording, the class will hear several ways of asking the time, some very polite and some more direct. These could be summarised in a table like this:

		Have you got the time,	
Steve,	excuse me,	What time is it,	please?
		What's the time,	

Write these different questions on the board and get learners to use them all in the exercise which follows.

Play the recording again, so that the class can complete the gapped sentences. Elicit answers.

Answer key

1. seven   2. five   3. one   4. four   5. eleven
6. twenty   7. two   8. twenty

Finally give the class some freer practice in asking and answering questions about the time. Tell each learner to write down five times, then use these as answers. Monitor, correcting where necessary and encouraging learners to use all the questions forms.

2 Times of day 🔲

Suggested steps

Start by checking that the class understands the language illustrated (*get up early and late / have breakfast / go to work / get home*), explain the listening activity, then play the recording.

Learners complete the table with the times they hear. (Since this is a listening comprehension activity, the answers can be written in numbers, rather than words.)

Play the recording again if necessary, then elicit answers for the man and the woman.

Tapescript

MAN: I get up at 6 o'clock in the morning.
WOMAN: Really? That's very early. I get up half past seven, and I have breakfast at 8 o'clock.
MAN: I have breakfast at a quarter to seven and go to work at a quarter past seven. What about you?
WOMAN: I go to work at twenty past eight.
MAN: I get home at eight o'clock.
WOMAN: Really? That's very late. I get home at half past five.

Answer key

	man	woman
1. get up	6.00	7.30
2. have breakfast	6.45	8.00
3. go to work	7.15	8.20
4. get home	8.00	5.30
or	20.00	17.30

Get learners to fill in the 'you' column in the table with their own times. They then use these times as the basis of their conversations in pairs.

Get the class to practise the conversation by repeating it after you, then start the pair work. Explain that they should write their partner's times in the 'friend' column in the table.

This activity can be extended by getting pairs to talk about the other times suggested (breakfast / lunch / dinner; English classes). They could do these with different partners.

Monitor all conversations, paying particular attention to how learners say the times.

Quick Check

Answer key

A
1. twenty-five to three   2. a quarter past ten
3. six o'clock   4. a quarter to twelve
5. five to one   6. half past one

B
1. 2.55   2. 12.05   3. 8.15   4. 3.30   5. 3.50

C
1. I get up at eight o'clock.   2. What's the time?
3. It's half past six.   4. It's a quarter to five.
5. Have you got the time?
6. I have breakfast at a quarter past seven.

Personal Study Workbook

4: the time

Before learners look at their books, introduce the topic of Lesson B by asking the class what jobs they do or hope to do. Start by saying: *I'm a teacher.* Then ask: *What's your job?* Don't spend time teaching the words in English for all the jobs that come up – there will be a chance for this later; if necessary, allow learners to use their own language. Spend no more than about five minutes on this, then go straight into the first activity.

1 What do you do? ▭

Suggested steps

Explain the activity and play the recording for the first time. Learners hear questions and answers about the jobs shown in the photos. The main purpose of the activity is for learners to pick out the job words from the list. Elicit the answers

Tapescript

1. A: What do you do?
   B: I'm a teacher.
2. A: What's your job?
   B: I'm a doctor.
3. A: What do you do?
   B: I'm a waiter.
4. A: What's your job?
   B: I'm an engineer.
5. A: What do you do?
   B: I'm a businesswoman.
6. A: What's your job?
   B: I'm a shop assistant.

Play the recording again and get the class to repeat, each *I'm a* (+ job) sentence.

> ### *Language Points*
> 1 Two different job questions are used in the recording: *What's your job?* and the more colloquial: *What do you do?*
> 2 Point out that the indefinite article, *a/an*, is used with job words in English.

Do this matching as a whole class exercise. The workplaces listed are shown in the photos. Many of the words may be known or will be guessable with help from the teacher.

Answer key

A an office (businesswoman) B a hospital (doctor)
C a school (teacher) D a restaurant a (waiter)
E a laboratory (engineer) F a department store (shop assistant)

2 Where do you work? ▭

The previous vocabulary exercise has prepared the class for this listening activity, which introduces the present simple tense. Speakers on the recording use the question forms: *Where do you work?* and *Do you work in a university?* and the answers: *I work in a (+ workplace noun)* and *I buy all my clothes there.*

Suggested steps

Explain the activity, then play the recording for the first time, pausing after each conversation.

It's up to you to decide whether or not learners should be able to refer to the lists of jobs and workplaces while they are listening. You could ask them to cover the lists and use them later to check their answers.

Play the recording again if necessary, then elicit answers. Make sure learners use the right article (*a* or *an*) when they answer.

Tapescript
See page 130.

Answer key

1. a businesswoman; an office (or offices in New York & London)
2. an engineer; a (small) laboratory
3. a doctor; a (large) hospital
4. a waiter; a (Greek) restaurant (in the town centre)
5. a shop assistant; a department store (in the town)
6. a teacher; a school (not a university)

Option

Ask the class more about the six people. Ask these questions to elicit the information in brackets in the Answer key above, then play the recording again.

1. Where are the offices?
2. Does the engineer work in a large laboratory?
3. Does the doctor work in a large hospital?
4. Does the waiter work in a French restaurant? Where is the restaurant?
5. Where is the department store?
6. Does the teacher work in a university?

1 What do you do?   `vocabulary`

CD Here are some people at work. Listen to the recording, look at the pictures and find the job words in the list. Tick the job word.

> a shop assistant   an engineer   a waiter   a teacher   a businesswoman   a doctor

A: ....

B: ....

C: ....

D: ....

E: ....

F: ....

Match each person with one of these workplaces. Write the place next to the pictures.

> a hospital   an office   a laboratory   a department store   a restaurant   a school

2 Where do you work?   `present simple; listening`

CD Listen to the interviews. Write a job word and a workplace word.

		job			*workplace*
1. I'm	a	businesswoman	I work in	an	office .
2.	a/an	....		a/an	....
3.	a/an	....		a/an	....
4.	a/an	....		a/an	....
5.	a/an	....		a/an	....
6.	a/an	....		a/an	....

Here are some more jobs and workplaces. Is your job here? No? Look in a dictionary or ask your teacher.

secretary (office)

lawyer (courtroom)

photographer (studio)

scientist (laboratory)

nurse (hospital)

Now make conversations, like this:

A: *What do you do?*
B: *I'm a teacher.*
A: *Where do you work?*
B: *I work in a primary school.*

HELP	In your language?
I work for (Kodak).	....

3 When do you start and finish work?   present simple; speaking

Listen and write the missing times. Write 24-hour clock times.

	1. teacher	2. waiter	3. shop assistant	4. businesswoman	5. engineer	6. doctor
Start	....	14.00	08.30	....	09.00	....
Finish	16.30	....	....	20.30	....	....

Ask five learners these questions and write their answers.

– When do you start work?   – When do you finish work?

✔ Quick Check

A Put the lines of this conversation in the right order.

A: you work Where do?
B: hospital I big work in a.
A: start you work When do?
B: morning the in o'clock eight At.
A: finish When you do?
B: in seven o'clock At the evening.

B Write one of these question words.

what   when   where

1. .... do you live?
2. ....'s your job?
3. .... do you finish work?
4. .... do you work?

C What are the missing words in this conversation? (There is ONE missing word in every line.)

A: What you do?
B: I'm engineer.
A: Where do work?
B: I usually work in laboratory.
A: What do you start?
B: About 9 o'clock in morning.
A: And do you finish?
B: I usually finish six o'clock at night.

The next set of illustrations presents more job and workplace vocabulary. Ask the class questions about the jobs and the places, and get them to practise correct pronunciation. (Insist on correct word stress, especially: **photographer** photographer and **secretary**.) secretary

Make sure every learner knows the words for his or her own job and workplace. It will be more interesting if this is done as a whole class activity, though learners could, if necessary refer to a dictionary. Write all the new job and workplace words on the board.

Learners can now practise conversations, following the example. Let them mingle, as if at a social gathering like a party, etc.

Note: Point out the Help box language: *I work for* (+ company name).

3 When do you start and finish work? 📼

Suggested steps

Revise *morning, evening, night* and teach *afternoon* in preparation for the listening exercise. Learners will have to write 24-hour clock times, so give them some practice in this. Get them to write times like these:

three o'clock in the afternoon	15.00
ten o'clock at night	22.00
half past eight in the evening	20.30
a quarter to four in the morning	03.45
twenty-five to five in the afternoon	16.35

Check that the class understands *start* and *finish*.

Clarify the activity: learners are going to hear the same six people again, this time talking about the times they start and finish work. Then play the recording for the first time, pausing after each conversation to allow thinking and writing time.

Play again, if necessary; allow learners to compare times, then elicit answers.

Tapescript

1. A: What do you do?
   B: I'm a teacher.
   A: What time do you start work?
   B: I start at a quarter to nine in the morning.
   A: And when do you finish?
   B: At half past four in the afternoon.

2. A: What's your job?
   B: I'm a waiter.
   A: What time do you start work?
   B: At two o'clock in the afternoon.
   A: And when do you finish?
   B: At one o'clock in the morning.

3. A: What's your job?
   B: I'm a shop assistant.
   A: What time do you start work?
   B: I start at half past eight in the morning.
   A: And when do you finish?
   B: I finish at half past five in the afternoon.

4. A: What do you do?
   B: I'm a businesswoman.
   A: What time do you start work?
   B: At about 6 o'clock in the morning.
   A: And when do you finish?
   B: I usually finish at about half past eight in the evening.

5. A: What's your job?
   B: I'm an engineer.
   A: What time do you start work?
   B: Nine o'clock in the morning.
   A: And when do you finish?
   B: I finish at six o'clock in the evening.

6. A: What do you do?
   B: I'm a doctor.
   A: When do you start work?
   B: This week, I start at 9 o'clock in the evening.
   A: And when do you finish?
   B: At 6 o'clock in the morning.

Answer key

	Start	Finish
1. teacher	**08.45**	16.30
2. waiter	14.00	**01.00**
3. shop assistant	08.30	**17.30**
4. businesswoman	**06.00**	20.30
5. engineer	09.00	**18.00**
6. doctor	**21.00**	**06.00**

Learners walk around and ask each other when they start and finish work. Monitor, listening for the correct use of present simple verbs and times with the expressions *in the morning/afternoon evening* and *at night*.

Option

If any learners do not go to work, suggest they talk about an equivalent routine, e.g. going to school, college or getting up and going to bed.

Quick Check
Answer key

A
A: Where do you work?
B: I work in a big hospital.
A: When do you start work?
B: At eight o'clock in the morning.
A: When do you finish?
B: At seven o'clock in the evening.

B
1. Where   2. What   3. When   4. Where

C
A: What **do** you do?
B: I'm **an** engineer.
A: Where do **you** work?
B: I usually work in **a** laboratory.
A: What **time** do you start?
B: About 9 o'clock in **the** morning.
A: And **when** do you finish?
B: I usually finish **at** six o'clock at night.

Personal Study Workbook

2: present simple verbs   7: vocabulary

This lesson of the unit presents and practises the *he/she* form of the present simple, as well as questions with *Do/Does* and short answer forms. All the forms of the present simple are included in the simple table on page 55 and are summarised in more detail in the Grammar Reference at the back of the Class Book.

1 She does but he doesn't! ▢

Elicit learners' ideas about the photographs. *Who are the people?*

Play the recording once while learners simply listen. Play the recording again, with pauses, and get the class to repeat.

Tapescript

CLARE: What do you do, John?
JOHN: I'm a waiter.
CLARE: Do you work in a café?
JOHN: No, I don't. I work in a restaurant.

CLARE: Do you know John?
SUE: No, I don't. What does he do?
CLARE: He's a waiter.
SUE: Does he work in a café?
CLARE: No, he doesn't. He works in a restaurant.

Present the third person verb form *works* like this:
- You say: *I'm a teacher. I work in a school.*
- Point to the photo in the Class Book and say: *He's a waiter. He works in a restaurant.*
- Ask: *Where does he work?* (*He works in a restaurant.*)
- Ask: *Does he work in a café?* (*No, he works in a restaurant.*)

Option

Take in pictures of people doing other jobs and ask: *Where does he/she work?*

Go through the present simple table in the Class Book.

Explain the three-person task to the class. **Note:** If the class doesn't divide into threes this task can be done equally well in fours or fives – but not pairs. Get the class to practise going through the sample conversation, then allow them time to talk to and about each other in their groups. Monitor, making sure you correct any present simple verb errors you hear.

1 She does but he doesn't! | present simple: questions and short answers |

CD Look at the pictures and listen to the conversations.

Do you work in a café?

No, I don't.

Does he work in a café?

No, he doesn't.

CD Listen again and repeat the conversations.

	Present simple	
Statements	**I/you/we/they work / don't work** in an office.	
	He/she works / doesn't work in a shop.	
Questions	**Do** you **work** in an office?	**Does she work** in a shop?
Answers	Yes, I **do**.	Yes, she **does**.
	No, I **don't**.	No, she **doesn't**.

Talk in threes. Ask and answer questions, like this:

A: *Do you work in an office?*
B: *No, I don't. I work in a shop.*
C: *Does B work in an office?*
A: *No, he/she doesn't. He/she works in a shop.*

2 What exactly do they do?

present simple: *he/she* form

Match the sentences with the pictures.

1. He **travels**.
2. She **writes**.
3. She **helps** people.
4. He **takes** money.
5. She **serves** customers.
6. He **buys**./She **sells**.
7. He **phones**.

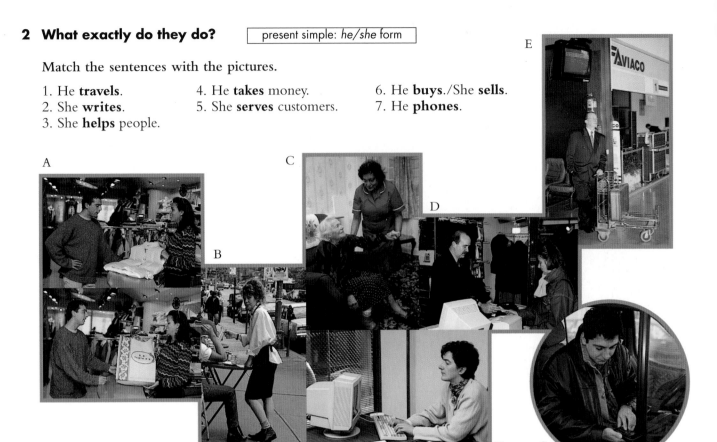

What do you think a waiter, a doctor, a shop assistant and a businesswoman do in their jobs?

Use these verbs: *buy, help, phone, sell, serve, take, travel, write.*

Talk to a partner and make lists, like this:

A waiter serves customers .....
writes bills .....
and takes money .....

⏭ Listen to the four people talking and check your ideas. Tick your list.

Talk to your partner about the four jobs.

Example: A: *Does the waiter serve customers?*
B: *Yes, he does. Does he write their bills?*
A: *No, he doesn't. Does he take their money?*
B: *Yes, he does.*

Now ask three other learners about their jobs. What exactly do they do?

3 Profiles

present simple; reading and writing

Read the text and answer these questions.

1. What is Katherine's job?
2. Where does she work?
3. What exactly does she do?

Write 30–40 words about one of the learners you talked to.

Katherine is a newspaper journalist. She works in New York. She writes about films and television. She takes her computer to the cinema. She watches films and writes about them. She often works in the evening and gets home late.

2 What exactly do they do? 〔⬚⬚〕

This first task presents some new verbs associated with work. Learners match the sentences with the appropriate illustrations. They may do this individually or in pairs. Elicit the sentences for each picture, checking the meaning and correcting pronunciation where necessary.

> ### Language Point
>
> When you are correcting pronunciation, pay particular attention to the sound of the final *-s* of the seven verbs:
> 1. travels (/z/) 2. writes (/s/) 3. helps (/s/)
> 4. takes (/s/) 5. serves (/z/) 6. buys (/z/);
> 7. phones (/z/)   sells (/z/)

Answer key

1. E 2. F 3. C 4. D 5. B 6. A 7.G

In the next part of this lesson learners suggest what the four people do in their jobs. Allow five or ten minutes for pairs to talk and write simple sentences, like those suggested. Now play the recording and get learners to check how many of their ideas are mentioned by the speakers. They can tick any of the ideas on their lists and then write any sentences they hadn't thought of.

Tapescript

1. A: John, you're a waiter – what do you do in the restaurant?
   JOHN: Well, I serve customers.
   A: Do you write their bills?
   JOHN: No, I don't. A computer writes the bills.
   A: Do you take their money?
   JOHN: Yes, I do.

2. A: What do you do in the hospital, Doctor Piper?
   DOCTOR PIPER: Well, I help people.
   A: Do you take money from them?
   DOCTOR PIPER: No, I don't, I write prescriptions.
   A: Do you travel in your job?
   DOCTOR PIPER: Yes, I do. I work in three hospitals.

3. A: Dave, you work – what do you do?
   DAVE: Well, I serve customers of course – I help them and I sell them things.
   A: Do you take their money?
   DAVE: Yes, I do.
   A: And do you travel in your job?
   DAVE: No, I don't.

4. A: You're a businesswoman, Caroline. What do you do in your job?
   CAROLINE: I travel a lot. I go to a lot of countries.
   A: Do you sell things?
   CAROLINE: I don't. I buy things for my company.
   A: Do you write letters and phone people?
   CAROLINE: I phone people, but my assistant writes my letters for me.

Answer key

1. A waiter: He serves customers and takes their money.
2. A doctor: She helps people. She writes prescriptions.
3. A shop assistant: He serves customers. He helps customers and he sells things. He takes their money.
4. A businesswoman: She travels. She buys things (for her company). She phones people.

Learners now talk in pairs about the four jobs, using the example conversation in their books as a model. Monitor, again paying careful attention to all present simple verbs.

Finally get learners in threes to ask and tell each other about their own jobs. This allows the possibility of *I/you* and *he/she* verbs. Monitor these conversations and be prepared to supply new verbs to enable learners to say exactly what they do.

3 Profiles

These activities give learners an opportunity to consolidate in writing what they have just been practising orally.

Suggested steps

Explain the activity, draw learners' attention to the three questions, then get them to read the text. Let learners compare ideas, then elicit answers.

Answer key

1. She is a newspaper journalist. She writes about films and television.
2. She works in New York.
3. She takes her computer to the cinema. She watches films and writes about them.

Learners now write about one of the people they talked to at the end of the last exercise. They should model their writing as closely as possible on the text about Katherine – 40 words long. If this writing is done in class, monitor and help where necessary. Correct all present simple verb errors.

4 In conversation ▭

As you play the recording for the first time, the class follows it in their books.

Before playing the recording again, ask the class how B feels about her job. Accept any answer which shows a basic understanding that she likes it a lot. (In fact she's *enthusiastic*, but don't use this word unless it is similar to the word in students' own language.)

Ask the class to repeat after you the last thing B says in the first two conversations: *It's great!* and *It's fantastic!* Learners should practise this until they really sound enthusiastic.

Now play the recording again and get the class to say B's words.

Note: Notice that the question *Do you like it?* is used in the first conversation. You could spend some time modelling and practising this now.

Finally get the class to ask and answer more questions to practise sounding enthusiastic. Here are some more possible questions and answers.

Where are you from?		
Is it a beautiful town?		*it's fantastic!*
What's your job?		*it's great!*
Is it an interesting job?	*Yes,*	*it's very interesting!*
Where do you work?		*it's brilliant!*
Is it a good company?		*I like it a lot!*
Do you like your job?		

Monitor conversations, reminding learners to sound enthusiastic.

Quick Check

Answer key

A
1. waiter; serves
2. shop assistant; sells
3. businessman; work; travel
4. doctor; works; writes
5. teacher; teaches

B
1. A: Do   2. A: Does
   B: don't   B: does
3. A: Does   4. A: Do
   B: doesn't   B: do

Personal Study Workbook

1: present simple verbs
3: present simple questions
5: vocabulary
6: prepositions
8: reading; times
9: listening and speaking
10: visual dictionary

4 In conversation `showing enthusiasm`

A 📼 Listen to the recording and read the conversations.

1. A: What's your job?
   B: I'm a journalist.
   A: Do you like it?
   B: Yes, **it's great!**

2. A: What exactly do you do?
   B: I go to the cinema and write about films.
   A: Is it an interesting job?
   B: Yes – **it's fantastic!**

3. A: What time do you get up?
   B: Five o'clock in the morning.
   A: That's very early.
   B: **It's terrible!**

B 📼 Listen again. A is on the cassette. You say B's words.

In pairs, ask and answer questions. Use expressions from the conversations.

✔ Quick Check

A Fill the gaps with a job word and one of the verbs.

Jobs: businessman   doctor   shop assistant   teacher   waiter
Verbs: sell(s)   serve(s)   teach(es)   travel(s)   work(s)   write(s)

1. He's a ....
   He .... customers in a restaurant.
2. She's a ....
   She .... shoes and clothes to customers.
3. I'm a ....
   I .... in an office and I
   .... to lots of countries.
4. He's a ....
   He .... in a hospital and
   .... prescriptions.
5. She's a ....
   She .... children in a primary school.

B Fill in the gaps with one of these words: *do, does, don't, doesn't.*

1. A: .... you work in a school?
   B: No, I ....
2. A: .... she travel to other countries?
   B: Yes, she ....
3. A: .... he serve customers?
   B: No, he ....
4. A: .... you like your job?
   B: Yes, I ....

PERSONAL STUDY WORKBOOK
- vocabulary of jobs and workplaces
- asking and saying what the time is
- listening to people talking about their work
- present simple verbs
- visual dictionary – jobs and time
- reading – episode 7 of *Lost in time*

REVIEW OF UNIT 5

1 Picture crossword [vocabulary]

Write the words in the crossword.

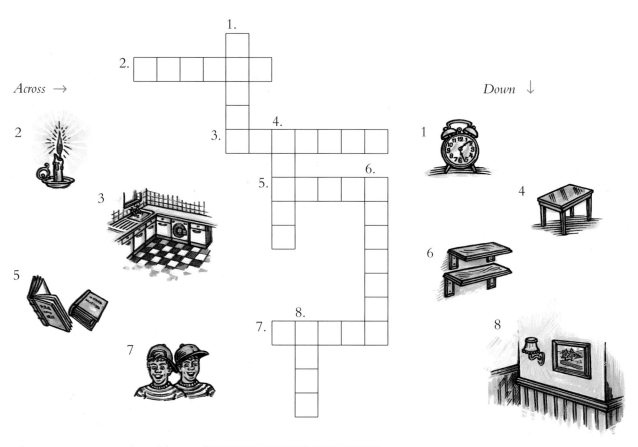

Across →

2
3
5
7

Down ↓

1
4
6
8

2 There's a pen under the ... [prepositions of place; writing]

There are four pens in this room. Find them. Write four sentences about the pens.

1. The first pen ....

2. The second pen ....

3. The ....

4. The ....

REVIEW OF UNIT 5

1 Picture crossword

Answer key

Across	Down
2 candle	1 clock
3 kitchen	4 table
5 books	6 shelves
7 twins	8 wall

2 There's a pen under the ...

Answer key (in any order)

1. The first pen is **by** / **next to** the computer.
2. The second pen is **under** a book.
3. The third pen is **on** a (mobile) phone.
4. The fourth pen is *in* a mug/cup.

REVIEW OF UNIT 6

1 Come to our English class

Answer key

Come to our English class …
Learn English with …
Enjoy …
Don't wait. Phone …
Don't forget …

2 At the travel agent's ☐☐

Learners could do this exercise individually or in pairs.

Tapescript

TRAVEL AGENT: Good morning. Come in and sit down.
CUSTOMER: Thanks.
TRAVEL AGENT: Which country are you interested in?
CUSTOMER: Greece. Do you have any information on holidays in Athens?
TRAVEL AGENT: Athens. Yes, I'm sure we have. Hang on. Yes, here you are.
CUSTOMER: Mm – lots of old monuments – and the sea is quite near.
TRAVEL AGENT: How about Italy? Florence is beautiful. Have a look at the brochure.
CUSTOMER: What's it like at this time of the year?
TRAVEL AGENT: It's fantastic!

Answer key

Come **in** and sit **down**
… interested **in**
information **on** holidays **in** Athens
Hang **on**. Yes, …
lots **of** old monuments
How **about** Italy? Have a look **at** the brochure.
What's it like **at** this time **of** the year?

Play the recording and let the learners check their answers.

Unit 7 Worksheet

Suggested steps

Individually, learners fill in the appropriate times for each of the actions for themselves and for someone in their family.

Learners then work in pairs. They ask each other questions and note down the answers in the spaces provided.

This activity practises *times* and these forms of the *present simple*:
Questions: *What time   do you get up?*
                           does s/he get up?
Statements: *I get up at …*
                      S/he gets up at …

REVIEW OF UNIT 6

1 Come to our English class | imperatives; writing |

Complete the advert for your English class with words in the HELP box.

C............... **to our English class in** ....(your city)**.**
L............... **English with some lovely people.**
E............................ (number) **hours a week with a**
.... (adjective) **teacher from** .... (country)**.**
D............ **w**................ **. P**.......................
.... (name of your school) **NOW!**

D..........................*f*..........................
English is the international language of travel!

Read your advert for a radio station.

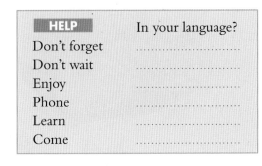

HELP	In your language?
Don't forget	....
Don't wait	....
Enjoy	....
Phone	....
Learn	....
Come	....

2 At the travel agent's | prepositions |

Read this conversation and try to fill the gaps with the right words.

in	on	down	about	of	at

TRAVEL AGENT: Good morning. Come .... and sit ....**.**

CUSTOMER: Thanks.

TRAVEL AGENT: Which country are you interested ....?

CUSTOMER: Greece. Do you have any information .... holidays .... Athens?

TRAVEL AGENT: Athens. Yes, I'm sure we have. Hang .... Yes, here you are.

CUSTOMER: Mm – lots .... old monuments – and the sea is quite near.

TRAVEL AGENT: How .... Italy? Florence is beautiful. Have a look .... the brochure.

CUSTOMER: What's it like .... this time .... the year?

TRAVEL AGENT: It's fantastic!

▱ Now listen to a recording of the conversation and check your answers.

8

INTERNATIONAL FOOD

Language focus:
expressing likes and dislikes: *like(s)/don't (doesn't) like*
asking about likes and expressing agreement:
Do you like ...? So do I. Me too.
conjunctions: *and* and *but*
question forms: *How long ...? How many ...?*
expressing lack of knowledge or information:
I don't know. I've no idea.
possessives: *'s*

Vocabulary:
food
months
language skills

A   I LIKE THAI FOOD ... SO DO I

1 Food from other countries   food vocabulary; nationalities

Name the restaurants for the meals A to G.

Example: *A is a meal from an Indian restaurant.*

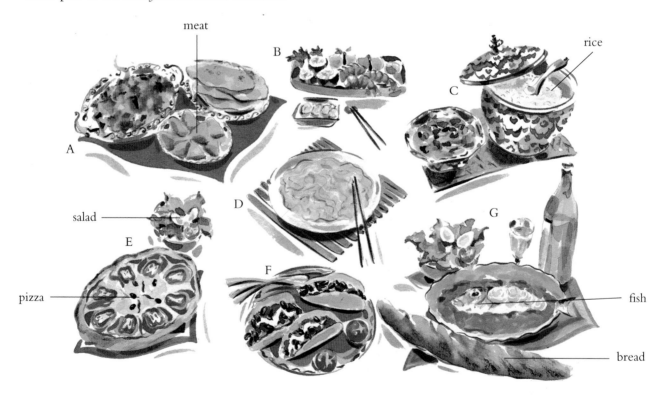

Look at the food words. Answer the questions.

1. What is white?
2. What is green?
3. What is cold?
4. What is hot?

Have you got restaurants from these countries in your town?

HELP
spicy
hot
cold

In your language?
....
....
....

INTERNATIONAL FOOD

Introduction to the unit

This unit continues the development of the present simple tense largely through the topic of food likes and dislikes.

Lesson A presents likes and dislikes (*like + noun* not *-ing* form) in the context of *international food*. The simple, but useful agreement expressions *so do I* and *me too* are also introduced and practised here. The theme of Lesson B is *sandwiches* and this provides learners with further practice of all forms of present simple verbs. Lesson C has more opportunities for speaking practice and includes a focus on the language of telephone conversations. The possessive *'s* and the questions *How long …?* and *How many …?* are also introduced. Finally learners are given the chance to assess their progress as learners of English.

A I LIKE THAI FOOD ... SO DO I

1 Food from other countries

Warm-up

It is often a good idea to use informal activities to establish the topic in a friendly way. Before you start this unit, maybe you could organise a coffee break with a few attractive, unusual snacks . This would enable target language e.g. *Do you like…? So do I/Me too* to occur naturally and would coincidentally consolidate good relations within the group. With larger classes, it would be necessary to go outside the class in smaller groups for a number of shared coffee breaks.

Suggested steps

Check the answers yourself first if any of the meals is unfamiliar.

Clarify the matching task and let learners try it in pairs. Use the example to model pronunciation and form. Elicit and check answers.

Answer key

A is a meal from an Indian restuarant.
B is a meal from a Japanese restuarant.
C is a meal from a Thai restuarant.
D is a meal from a Chinese restuarant.
E is a meal from an Italian restuarant.
F is a meal from a Mexican restuarant.
G is a meal from a French restuarant.

White: rice
Green: salad
Cold: sushi, salad, wine
Hot: meat: rice, fish, noodles, pizza, tacos

Option

Use a pyramid approach. Each pair takes their answers to another pair and negotiates an agreed set of answers. The four then go to another four and do the same until the class has one set of answers agreed and accepted by everyone. Then the teacher elicits these and compares with her own.

Build the vocabulary of the labelled food items, using the questions, e.g. *What is white?* etc. Let learners ask and answer in pairs to maximise participation. Monitor pronunciation.

Use the Help box to establish spicy (remember sometimes English speakers use the expression *hot* to mean spicy rather than the opposite of *cold*).

Recycle *Is there …?* for the final questions about the learners' own towns or suburbs, e.g. *Is there a Mexican restaurant in … ?* Again, do the activity in pairs if learners come from different towns or suburbs.

1 Sandwich? No, thanks, John! | reading; vocabulary; *she/he likes/loves* |

Which title is for which text?

A sandwich? –
It's so simple

Sandwich? –
No, thanks, John

Sandwich? – *I'm in the international club*

Read one text. Tell a partner about it.

1. John is from Brisbane in Australia. He loves sandwiches! His sandwiches are interesting! He likes jam with cheese sandwiches, and meat sandwiches with fruit.

strawberry
banana } fruit
orange

jam
meat
cheese

2. Veronique is from France. In France people eat simple sandwiches. French bread with ham is a good example. A simple ham sandwich with a good, black coffee ... and no sugar... is wonderful.

3. Nobihiro is from Japan. He travels a lot to new countries. In international hotels he likes a good club sandwich. It's not Japanese, but chicken with bacon, fries and salad is nice and tasty.

bacon
fries

Ask and answer.

1. Does John like jam with cheese?
2. Does John like interesting sandwiches?
3. Does Veronique like coffee with sugar?
4. Does Nobihiro like sandwiches in Japan?

What about you? Do you like sandwiches?

HELP	In your language?
I don't know.	....
They're all right sometimes.	....

Language Point

Learners may be confused by the short response forms *Yes, I do/No, I don't*. Explain that when you want to give a more elaborate answer you often say things like: *Yes, I do like Greek food but only when it's fresh ...* or *No, I don't like Thai food, it's too spicy for me*; when you only want to tell your questioner that your answer is simply *yes* rather than *no* then *Yes, I do/No, I don't* are the alternatives to *Yes/No*.

You can't say *Yes, I like* or *Yes, I do like* as a simple answer.

Answer key

Version 1
Stefan likes Italian food.
The teacher likes Thai food.

Version 2
His sister likes Chinese food.
Her brother likes Indian food, spicy food.

Quick Check

Answer key

A
French, Italian, Spanish, Chinese, Indian, Thai, American, Japanese, Greek

B
He **likes**; She **likes**; Do you **like**

C
1. ... she **likes** salad.
2. Miguel **likes** rice and so **do** I.
3. **Do** you **like** Italian food? Yes, I **do**, of course, and my wife **likes** Italian coffee. Mm so **do** I, and I like Brazilian coffee. **Me** too.
4. Do you like Chinese food? No, I **don't**.

D
1. drinks   2. food   3. countries

Personal Study Workbook

1: *like/likes*
2: present simple in mini conversations
7: listening

1 Sandwich? No, thanks, John!

Warm-up

Make cards, each showing outlines of the territorial boundaries of a range of countries. Put the class into groups. Ask each group to name each country and one food that each named country has given to the world. They can use a dictionary.

Suggested steps

Demonstrate what a sandwich is by using actual examples or pictures. Practise pronunciation by naming types of sandwich, e.g. cheese sandwich, ham sandwich, club sandwich.

Let learners match texts and titles on their own first, then check their answers in pairs.

In the same pairs let the learners read the texts and then ask and answer the questions alternately. Monitor and assist where necessary. Elicit the question *Do you like sandwiches?* from the learners. Model a range of answers including answers in the Help box. Put pairs together with other pairs for personalised *Do you like sandwiches?* conversation.

Monitor and encourage the use of the *What about you?* form as an alternative to repeating the *Do you like ...?* question.

Answer key

1. Sandwich? – No, thanks, John 2. A sandwich? – It's so simple. 3. Sandwich? – I'm in the international club.
1. Yes   2. Yes   3. No   4. No

2 I don't like coffee with sugar 🎧

Suggested steps

Use the pictures to elicit guesses for the missing expressions in the speech balloons.

Draw attention to the form and pronunciation of the negative forms *don't/doesn't like*.

Try to elicit the function of *but*; contrast it with *and*. Establish the context of the recordings (acquaintances talking) and clarify the listening task. Learners listen and try to complete the missing words in the balloons. Play the recording in sections.

Tapescript

A: Do you like coffee?
B: Good coffee, yes, but I don't like coffee with sugar. It's awful.
A: What about your husband?
B: Oh, he doesn't like coffee, but he loves tea – tea at eight, nine, ten, eleven – he likes tea all the time!
A: Really?
B: Mm, and he likes it with lots of sugar. It's not good!
C: Do you like sandwiches?
D: We don't eat sandwiches much in our country but we like sandwiches in England.
C: Do you like simple sandwiches or sandwiches with lots of different things inside?
D: I like simple sandwiches – ham on fresh bread for example, but my wife likes sandwiches with different things in. She likes meat, salad and fruit jam sandwiches, for example.
C: Really?
D: Mm, our friends in England make lots of interesting sandwiches for her. But we don't like the sandwiches in some of the coffee shops: the bread isn't very nice.

Learners compare their answers in pairs.

Play the recordings again, asking learners to listen for additional information and for the different forms *don't/doesn't*.

Model the conversation about food and drink *you/a friend like/don't like*. Let the learners sit in new pairs or groups to talk about food. Elicit feedback from the groups; check the verb forms.

Answer key

… but I don't like **coffee** with **sugar**.

I like simple **sandwiches**, but my wife **likes** sandwiches with different things in. But we **don't** like the sandwiches in some of the coffee shops.

3 In our family we like …

Suggested steps

Establish that the text is part of a letter to a friend in England and that this section of the letter is about food.

Look at some of the spaces and ask learners what kinds of expressions they think could go there.

Let the learners write their letters individually on pieces of paper. Collect the letters and let different learners take one each, read it out and guess who wrote it.

If there is time, you might like to establish or re-establish that letters are usually begun with *Dear …* followed by the first name if it is a friend.

Quick Check
Answer key

A
1. I **don't** like coffee. = I do **not** like coffee.
2. She **doesn't** like meat. = She **does** not like meat.
3. **That's** terrible. = That **is** terrible.
4. **They've** got some sandwiches. = They **have got** some sandwiches.
5. They **don't** like the bread. = They **do** not like the bread.

B
1. but   2. and   3. and   4. but   5. and

C
1. orange, strawberry   2. ham, chicken
3. coffee, tea, beer   4. an Indian curry

Personal Study Workbook

3: reading
4: *and* or *but* in letter writing to friends

2 I don't like coffee with sugar

listening; don't/doesn't like; and/but

Listen and complete.

Do you like coffee?

Good coffee, yes, but I don't like ....
with ....
My husband doesn't like ....
but he loves ....

Do you like sandwiches?

I like simple .... but my wife ....
sandwiches with different things in. But we ....
like the sandwiches in some of the coffee shops.

Talk about:

– food/drink you don't like (*I don't like …*)
– food/drink a friend, husband or wife doesn't like (*My friend doesn't like …*)

3 In our family we like ...

writing with *I/we like*

This is part of a letter from you to a friend in England. Complete the sentences about food and (1) your friend, (2) your family, (3) people in your country. Use a dictionary.

> My friend, _____, likes_____
> with _____ but I don't like _____ .
> My (mother) doesn't like _____ .
>   In our family we don't like _____ but
> we eat a lot of _____ . People in our country
> love _____ .
>   See you in July,

✓ Quick Check

A Write in the five apostrophes ('). Complete the long form of the verbs.

1. I dont like coffee. = I do .... like coffee.
2. She doesnt like meat. = She .... not like meat.
3. Thats terrible. = That .... terrible.
4. Theyve got some sandwiches = They .... some sandwiches.
5. They dont like the bread. = They .... not like the bread.

B Write *and* or *but*.

1. I like meat .... I don't eat fish.
2. He likes coffee .... cheese.
3. We love bread .... we love rice.
4. They like bread .... not sandwiches.
5. I don't like wine .... I don't like tea.

Write Sentence B3 in your language.

C Give an example of:

1. a fruit ....
2. meat ....
3. a drink ....
4. a meal ....

1 In conversation | possessive 's; *I don't know/I've no idea* |

Study this sentence:

My tea, your tea, Miguel's tea and my mother's tea are in the kitchen.

Complete these sentences.

1. Miguel's tea means the tea of ....
2. My mother's tea means the tea of ....

📼 Listen and read this conversation.

VACLAV: When's Jana's dinner party?
HELEN: Er, sorry, I've no idea.
VACLAV: Is it on Saturday, do you think?
HELEN: I don't know. Ask Tomo, he's Jana's friend.
VACLAV: OK, thanks, bye.
HELEN: Bye.

Tick the correct box or answer the question.

1. Vaclav and Helen are probably friends. Yes ☐ No ☐
2. What's the name of Jana's friend? ....
3. Is Jana's party on Saturday? Yes ☐ No ☐ I'm not sure ☐
4. I've no idea = I don't know. Yes ☐ No ☐

Practise the conversation with different names.

2 Phone language | listening for sounds; phone vocabulary |

A 📼 Listen and say these names.

– Smith's restaurant – Schmidt's restaurant – Smee's restaurant

B 📼 Listen. What is the name of the restaurant in this phone conversation?

WOMAN: Is that (*name*)?
MAN: Sorry? What? It's a bad line.
WOMAN: Is that (*name*)?
MAN: I'm sorry ... is that who?
WOMAN: (*name*).
MAN: What number do you want?
WOMAN: 288 40212.
MAN: You've got the wrong number; this is 288 40202.
WOMAN: Oh, I'm sorry.
MAN: That's OK, bye.

C 📼 Listen to the conversation on a good line. Check your answer.

Practise the conversation.

1 In conversation 🔲

Suggested steps

Let learners sit in pairs to study and complete the sentences with the possessive *'s*. Check their understanding and pronunciation.

Let the same pairs read the conversation, answer the questions and try to mark the main stressed syllables.

Check meaning is understood for *I don't know/I've no idea/dinner party/ask*.

Play the recording; let the learners check the stressed syllables.

Set up mini role play pairs, handing out different days of the week and different names to different pairs.

Let the pairs practise the conversation; circulate and help with their pronunciation. If it is practical, set up a simple stage (table, chairs).

Ask for pairs to volunteer to perform their conversations without the book.

Discuss body language and facial expressions as cultural factors in conversations to see if learners are aware of how British or American speakers might be different in terms of their gestures and signals; talk about how tone of voice can communicate different things to the other person, e.g. flat voice communicates boredom; too much stress might communicate annoyance or aggression to a native speaker of English.

Answer key

1. Miguel's tea means the tea of **Miguel**.
2. My mother's tea means the tea of **my mother**.
1. Yes   2. Tomo   3. I'm not sure   4. Yes

2 Phone language 🔲

Suggested steps

This is an activity to illustrate how single sounds misheard on a bad phone line can lead to confusion.

Play the recording and stop after each name for the class to repeat.

Write the three restaurant names on the board. Ask someone to say one of the names and ask another learner to point to the name they heard.

Tapescript

A
1. Good evening, Smith's restaurant.
2. Hello, Schmidt's restaurant.
3. Hello, Smee's restaurant, can I help you?

Clarify the listening task. Learners have to try to distinguish the name of the restaurant on a bad phone line.

Play the recording once only. Ask learners to put their hand up if they thought it was one or other of the three names. Write the number of votes for each name. Play the second recording. Ask again for the name.

Tapescript

B
WOMAN: Is that Smith's?
MAN: Sorry? What? It's a bad line.
WOMAN: Is that Smith's restaurant?
MAN: I'm sorry ... is that who?
WOMAN: Smith's.
MAN: What number do you want?
WOMAN: 288 40212.
MAN: You've got the wrong number. This is 288 40202.
WOMAN: Oh, I'm sorry.
MAN: That's OK, bye.

C
WOMAN: Is that Smith's?
MAN: I'm sorry?
WOMAN: Is that Smith's restaurant?
MAN: What number do you want?
WOMAN: 288 40212.
MAN: I think you've got the wrong number. This is 288 40202.
WOMAN: Oh, I'm sorry.
MAN: That's OK, bye.

Let the learners practise the conversation with the script back-to-back in pairs.

Listen to pairs and make a note of any points that might need further practice at a later stage. Encourage and give positive feedback where appropriate.

Answer key

Smith's restaurant

3 Two hours a week for three months
ᗑ

Suggested steps

Practise saying the names of the months and then drill by recycling *first, second,* etc. (*What's the fifth month? What's the tenth month?*)

Clarify the listening task. Which two months are in the wrong order?

Tapescript

A

January
February
March
April
May
June
July
August
October
September
November
December

The follow-up listening activity revises months, weeks, days in the context of an interview with a student. To set a context, tell learners that the student is being interviewed for a student newspaper.

Clarify the task. Learners have to complete the missing details.

Let the learners read the box with Ludmila's information. Check their understanding by asking specific questions, e.g. *How many hours are there in a day? What is after a.m.?*

Play the recording. Let learners check their answers in pairs and then with other pairs if necessary.

Tapescript

B

LUDMILA:	Hi, I'm Ludmila.
INTERVIEWER:	Oh, hello, thanks for coming. I've got one or two questions about your course, OK?
LUDMILA:	Yes, fine.
INTERVIEWER:	OK. How long is your English course?
LUDMILA:	Er, three months – July, August and September.
INTERVIEWER:	How many weeks is that?
LUDMILA:	Er, 12 weeks, I think, yeah, 12.
INTERVIEWER:	How many hours a week are you in class?
LUDMILA:	Four hours per week.
INTERVIEWER:	What days and times?
LUDMILA:	Tuesday and Thursday from 7 till 9.
INTERVIEWER:	Seven till 9 p.m.?
LUDMILA:	Yes, 7 till 9 in the evening after work.
INTERVIEWER:	What week of your course is this week?
LUDMILA:	Week ten ... mm, the tenth week.

INTERVIEWER:	And is the course OK?
LUDMILA:	Yes, it's fine, but I don't like listening, it's very fast for me.
INTERVIEWER:	OK ... well, thanks, Ludmila.
LUDMILA:	You're welcome.

Ask learners to complete the information for their own course. (This could be done before the listening if preferred.)

Establish the meaning of *progress*. Let the learners complete the progress box at home on a photocopy. You might like to use it as a basis for talking to each learner about their progress and strategies for improvement.

Answer key

September and October; the sixth month is June and it's got 30 days

three months (July, August, September); 12 weeks; 4 hours per week; Thursday 7 – 9 p.m.; week 10

3 Two hours a week for three months

winter in Britain

summer in Britain

January	February	March	April	May	June
1 2 3 4 5 6 7	1 2 3 4 5 6 7	1 2 3 4 5 6 7	1 2 3 4 5 6 7	1 2 3 4 5 6 7	1 2 3 4 5 6 7
8 9 10 11 12 13 14	8 9 10 11 12 13 14	8 9 10 11 12 13 14	8 9 10 11 12 13 14	8 9 10 11 12 13 14	8 9 10 11 12 13 14
15 16 17 18 19 20 21	15 16 17 18 19 20 21	15 16 17 18 19 20 21	15 16 17 18 19 20 21	15 16 17 18 19 20 21	15 16 17 18 19 20 21
22 23 24 25 26 27 28	22 23 24 25 26 27 28	22 23 24 25 26 27 28	22 23 24 25 26 27 28	22 23 24 25 26 27 28	22 23 24 25 26 27 28
29 30 31		29 30 31	29 30	29 30 31	29 30

summer in Britain

winter in Britain

July	August	September	October	November	December
1 2 3 4 5 6 7	1 2 3 4 5 6 7	1 2 3 4 5 6 7	1 2 3 4 5 6 7	1 2 3 4 5 6 7	1 2 3 4 5 6 7
8 9 10 11 12 13 14	8 9 10 11 12 13 14	8 9 10 11 12 13 14	8 9 10 11 12 13 14	8 9 10 11 12 13 14	8 9 10 11 12 13 14
15 16 17 18 19 20 21	15 16 17 18 19 20 21	15 16 17 18 19 20 21	15 16 17 18 19 20 21	15 16 17 18 19 20 21	15 16 17 18 19 20 21
22 23 24 25 26 27 28	22 23 24 25 26 27 28	22 23 24 25 26 27 28	22 23 24 25 26 27 28	22 23 24 25 26 27 28	22 23 24 25 26 27 28
29 30 31	29 30 31	29 30	29 30 31	29 30	29 30 31

A 📖 Listen and tick the months. Two are in the wrong order. Which two?
What is the sixth month? How many days has it got?

a month   a week

B 📖 Listen and complete the information for Ludmila.
Write the information for your course.

Ludmila's English Course

How long is your English course?   ..3 months. – July,.
.... How many weeks? .... weeks
How many hours a week? .... hours per week
What are the days and times a week? Tuesday and
.... from .... till........... **9** p...........
What week of your course is this week? ....

My English Course

How long is your English course? ....
How many weeks? .... weeks
How many hours a week? .... hours per week
What are the days and times a week? ....
.... from .... till ....
What week of your course is this week? ....

Tick the boxes for you.

My Progress in English

	Good progress	OK	Slow progress
Listening	☐	☐	☐
Speaking	☐	☐	☐
Reading	☐	☐	☐
Writing	☐	☐	☐
Vocabulary	☐	☐	☐
Grammar	☐	☐	☐
Pronunciation	☐	☐	☐
English homework	☐	☐	☐

A Answer the questions.

1. Put the months in order from 1–12. Start with January.
2. How many days are there in one week?
3. How many days are there in June?
4. How many days are there in March?
5. What is the second month?
6. What is the fifth month?
7. Is August a summer month in Australia?
8. There are 24 hours in one ....
9. When is your birthday?
10. When is your teacher's birthday?

B Rewrite these with 's.

1. The birthday of my sister
   = My ....
2. The birthday of Karel
   = ...

3. The birthday of his father
   = His ....
4. The birthday of John's grandmother
   = John's ....

C Put the words in the right order in some of the lines (★) of the conversation.

★A: Hi, there John is?
★B: Sorry, want to to you who speak do?
 A: John.
★B: who John?
 A: John Smith.
★B: number got you've wrong the Sorry.
★A: sorry, I'm bye.
 B: Bye.

🔲 Listen and check.

PERSONAL STUDY WORKBOOK

- reading an airline menu
- *to like* practice
- *and/but* in a letter

- visual dictionary – food
- reading – episode 8 of *Lost in time*

D REVIEW AND DEVELOPMENT

REVIEW OF UNIT 6

Please come   vocabulary: days of the week; speaking

Complete the conversation. Use the sentences in the Sorry box and write some others.

A: Come on Monday.
B: Sorry, I've got an English class on Monday.
A: How about Tuesday?
B: Sorry, I've got a meeting.
A: OK. How about Wednesday?
B: Sorry, ...
A: Mmm. How about Thursday?
B: Sorry, ...
A: OK How about Friday?
B: I'm sorry I'm ...
A: How about Saturday?
B: Sorry, I'm ...
A: How about Sunday?
B: Mmm. Yes, that's fine.
A: Is it? Are you sure?
B: Mmm.
A: Great!!!!
B: Oh! Sorry, I've got a ...

SORRY BOX

Sorry, I've got an English class on Monday.

I've got a conference.

I'm at the library.

I'm in Scotland.

I'm at work.

....

....

(Write one or two.)

Say the conversation with a partner. Record your conversation and listen to it.

Answer key

A

1. January, February, March, April, May, June, July, August, September, October, November, December
2. 7   3. 30   4. 31   5. February   6. May   7. No
8. day

B

1. My sister's birthday   2. Karel's birthday
3. His father's birthday   4. John's grandmother's birthday

C

A: Hi, is John there?
B: Sorry, who do you want to speak to?
A: John.
B: John who?
A: John Smith.
B: Sorry, you've got the wrong number.
A: I'm sorry, bye.
B: Bye.

Personal Study Workbook

5: forming questions
6: pronunciation: question intonation
8: visual dictionary

REVIEW OF UNIT 6

Please come

Suggested steps

Establish the context of the conversation: it is a man and a woman who know each other; the man is asking the woman to go out with him; she's busy most days; he is persistent.

Look at the key language: *How about ...? / I'm sorry, I've got /I'm.*

Get the class to try to ask you out. Elicit *How about ...?* from different learners or chorally; reply with *sorry* and a reason. Focus on stress and intonation.

Ask pairs to suggest one day to go out and reply with a reason or excuse. There are ideas in the Sorry box.

Ask the same pairs to try to prepare the whole conversation as a role play. If you can, organise for the pairs to record their conversations.

Use the recordings for learners to diagnose areas for improvement, perhaps using a diagnostic sheet prepared by you.

Encourage this sort of self assessment as part of the development of learner independence if this is appropriate in your teaching situation.

MONEY! MONEY! MONEY!

Language focus:
talking about prices: *How much ...?*
asking for things in shops: *I'd like ...*
asking someone to repeat something: *Pardon? Sorry?*

Vocabulary:
presents
money and currencies
electrical goods

A SHOPPING

1 Shops   vocabulary

You are at the airport. Where can you buy these things? Find the right shop, A, B, C,
D, E or F.

earrings .... camera .... CDs .... personal stereo ....

television .... T-shirt .... jeans .... necklace ....

shoes .... newspapers .... postcards .... things for children ....

What other things are in these shops? Write lists.

2 At the airport   listening; vocabulary

A ▢ Listen to some people at an airport. They are on their way home. Which shops
are they in? Fill in the spaces.

Which shop? (A–F)	*What do they buy?*
1.	....
2.	....
3.	....
4.	....
5.	....

MONEY! MONEY! MONEY!

Introduction to the unit

This unit focuses on a variety of themes related to money. Lesson A starts with buying presents for friends and family and includes shop conversations and descriptive vocabulary. Lesson B introduces different currencies and moves on to prices, and the questions: *How much is it? / are they?* Lesson C moves on to ordering things by telephone from a catalogue. In addition to consolidating the language points from lessons A and B, this last lesson provides reading and writing practice and includes an *In conversation* exercise which introduces ways of asking someone to repeat what they have just said – language which is especially useful in phone conversations.

Warm-up

Start by focusing on the concept of *presents*. Teach the word by bringing in one or two of your possessions that you were given as presents. Have a short discussion about presents; here are a few question ideas to start with:

1. When do you give presents? (e.g. birthdays)
2. What kind of presents do you like to get and give?
3. Has anyone got with them something somebody gave them? (e.g. clothes, jewellery, etc.)

A SHOPPING

1 Shops

Suggested steps

Make sure learners understand the word *airport*, explain the task, then let them work, individually or in pairs matching the things with the shops. You may wish to pre-teach these words from the list which may be new to learners - *personal stereo, necklace, T-shirt, shoes*. You may also wish to check that learners understand the shop names, although this should be self-evident from the illustrations.

Elicit the answers.

Answer key

A. Jewellery: earrings, necklace
B. Hi-tech: camera, television
C. Clothes: jeans, T-shirt, shoes
D. Music: personal stereo, CDs
E. Toys: things for children
F. Books: postcards, newspapers

Elicit the names of other things in the shops illustrated.
Note: You should decide for yourself how much of this vocabulary your class can cope with at this stage.

Answer key:

A. Jewellery: watch, wallet, handbag
B. Hi-tech: video camera, mobile phone, video machine, radio
C. Clothes: scarf, hat, tie
D. Music: cassettes, posters
E. Toys: car, doll, bike, teddy bear, train
F. Books: magazine, book, chocolate, etc.

2 At the airport 🔲

Suggested steps

Make sure the class understands the context for this task – people are at an airport on their way home from a holiday or a business trip. They are in the airport shops making last minute purchases.

Play the recording for the first time, pausing after each conversation. The class listens to the conversations and decides which shops they relate to.

Play the recording a second time, again with pauses. This time they listen specifically for what the people buy. Point out that they should choose from the list in their books. (Some things are not mentioned in the conversations.)

Get learners to compare answers in pairs, then, if necessary, play the recording for a third and final time, then elicit answers.

Tapescript

See page 130.

Answer key

Conversation 1: C a dark blue T-shirt with the words
I love Australia on it

Conversation 2: A a necklace

Conversation 3: B a small black television (the same
size as a camera)

Conversation 4: D some (unnamed) CDs and two
new Phil Collins CDs

Conversation 5: E a teddy bear – not too big

Note: Nobody buys a small camera, cassettes,
earrings, a magazine or shoes.

The class is going to hear the same conversations
again, but this time the customers say who they are
buying the things for. Explain the task, if necessary
checking learners' understanding of *partner, boyfriend,
girlfriend, grandson, granddaughter*. (The rest of the
family words were introduced in an earlier unit.)

Play the recording, once or twice, as necessary. Elicit
the answers.

Tapescript

See page 130.

Answer key

Conversation 1: The T-shirt is for the man's **wife**.

Conversation 2: The necklace is for the woman's
daughter.

Conversation 3: The television is for the man's
girlfriend.

Conversation 4: One CD is for the woman's **sister**
and the other is for her **husband**.

Conversation 5: The teddy bear is for the man's (10-
week-old) **grandson**.

3 Presents

This task gives learners the chance to practise shop
conversations.

Suggested steps

Read through the *Presents to buy* list with the class.
Check their understanding of the words and ask a few
comprehension questions.
Examples: *Do you buy earrings at a toy shop?   Do you
buy T-shirts at a book shop?   What does this person buy
for his or her friend?*

Get learners to make their own present lists, including
any words they know. They will use these lists as the
basis for the conversations which follow.

Read through the example conversation with the class,
then build another dialogue like this, eliciting ideas
from the class. Finally, let learners make their own
conversations in pairs. Monitor their conversations,
correcting selectively. Listen particularly for the correct
use of the short form *I'd like ... .*

Option

As a round-up to this exercise, ask one or two pairs to
redo their conversations for the whole class.

4 Questions

This is revision of some of the questions that have
occurred in the unit so far.

Suggested steps

Learners read through the questions and answer them
for themselves in writing. They then work in pairs. It
will probably work best if A asks B all the questions
and notes down the answers, then B asks A.

Monitor the conversations, checking spoken and
written language.

Quick Check

Answer key

A

1. C: *Can I have this necklace, please?*
   or
   Please can I have this necklace?
   A: *Yes, of course. Is it a present?*
2. C: *Have you got a green T-shirt?*
   A: *Yes, we have. Large or small?*
3. A: *Can I help you?*
   C: *I'd like that small Japanese camera, please.*
4. C: *I'd like an umbrella, please.*
   A: *Is it for a man or a woman?*

B

1. It's = **It is**
2. I'd = **I would**
3. We've = **We have**
4. It's = **It is**; He's = **He is**
5. They're = **They are**

C

Note: Point out that some nouns can go with more
than one verb.

You can *listen to*: *a cassette / a CD / a film / a football
match (on the radio), a personal stereo,
a television*

You can *read*: *a book / a magazine / a newspaper*

You can *watch*: *a film / a football match / television*

> ### Language Point
>
> The subject of the order of adjectives before a
> noun is much too complicated to go into in any
> detail at this level, but the phrase *a small Japanese
> camera* occurs in answer A3 and may provoke
> questions from the class. If learners ask *Why can't
> you say a Japanese small camera?*, you could give
> them this pattern to follow.
>
> | | size | colour | country | noun |
> |---|------|--------|---------|------|
> | *a* | *small* | *red* | *German* | *car* |
> | *a* | *big* | *blue* | *Japanese* | *television* |

B 🔲 Listen again. What do the people buy? Choose from the list and fill the spaces.

a small camera   cassettes   CDs   a pair of earrings   a magazine   a necklace
a pair of shoes   a T-shirt   a teddy bear   a television

C 🔲 Who do they buy things for? Listen and choose a person for each conversation.

partner (= husband or wife/boyfriend or girlfriend)   brother   sister   son
daughter   grandson   granddaughter   friend

1. ....   3. ....   5. ....

2. ....   4. ....

3 Presents | *I'd like...; speaking* |

You want to buy some presents for your family and friends.
Choose things from the shops. Write a list, like this:

Work in pairs. Make conversations, like this:

ASSISTANT: *Can I help you?*
CUSTOMER: *Yes, I'd like some earrings, please.*
ASSISTANT: *Are they a present for someone?*
CUSTOMER: *Yes, they are. They're for my mother.*

4 Questions | speaking; writing |

Answer these questions.

1. Have you got an umbrella?
2. What colour is it?
3. Have you got a TV?
4. Is it big or small?
5. Would you like a new T-shirt?
6. What colour would you like?

Now ask another learner the questions and write his or her answers.

Presents to buy

mother: earrings

partner: watch

son or daughter: CD

brother or sister:
red T-shirt

friend: cassette

✔ Quick Check

A Write the words in the correct order.

1. CUSTOMER: have this please can I necklace?
   ASSISTANT: course yes of present it a is?
2. CUSTOMER: T-shirt got a have you green?
   ASSISTANT: have we yes or small large.
3. ASSISTANT: you help can I?
   CUSTOMER: please that camera Japanese small
   like I'd.
4 CUSTOMER: umbrella I'd please an like.
   ASSISTANT: a for a man woman is it or?

B What are the long forms?

1. It's for my daughter.
2. I'd like a small television.
3. We've got black, white or red.
4. It's for my son. He's only five weeks old.
5. They're for my mother.

C What can you listen to, what can you read, what can you see? Match the verbs with the nouns.

Verbs: listen to   read   watch
Nouns: book   cassette   CD   film   football match
magazine   newspaper   personal stereo   television

1 Prices   vocabulary; listening

Where is the money from?
Match the countries and the currencies.

Australia   lira
Britain   drachma
Germany   yen
Greece   dollar
Italy   pound
Japan   dollar
Spain   deutschmark
United States   peseta

☐☐ Listen and write the prices.

1. .... yen   3. .... pounds   5. .... pesetas   7. .... dollars
2. .... lire   4. .... drachma   6. .... deutschmarks   8. .... dollars

2 Souvenirs   prices; listening

A ☐☐ Four people talk about their holiday souvenirs. Listen for the name of the country and the souvenirs. Fill in the spaces.

	Example	1.	2.	3.	4.
Country	*Japan*	....	....	....	....
Souvenir	*camera*	....	....	....	....

B ☐☐ Listen to the conversations and write the prices of the souvenirs in the price tags.

HELP	In your language?
How much is it?	....
How much are they?	....

1 Prices 🔲

Suggested steps

Before learners open their books, write the names of a few countries on the board and ask: *What is their money?* Elicit the names of the currencies.

Option

Ask if any learners know the current exchange rates between their currencies and major world currencies (dollar/pound/mark/yen, etc.)

Learners can work individually or in pairs on the matching exercise.
Elicit the answers.

Answer key

Australia – dollar	Britain – pound
(Australian dollar)	Greece – drachma
Germany – deutschmark	Japan – yen
Italy – lira	United States – dollar
Spain – peseta	(United States dollar)

Explain that learners are going to hear some prices in different currencies. Play the recording, pausing after each price. Play again, if necessary. Allow learners to compare answers, then elicit answers.

Tapescript

1. That's seven hundred and fifty yen.
2. 40,000 lire, please.
3. Ninety pounds? That's really expensive!
4. They're 300 drachma each.
5. That's about 200 pesetas.
6. It's seventeen deutschmarks.
7. Hmm. Eighty dollars – that's quite cheap.
8. I think it's eighteen dollars.

Answer key

1. seven hundred and fifty yen (750)
2. forty thousand lire (40,000)
3. ninety pounds (90)
4. three hundred drachma (300)
5. two hundred pesetas (200)
6. seventeen deutschmarks (17)
7. eighty dollars (80)
8. eighteen dollars (18)

Option

Get the class to practise saying numbers by repeating each price phrase from the recording. Point out the contrast between **eighteen** and **eighty**, and give more examples of this difference if you wish.

2 Souvenirs 🔲

This activity provides further listening practice related to prices, souvenirs and places.

Suggested steps

Explain the activity and play the recording for the first time, pausing after each conversation.

Give learners a chance to compare answers with a partner, then, if necessary, play the recording again.

Tapescript

See page 131.
Elicit answers.

Answer key

	1.	2.	3.	4.
Country	Italy	United States (America)	England	Spain
Souvenir	shoes	painting	umbrella	sunglasses

Option

Ask learners for other information from the conversations. Here are some possible questions:
1: Where are the shoes from?   Which city?   *Rome*
2: Where is the painting from?   Which city?   *New York*   Is the painting old?   *No, it's modern.*
3: Where is the umbrella from?   Which city?   *London.*

Explain that learners are now going to hear the four people buying the souvenirs they have just heard about. They should listen for the prices and complete the empty price tags in the illustration.

Play the recording, allowing time for learners to compare answers. Play the recording again, then elicit the answers.

Tapescript

See page 131.

Answer key

A. 200,000 lire
B. £15
C. $200
D. 800 pesetas

Language Point:

Draw attention to the questions: *How much is?* and *How much are?* in the Help box. Provide extra practice of these by writing a mixture of singular and plural nouns on the board, and eliciting the appropriate questions from the class. Example:

> You point to a plural noun on the board e.g. *books* and say to a learner: *Ask me a question.*

The learner should say: *How much are the books?*

---

3 Prices

Suggested steps

Explain the activity, and get pairs of learners to read the example conversation aloud.

Each individual then decides, secretly, what each of the things illustrated costs.

Referring to their own prices, learners have conversations in pairs. Monitor, paying particular attention to the *How much?* expressions. Check particularly that learners are using *How much is?* with singular nouns and *How much are?* with plural nouns.

Quick Check

Answer key

A
1. Spain **is** a very nice country.
2. **That's** / That **is** really expensive.
3. That teddy bear is two **hundred** (NOT hundreds) pounds.
4. My shoes **are** from London.
5. We really like **modern** (NOT moderns) paintings.
6. How much **is** this necklace?

B
1. on   2. for   3. from   4. in   5. to

C
1. d   2. a   3. f   4. c   5. b   6. e

Personal Study Workbook

2: conversation

3 Prices | *How much?* speaking |

How much are these things? Write a list of prices in your money and in pounds or dollars. Don't show other people.

Make conversations in pairs, like this:

A: *Hello. Can I help you?*
B: *Yes, how much is this necklace?*
A: *It's a hundred pounds.*
B: *That's very expensive!*

✔ Quick Check

A Correct the mistakes.

1. Spain are a very nice country.
2. That really expensive.
3. This teddy bear is two hundreds pounds.
4. My shoes is from London.
5. We really like moderns paintings.
6. How much are this necklace?

B Fill the gaps in these sentences with one of these words: *for, from, in, on, to.*

1. My T-shirt's got my name .... it.

2. I've bought a present .... my best friend.

3. My shoes are .... Italy.

4. Have a nice holiday .... France.

5. Welcome .... New York.

C Find the right answers to the questions.

1. How much is that T-shirt?
2. Have you got any postcards?
3. How much are these shoes?
4. Who are the sunglasses for?
5. Where are you from?
6. Who's the necklace for?

a. No, we haven't.
b. I'm from Scotland.
c. They're for my little sister.
d. It's twenty pounds.
e. It's for my mother.
f. They're £100.

1 Things in a catalogue   reading; vocabulary

Read these descriptions of things in a catalogue. Match them with the photographs.

WALLET
Black or brown.
Real leather.
For notes and credit cards.
CODE: MLW66

MICRO RECORDER
Two-speed micro-cassette recorder.
Two hours of recording time. Speak
and the recorder starts.
CODE: MCR22

NIGHT WATCH
Quartz watch. White face and
large black numbers. Silver
hour and minute hands and
red second hand.
CODE: WWN 2

DESK FAX
Answer machine and fax in one.
Black or green.
CODE: DFX–33

2 On the phone   listening

Listen to the telephone conversation and complete this form.

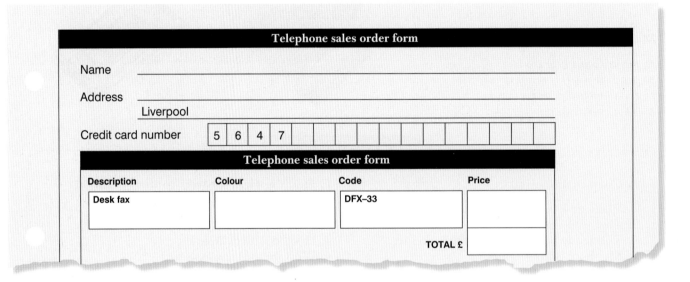

Telephone sales order form			
Name			
Address			
Liverpool			
Credit card number 5 6 4 7			

Telephone sales order form			
Description	**Colour**	**Code**	**Price**
Desk fax		DFX–33	
		TOTAL £	

3 Role play   speaking

In pairs, take turns to be the customer and the assistant. Use some of these questions.

Customer: *Have you got a ...?*   *Can I have ...?*   *How much is ...?*
Assistant: *What colour ...?*   *What's your name/address/card number?*

Partner A (Customer):   Find the price of the watch, then order it.
Partner B (Sales assistant): Tell the customer the price of the watch (you decide), then ask for
his or her name and address.

Partner A (Customer):   Find the price of the wallet, then order it. (You want a brown wallet.)
Partner B (Sales assistant): Tell the customer the price of the wallet (you decide), find out the
colour he or she wants, then ask for his or her name and address.

1 Things in a catalogue

Suggested steps

Before learners open their books, do a quick class survey to find out how many people regularly order things from catalogues. What kinds of things?

Explain the task: to match the descriptions with the illustrations. Point out, in the learners' own language if appropriate, that there are a lot of new words in these descriptions, but that it is not necessary for them to know them all.

The matching should not take more than a few seconds, so do it as a whole class activity. Elicit the answers.

Answer key

A. Desk fax   B. Night watch   C. Micro recorder
D. Wallet

2 On the phone 📖

The class now hears a conversation in which someone telephones the catalogue company to order two items described in Exercise 1. They complete the form in their books with the information they hear.

Suggested steps

Clarify the task. If you wish, you could tell learners to imagine they work for the catalogue company and take orders from telephone customers.

Pre-teach or check learners' understanding of these words and phrases from the printed form: *telephone sales order form; credit card number; code; total.*

Play the recording for the first time. There is repetition in the conversation, so try playing it without pausing. If learners find it very difficult, play it a second time with pauses.

Give the learners time to compare completed forms in pairs, then elicit the answers.

Tapescript

A: Hello. Telephone sales. Can I help you?
B: Oh yes, hello. I'd like some things from the catalogue.
A: Yes, what would you like?
B: The desk fax.
A: What's the code number?
B: It's DFX–33.
A: DFX–33. That's £284. Do you want black or green?
B: Green, please.
A: Green. Yes?
B: And the night watch. That's WWN2.
A: The night watch. Yes. That's £29.99. Anything else?
B: No, that's all thanks.
A: Right. That's the desk fax and the night watch. That's £313.99. How do you want to pay?
B: Credit card. Is that OK?
A: Fine. What's your card number, please?
B: 5647 2165 4583 2409.
A: And your name and address, please?
B: Paul North ...
A: Paul North.
B: 17, London Road, Liverpool.
A: Thank you, Mr North.

Answer key

Name:		Paul North	
Address:		17, London Road, Liverpool	
Credit card number:	5647 2165 4583 2409		
Description	Colour	Code	Price
Desk fax	green	DFX - 33	£284.00
Night watch	X	WWN 2	£29.99
		TOTAL	£313.99

3 Role play

This role play activity can be done face-to-face as a shop conversation or back-to-back as a telephone conversation. The watch and the wallet mentioned are those in the illustrations of the catalogue items. The prices should be decided by the learner being the assistant in each case. If it is done as a telephone conversation, the assistant could write down the details on a copy of the telephone sales order form.

Suggested steps

Explain the task, then monitor conversations and check written notes.

Option

Round off the activity by asking one or two pairs to 'perform' their conversations to the rest of the class.

4 In conversation 💬

Suggested steps

Option

A way of introducing the task would be to say something to the class that they cannot understand or hear, e.g. you could whisper something, say something in very advanced English or say something in another foreign language. Then ask the questions: *Do you understand me? No? What do you say?*

Whether or not you use the above idea, tell the class that they are going to hear a conversation in which one person doesn't understand what the other person is saying. Ask them to listen to the conversation, follow the text in their books and pick out the (three) questions Maria uses to ask for something to be repeated.

Play the recording, and elicit the words and phrases: *What did you say? Pardon? Sorry?*
Play the recording again and ask learners to repeat Maria's words.

Finally, get the class to make similar conversations related to two new catalogue items: a digital diary and a mini-fridge. Monitor but do not interrupt the conversations.

> #### Language Point
> One of the phrases in the recording, *What did you say?* contains a past tense question. It is advisable, at this stage, to treat this simply as a useful phrase, rather than drawing attention to the past tense.

Quick Check
Answer key
A
1. d   2. e   3. b   4. a   5. c
B
1. the night watch
2. small
3. sixty
4. 6 (white, black, silver, red, green, brown)
5. micro and mini

Note: *micro* and *mini* are really prefixes rather than words in their own right, since they are not normally used as adjectives.
C
Obviously, there are no specific answers for this. Look at each individual learner's writing and correct errors.

Personal Study Workbook

1: vocabulary	6: reading
3: question words	7: reading and writing
4: vocabulary	8: listening
5: vocabulary	9: visual dictionary

4 In conversation | asking someone to repeat something |

📖 **Listen and read.**

POLLY: Look at this micro recorder.
  It's a very small cassette recorder.
MARIA: What did you say?
POLLY: This is a very small cassette recorder.
  You speak and the recorder starts.
MARIA: Pardon?
POLLY: You speak and it starts.
MARIA: Is it expensive?
POLLY: About £300, I think.
MARIA: Sorry?
POLLY: About £300.

Work in pairs. Have conversations like this about the digital diary and the mini-fridge.

DIGITAL DIARY
Small screen with clock and
alarm. Keep your addresses and
telephone numbers in one place.
500 names and numbers.
£30

CODE: DD1X

MINI-FRIDGE
For offices or small shops.
Keep snacks and drinks cold.
486 mm x 502 x 564
£200

CODE: MFW–101

✔ Quick Check

A Match the questions and answers.

Questions
1. What would you like?
2. What's the code number?
3. What colour do you want?
4. How do you want to pay?
5. What's your card number?

Answers
a. By credit card.
b. Black, please.
c. 3247 9572 6129 3726.
d. I'd like a mini-TV, please.
e. It's MTV32.

B Look at the catalogue descriptions and answer these questions.

1. What has a face and three hands?
2. What is the opposite of *large*?
3. How many minutes are there in one hour?
   Write a word.
4. How many words for colours are there in the
   six descriptions?
5. Find two words for very *small*.

C Write a catalogue description of one of your things, for example a watch, a pen, glasses, a radio. Write like this:

WALLET
– Black or brown.
– Real leather (not plastic).
– For notes and credit cards.
  CODE: MLW66

PERSONAL STUDY WORKBOOK
- vocabulary of money, prices and shopping
- listening to people buying things
- reading descriptions in a catalogue
- ordering things by telephone: listening and speaking activities
- visual dictionary – a student's room
- reading – episode 9 of *Lost in time*

REVIEW OF UNIT 7

1 Departure times |times; speaking|

Fill the spaces with one of these times. Don't show other people.

06.30	07.05	09.15	10.50	11.45	13.50	14.25	16.20	18.00
20.05	22.10	23.30						

International departures

Destination	Flight	Time	Gate
Madrid	IB632	....	16
Perth	QF235	....	10
Istanbul	BA39	....	17
Bangkok	MAS724	....	22
Berlin	LH212	....	12
Tokyo	JAL831	....	18

Have conversations with another learner, like this:

A: *What time is the flight to Madrid?*
B: *It's half past six in the morning.*

2 Verb endings |pronunciation|

🔊 Listen. What are the sounds at the end of these verbs, /s/, /z/ or /ɪz/?

1. **works**   He works in a café.
2. **teaches** She teaches in a primary school.
3. **goes**   He goes to school at 8 o'clock.
4. **finishes** She finishes work at 6 o'clock.
5. **helps**   He helps his brother.
6. **watches** She watches television in the evening.
7. **phones**   He phones his sister every day.
8. **writes**   She writes postcards to her family.

🔊 Listen again and check.

REVIEW OF UNIT 7

1 Departure times

Suggested steps

Explain the activity: each learner fills in the flight departure table with times from the list and then uses this table to answer a partner's questions about flight times.

Monitor the conversations, listening particularly to the correct time expressions.

Option

The main purpose of this exercise is to revise and practise saying the time. If the class finds this very easy, suggest extending the conversations to include flight numbers and gate numbers.
Example:

> A: *What time is the flight to Madrid?*
> B: *It's half past six in the morning.*
> A: *What's the flight number?*
> B: *It's IB632.*
> A: *And the Gate number?*
> B: *It's Gate sixteen.*
> A: *Thank you very much.*

More advanced learners might also include the questions from Exercise 4 in Lesson C: *Pardon? Sorry? What did you say?*

2 Verb endings ▭

This pronunciation exercise draws learners' attention to the three different endings of the third person singular of present simple verbs.

Suggested steps

Explain the task, making sure that learners understand and can hear the differences between the three endings. Use these verbs, if you need examples not in the exercise:
wash/washes /ɪz/;   *listen/listens* /z/;   *start/starts* /s/

Play the recording, then allow learners to compare answers in pairs.

Play once or twice more as necessary, then elicit the answers.

Answer key

1. works /s/   2. teaches /ɪz/   3. goes /z/
4. finishes /ɪz/ 5. helps /s/   6. watches/ɪz/
7. phones /z/   8. writes /s/

Finally, get learners to listen to the recording again and repeat each sentence.

REVIEW OF UNIT 8

1 Do you like international fast food?

This is a free speaking activity.

Suggested steps

You could start this off as a whole class activity, eliciting the names of a few fast food restaurants and the types of food they sell and listing them on the board. Once learners understand what is required, let them continue compiling lists individually.

After about two minutes stop this listing activity and get learners to work in pairs, telling each other about their restaurants.

2 Seasonal geography

Explain the activity: to talk about when the seasons are in different cities of the world.

Suggested steps

Learners work out the answers to the questions about seasons. This is probably best done as a class activity. Elicit the answers:

Answer key

Winter in Buenos Aires: June, July, August
Summer in Oslo: June, July, August
Spring in Melbourne: September, October, November
Autumn in Edinburgh: September, October, November

Learners then ask each other about other cities or countries. Again this could be done as a whole class activity.

Unit 9 Worksheet

This is a simple information gap activity in which learners have to ask each other the prices of items they have chosen from a catalogue book.

Suggested steps

Individually, learners choose and list five items to buy for friends. They then ask their partner how much these five items cost and note down the prices.

Finally, they have shop conversations, taking turns to be the shopkeeper and the customer.

REVIEW OF UNIT 8

1 Do you like international fast food? $\boxed{\text{vocabulary; speaking}}$

What international fast food restaurants are there near your home or in your part of the city? Write a list of the names and the type of food.

Do you like these restaurants? Tell a partner about the good and bad restaurants.

Examples: *I like … a lot.*
I don't know that restaurant.
The service is quick/good/awful.
The food is cheap/expensive/fresh.
My son/daughter likes … but I …

2 Seasonal geography $\boxed{\text{months and seasons; speaking}}$

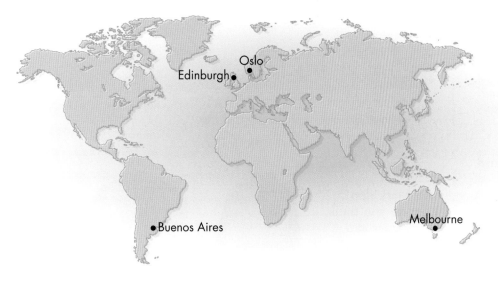

Write the names of the months for the seasons in these cities.

Winter in Buenos Aires   ....
Summer in Oslo   ....
Spring in Melbourne   ....
Autumn in Edinburgh   ....

Ask a partner questions about other cities.

Example: *What are the (spring) months in (Paris)?*

CLOTHES FOR WORK AND PLAY

Language focus:
questions: *whose?/which?*
possessive *'s*
too + adjective
compliments: *I like your ... It suits you.*

Vocabulary:
clothes
jobs

A   WORK AND CLOTHES

1   What do people wear for work?   present simple; frequency adverbs; reading

Match the four people with their words.

I often wear a skirt, a pullover and flat shoes.

I always wear a suit, a white shirt and a tie.

I usually wear jeans, a shirt and a jacket. I never wear a tie.

I always wear a suit, a white blouse and high-heeled shoes.

1. Pierre, 22, is a photographer.

2. Monica, 39, is a university teacher.

3. Angela, 24, works for an international company.

4. Mark, 42, is director of a German computer business.

2   At the weekend   present simple; listening

Pierre, Monica, Angela and Mark don't work at the weekend. What do you think they wear? Talk to another learner and then write lists.

pullover

sweatshirt

blouse

T–shirt

shoes

evening dress

skirt

trousers

jeans

shorts

sandals

cap

CLOTHES FOR WORK AND PLAY

Introduction to the unit

The main topic focus of this unit is clothes. Lesson A contrasts people's work and weekend clothes and introduces more frequency adverbs used with present simple verbs. Lesson B starts with the theme of uniforms and presents the language of possession: *whose?* and the genitive – *'s*. The theme widens to include other possessions and the question word *which?* is introduced. The main focus in Lesson C is the language of paying compliments, a useful social skill; reading and writing skills are also practised.

Warm-up

Instead of using the illustrations in the Class Book to present clothes vocabulary, use your own flash cards or the clothes learners themselves are wearing. Limit the number of nouns in the first instance to those presented in Lesson A of the unit, but extend the list later if the class can cope with more.

Point to pictures or real clothes and try to elicit the vocabulary. Example questions and possible answers:

What's this?	*It's a jacket.*
What are these?	*They're jeans.*
What colour is it?	*It's blue.*
What colour are they?	*They're blue.*

A WORK AND CLOTHES

1 What do people wear for work?

If you have already presented the clothes vocabulary to the class as suggested above, Exercises 1 and 2 will revise this vocabulary, leaving you free to focus on the use of the frequency adverbs.

Suggested steps

Ask learners to look at the illustration and match the speech bubbles with the people. You could read the speech bubbles out in a random order, stressing the frequency adverbs.

Elicit answers from the whole class.

Answer key

I always wear a suit ...	4 - Mark
I usually wear jeans ...	1 - Pierre
I often wear a skirt ...	2 - Monica
I always wear a suit ...	3 - Angela

If learners do not already know this clothes vocabulary, teach it, first from the illustration of the four people, then, if possible using real examples from the class.

Practise by asking more questions. Examples:
> *What does Mark wear at work?*
> *Does Pierre wear a suit at work?* etc.

Learners could ask and answer questions like this in pairs, as well as answering your questions. Do not insist on the use of frequency adverbs at this stage.

Option

You could use the details of the four people for further practice of questions. Examples:
How old is Angela? What does Mark do?
Who is a photographer? Where does Monica work?

Now focus on frequency adverbs by asking questions like this about the four people:
Does Mark usually wear a suit for work?   *No, he **always** wears a suit ...*

Then elicit the difference in meaning between always, usually and often. If this is a problem, show the frequency using percentages, like this:

always =	100%	= every day
usually =	80%-99%	= 5 or 6 days a week
often =	about 50%-79%	= 4 or 5 days a week
sometimes =	1% – 49%	= 1 – 3 days a week
never =	0%	= no days

Note: This information is included in the Grammar Reference at the back of the Class Book.

> ### Language Point
>
> At this stage teach the class that the position of frequency adverbs is immediately before the main verb. Only practise them with present simple questions and statements. (i.e. do not use them with the verb *be*.) Examples:
> *What do you **usually** wear for work?*
> *I **never** wear a suit for work.*
> *I don't **always** wear a tie for work.*

2 At the weekend 🔲

Suggested steps

Learners guess what each of the four people wears at the weekend. They choose from the items in *both* illustrations on page 76 of their books and write lists. This could be pair work or a class activity. The lists give them a reason to listen to the next recording.

> ### Language Point
>
> Point out that in English these words are always plural: *shorts, trousers, jeans.*
> This point could be practised by getting learners to ask and answer questions like this:
> *What colour are your jeans?*   *They're blue.* etc.

Clarify the task: learners listen to the recording and check to see how many of their guesses were correct. **Note:** The speakers' names are mentioned in the conversations. They speak in this order: Mark, Monica, Angela, Pierre.

Play the recording, once or twice as necessary and elicit the answers. *Who wears what at the weekend?*

Tapescript

1. INTERVIEWER: Mark, what do you wear at the weekend?
   MARK: I usually wear trousers – not jeans – and a shirt. I sometimes wear a pullover.
   INTERVIEWER: Do you wear a hat?
   MARK: No, I don't.

2. INTERVIEWER: Monica, what do you wear at the weekend?
   MONICA: Mmm, I usually wear just jeans and a sweatshirt. And sandals – I love my sandals.

3. INTERVIEWER: Angela, what do you wear at the weekend?
   ANGELA: Well, I love long dresses, especially for parties. My favourite dress is black at the moment. And at discos, I usually wear a mini-skirt and a bright blouse.

4. INTERVIEWER: What do you wear at the weekend, Pierre?
   PIERRE: Shorts and a T-shirt. On the beach I sometimes wear a baseball cap and sunglasses.

Answer key

Mark: trousers (not jeans), a shirt, a pullover
Monica: jeans, sweatshirt, sandals
Angela: evening dress (long black dress) / mini-skirt, bright blouse
Pierre: shorts, T-shirt, baseball cap, sunglasses

Play the recording again – learners fill the gaps in 1 – 4 with clothes words. Allow learners to compare answers, play again if necessary, then elicit the answers.

Answer key

1. jeans, pullover, hat
2. sweatshirt, sandals (x 2)
3. mini-skirt
4. T-shirt, sunglasses

In pairs, learners now ask and answer questions about the four people. Get the class to repeat the example conversations.

> **Language Point**
> Notice the short answer in the second conversation: *Monica does.* Point this out to the class and make sure they realise it is short for *Monica wears sandals at the weekend.*
> Make it clear that *Monica wears.* is not correct.
> Practise this point further by asking the class about themselves. Example:
> *Who wears jeans? I do / You do / Juan does.* etc.

3 Survey

Suggested steps

This is a personalised activity in which learners ask each other what they do and what they wear at the weekend.

Work through the lists of useful vocabulary, checking understanding. (Learners might be able to add to these lists.) Explain that each learner should question at least three others and note down their details in a chart like the one in their books.
Monitor conversations, supplying any new vocabulary that might be necessary for learners to talk accurately about their weekends.

Quick Check

Answer key

A
1. What do you (usually) wear for work?
2. Do you wear high-heeled shoes at the weekend?
3. Is this/that your cap?
4. Is this/that your pullover?
   Is your pullover red/white/green/blue, etc.?
5. What do you wear at the weekend?

B
Men's clothes: *shirt/tie*
Women's clothes: *blouse/dress; high-heeled shoes; skirt*
Men's and women's clothes: *cap/jacket; jeans; pullover/sandals/shorts; suit/sweatshirt/T-shirt/trainers;*

Note: Of course anybody can wear any clothes they like. The key word in the rubric is *usually*.

C
Each individual will have different answers for this exercise.

Personal Study Workbook

1: present simple; frequency adverbs
4: vocabulary
6: vocabulary

📼 Listen to the four people talking. Check your guesses.

📼 Listen again and fill the spaces with a clothes word.

1. MARK: I usually wear trousers – not .... – and a shirt. I sometimes

wear a ....

INTERVIEWER: Do you wear a .... ?

2. MONICA: I usually wear just jeans and a .... And .... – I

love my ....

3. ANGELA: And at discos, I usually wear a .... and a bright blouse.

4. PIERRE: Shorts and a .... On the beach I sometimes wear a baseball

cap and ....

Ask another person questions about the four people, like this:

A: *What does Monica wear at the weekend?*   B: *She wears sandals.*
or
A: *Who wears sandals at the weekend?*   B: *Monica does.*

3 Survey [speaking]

Ask other learners *What do you wear at the weekend?*

Write their answers in the table. Look at the example.

Name	*What do you wear at weekends?*	*What do you do?*
Laura	**jeans, T-shirt, sandals**	**cinema/parties**
1.	....	....
2.	....	....
3.	....	....

Ask *What do you do at the weekend?* Use words from the lists. Write the answers in the spaces.

play	*go to*	*watch*		*work*
sports (football/ tennis/golf) games	the shops the beach the swimming pool the cinema parties concerts	TV	sport	at home in the garden

✓ Quick Check

A Here are some answers. **What are the questions?**

1. I usually wear a suit and tie for work.
2. No, I wear flat shoes at the weekend.
3. No, it's not my cap.
4. No, my pullover's black.
5. I always wear jeans and a T-shirt at the weekend.

B Who usually wears these clothes – men, women or men and women? Make three lists.

blouse   cap   dress   high-heeled shoes   jacket   jeans pullover   sandals   shirt shorts   skirt   suit sweatshirt   T-shirt   tie trainers

C What do you wear for work? Write lists of the clothes you wear:

– in the summer;
– in the winter.

1 Uniforms   `whose?, which?`

Look at these photos of people in uniforms. Match the photos with the words for their jobs.

| fire fighter | baseball player | nun | soldier | racing driver | nurse | school student |

Tom

Jenny

Brendan

Michael

Maria

Dave

Jerry

Now look at these small pictures.

Talk in pairs. Ask questions, like this:

A: *Whose dress is this?*   B: *It's Jenny's dress./It's the nurse's dress.*
or
A: *Which dress is Jenny's/the nurse's?*   B: *This dress (is Jenny's).*

Possessions
Question: **Whose** cap is this?   Question: **Which** cap is **Jerry's**?
Answer: It's **Jerry's** cap.   Answer: This cap is **Jerry's**.
           It's **Jerry's**.
Notice the 's in Jerry's.

1 Uniforms

Suggested steps

Even though these job words may be new to the class, they may be able to work some out by a process of elimination. Give the class two or three minutes to match the photos with the job words, then elicit answers.

Answer key

Tom: school student Jenny: nurse Brendan: soldier
Dave: fire fighter Maria: nun Michael: racing driver
Jerry: baseball player

As you elicit the words, get the class to pronounce them correctly.

Learners now look at the photos of clothes and try to work out which item belongs to which of the seven people. Make this into a quiz. Start by asking questions like this:
What's this? It's a tie.
Then work gradually towards the possessive language with sets of questions like these:
Is it Jerry's tie? No, it isn't. It's Tom's tie.
Whose tie is it? It's Tom's tie.
Is it Dave's tie? No, it's Tom's.

Introduce the question *Which?* in a similar way.
Example questions:
Is this Maria's dress? No, it isn't. It's Jenny's (dress).
Which dress is Maria's? This dress (is Maria's).

In pairs, learners ask and answer more questions like these. Monitor conversations listening carefully for the correct possessive language.

Finally draw learners' attention to the language box which summarises the use of *Whose? Which?* and the apostrophe – *'s*.

2 Discussion

This is a free speaking activity which gives the class the chance to express their personal ideas and feelings on the subject of uniforms. You may like to precede and/or round off the pair or group conversations with a short whole class discussion of this subject.

3 Famous faces

Suggested steps

Clarify the activity, do an example with the whole class, then let learners talk in pairs. Monitor conversations and insist on full *Whose* questions and answers which include *-'s*.

Play the recording for learners to check their ideas, then elicit answers. Insist on full answers including the possessive language.

Tapescript

OK here are the answers.
Mouth A is Nelson Mandela.
Mouth B is Pope John Paul II.
Mouth C is Tiger Woods.
Mouth D is Martina Hingis.
Mouth E is Cindy Crawford.
Mouth F is John Lennon.
How many have you got right?

Answer key

Mouth A: *It's Nelson Mandela's.*
Mouth B: *It's Pope John Paul II's. It's Pope John Paul's.*
Mouth C: *It's Tiger Woods's.*★
Mouth D: *It's Martina Hingis's.*★
Mouth E: *It's Cindy Crawford's.*
Mouth F: *It's John Lennon's.*

★ **Note:** Point out pronunciation of *-'s* in names which end with the letter *s*. Tiger Woods's (/wʊdzɪz/) and Martina Hingis's (hɪŋgɪsɪz).

Option

If time allows, get learners to say what they know about the nine people listed. Ask questions like these: *Who is Nelson Mandela? Where is he from? How old is he?*

4 Your possessions

Suggested steps

Explain this game to the class. It is important that no one sees what each learner puts on the table. Once there are enough things on the table, the conversations can start. Monitor the activity, listening carefully for the use of the possessive *-'s*.

An alternative to this group work arrangement is for everyone in the class to put something into a large bag and for the bag to be passed round. Each learner in turn takes an object out of the bag and says: *Whose … is this?* Other learners suggest names: *I think it's Paul's*, etc.

2 Discussion | speaking |

Talk in twos or threes.

– Do you wear a uniform in your job?   – Do you like uniforms?   – Which uniform would you like to wear?

3 Famous faces | whose?, which?; speaking |

Here are six famous mouths. Whose mouths are they? Ask each other questions.
Can you agree?

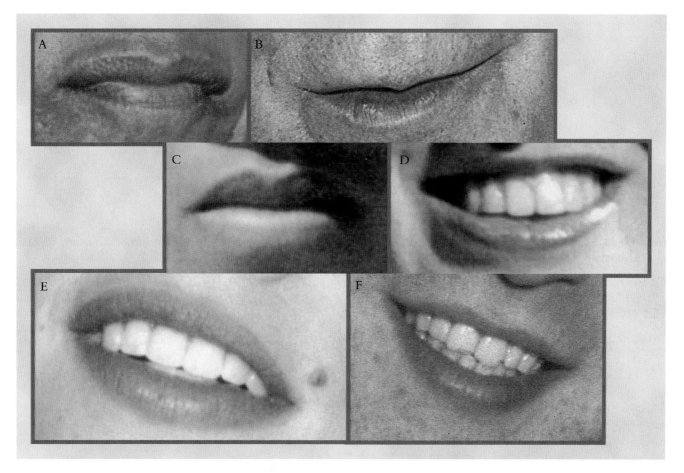

Brad Pitt   Margaret Thatcher   Tiger Woods   John Lennon   Martina Hingis
Catherine Deneuve   Nelson Mandela   Cindy Crawford   Pope John Paul II

🔲 Listen and check your answers. Have you got the same answers as other people in the class? Check, like this:

A: *Which mouth is Cindy Crawford's?*   B: *This mouth is (Cindy Crawford's).*

4 Your possessions | vocabulary; speaking |

Work with three or four other people. Close your eyes, then put something of yours on the table. Guess who the things belong to.

Example: A: *Whose bag is this?*
B: *I think it's Paul's.*
C: *I think it's Maria's.*
A: *Maria, is it your bag?*
D: *No, it isn't.*
B: *Is it your bag, Paul?*
E: *Yes, it is.*

A Which question words are missing?

what   which   who   whose

1. A: ....'s that?

   B: It's my father.

2. A: .... pullover is this?

   B: It's Tony's.

3. A: .... does a policeman wear on his head?

   B: A helmet.

4. A: .... dress is Sarah's?

   B: The red dress.

5. A: .... jacket is this?

   B: It's my jacket.

6. A: .... shoes do you wear at the weekend?

   B: I usually wear sandals.

B *'s* or *s*? Choose the right word.

1. Nurse's/Nurses wear uniform's/uniforms.
2. This is my father's/fathers jacket.
3. Are you Paul's/Pauls brother?
4. Do racing driver's/drivers always wear helmet's/helmets?
5. These boot's/boots are my brother's/brothers.

C Which word is different? What are the other two words?

Example: helmet, cap, shoe
Shoe is different. The other two words are hats.

1. nurse, soldier, doctor
2. student, baseball player, footballer
3. trousers, pullover, shorts
4. boots, sandals, jacket
5. dress, shirt, tie

C   IT'S LOVELY

1   Conversations | *too*; listening |

Listen to four conversations. Who are the people?

Match a person from List A with a person from List B.

A	B
boy	daughter
shop assistant	manager
waiter	customer
mother	boyfriend
girl	father

It's **too** expensive.

Listen to Conversations 2, 3 and 4 again and find the right picture: A, B or C.

Conversation 2

A   B   C

Conversation 4

A   B   C

Conversation 3

A   B   C

Answer key

A
1. Who's 2. Whose 3. What 4. Which
5. Whose 6. Which/What

B
1. Nurses; uniforms 2. father's 3. Paul's
4. drivers; helmets 5. boots; brother's

C
1. *soldier* is different. The other two work in hospitals.
2. *student* is different. The other two play sports.
3. *pullover* is different. The other two cover your legs.
   The other two are plural words.
4. *jacket* is different. The other two are for your
   feet.
5. *dress* is different. The other two are men's
   clothes.

Personal Study Workbook

2: whose; possessive *'s*
5: vocabulary

C IT'S LOVELY

1 Conversations 🔲

The four conversations the class is going to listen to
contextualise the *too* + adjective expressions.

Suggested steps

Explain the first listening task: learners identify the
two speakers they hear in each of the four
conversations. For each conversation, they should
match a person from List A with a person from List B.

Play the recording, pausing after each conversation to
give learners time to think about their answers. Elicit
the answers.

Tapescript

1. BOY: Dad, can I have some new shoes?
   FATHER: Yes, OK.
   BOY: I like the black shoes in the window.
   FATHER: No, I'm sorry, they're too expensive.

2. GIRL: Do you like my new jeans, Mark?
   BOY: They're OK.
   GIRL: What do you think of the colour?
   BOY: It's lovely. Yellow really suits you.
   GIRL: So, what's the problem?
   BOY: They're too bright. Your mum doesn't like
         bright clothes.

3. ASSISTANT: Hello, can I help you?
   ASSISTANT: Yes, I'd like to change this jacket.
   ASSISTANT: What's the problem?
   ASSISTANT: It's too big for me.

4. MOTHER: That skirt is very short.
   GIRL: It's a mini-skirt, Mum. Mini-skirts are always
          short.
   MOTHER: But it doesn't suit you. It's too short for you.

Answer key

Conversation 1: boy and father
Conversation 2: girl and boyfriend
Conversation 3: shop assistant and customer
Conversation 4: mother and daughter

Clarify the next listening task: learners find the
appropriate picture, A, B or C for Conversations 2, 3
and 4. Play the recording, pausing after each
conversation, give the class time to think about their
answers, then elicit answers.

Answer key

Conversation 2: Picture B – colour of jeans (yellow)
                too bright
Conversation 3: Picture A – jacket too big
Conversation 4: Picture A - skirt too short

Now check learners understand the word *too*. Point to
the pictures in turn and ask questions like these:
What's wrong with these jeans? They're too bright.
Are they too big?   *No, the colour is too bright.*

2 In conversation 〔▭▭〕

Suggested steps

Explain that learners should follow the conversation as the recording is being played. As they listen, they should answer this question: *Does B like A's hair?*

Play the recording, then elicit the answer to the while-listening question: *Yes, B likes A's hair.*

Ask the class which expressions show that B likes A's hair. Elicit the compliments from the conversation: *I like your hair. / it's great. / It really suits you. / it looks lovely.*

Now play the recording again and get the class to say B's words. Repeat this until B's compliments sound genuinely complimentary.

Learners now have their own conversations in pairs. They should take turns to compliment each other on one of the things listed in their books: hair, clothes, etc. A short list of adjectives is provided to help. Monitor conversations.

3 A letter from Florida 〔▭▭〕

This letter recycles language and vocabulary from this unit.

Suggested steps

Clarify the task: learners read the letter and fill the gaps with words from the list. Allow time for them to compare ideas with a partner, then play the recording, pausing from time to time to allow learners to check their answers.

Tapescript

I'm on holiday in Florida. I love America, but there are problems. There is a nightclub near the hotel – the music is too loud. And I don't like the weather. It's too hot for me.
Here's a photo of me in my holiday clothes. Do you like my T-shirt? And what about my hat? Do you think it's too big for me? I think it's fantastic! Don't worry, I only wear it on the beach.
See you next week.
Love,
Paula

Answer key

I'm on holiday in Florida. I love America, but there are problems. There is a **nightclub** near the hotel – the music is too **loud**. And I don't like the weather. It's too **hot** for me.
Here's a **photo** of me in my holiday clothes. Do you **like** my T-shirt? And what **about** my hat? Do you think it's too **big** for me? I think it's fantastic? Don't worry I only **wear** it on the **beach**.
See you next week. Love, Paula

Learners now write their own letters, using the letter in their books as a model. This could be set as a homework exercise.

Before you take this writing in for marking, get learners to exchange letters and read and correct each other's work.

2 In conversation — compliments; listening and speaking

A 📼 Listen and read this conversation.

A: Hi! How are you?
B: Fine. I like your hair!
A: Do you really?
B: Yes, it's great!
A: What about the colour?
B: It really suits you.
A: Do you think it's too short?
B: No, it looks lovely.

B 📼 Listen again. A is on the cassette.
You are B. Say B's words.

Make similar conversations with other learners. Talk about hair, clothes, jewellery, shoes or other things. Use some of these words:

red	blue	yellow	big	small	long	short	bright

3 A letter from Florida — reading and writing

Here is part of a letter from a friend. Fill the gaps with one of these words.

about	beach	big	nightclub	hot	like	loud	photo	wear

I'm on holiday in Florida. I love America, but there are problems. There is a .... near the hotel — the music is too .... And I don't like the weather. It's too .... for me. Here's a .... of me in my holiday clothes. Do you .... my T-shirt? And what .... my hat? Do you think it's too .... for me? I think it's fantastic! Don't worry, I only .... it on the ....

See you next week.

Love,
Paula

It's too loud!

📼 Compare answers with another person, then listen and check.

Write a letter like this to a friend.

A Fill the gaps in these sentences with *to* or *too*.

1. She wants .... go .... Turkey.
2. This jacket is .... expensive.
3. I usually go .... the beach on Sunday mornings.
4. A: The plane leaves at ten o'clock.
   B: That's .... late for me.
5. That cap belongs .... me.

B All the lines have *one* word missing. What is the word and where does it go?

1. A: You like my new shoes?
   B: Yes, do.
2. A: What do you think the colour?
   B: I like it. Red suits.

3. I'd like buy these shoes, please.
4. This T-shirt is too small me.
5. I like your jeans – look fantastic!

C Somebody says these things to you. Are they good or bad? Put ✓ or ✗.

1. Your shoes are too big for you.   ....
2. Your hair looks lovely.   ....
3. I really like your earrings.   ....
4. White jeans don't really suit you.   ....
5. Your jacket's too small.   ....
6. That uniform suits you.   ....

PERSONAL STUDY WORKBOOK

- vocabulary of clothes and uniforms
- saying nice things to other people: listening and speaking activities
- pronunciation work
- visual dictionary – clothes
- reading – episode 10 of *Lost in time*

D REVIEW AND DEVELOPMENT

REVIEW OF UNIT 8

1 I eat a lot of pasta | present simple; vocabulary; speaking |

Look at this 'pizza' diagram for the things this man eats.

Draw a pizza for you. Write the names of the foods.

Talk to a partner about the things you eat.

Example: *I eat a lot of (vegetables).*
          I don't eat a lot of (meat).

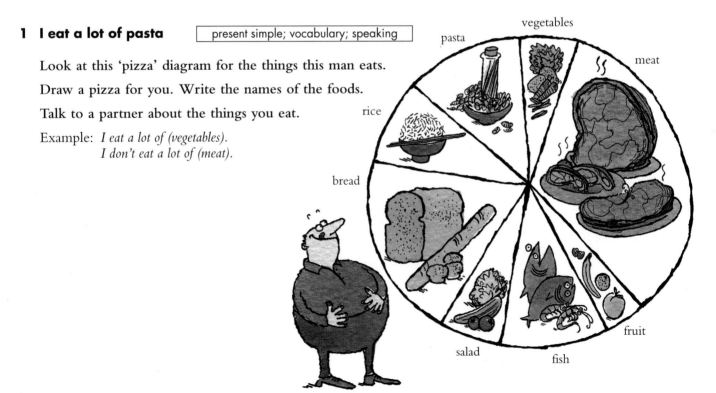

pasta
vegetables
meat
rice
bread
fruit
salad
fish

Answer key

A

1. to; to   2. too   3. to   4. too   5. to

B

1. A: **Do** you like my new shoes?
   B: Yes, **I** do.
2. A: What do you think **of/about** the colour?
   B: I like it. Red suits **you**.
3. I'd like **to** buy these shoes, please.
4. This T-shirt is too small **for** me.
5. I like your jeans – **they/you** look fantastic!

C

1. ✗ (It's not good for shoes to be too big.)
2. ✓
3. ✓
4. ✗ (It's not good if things don't suit you.)
5. ✗ (It's not good for clothes to be too small.)
6. ✓

Personal Study Workbook

 3: compliments
 7: reading
 8: listening
 9: writing
10: pronunciation
11: visual dictionary

REVIEW OF UNIT 8

1 I eat a lot of pasta

Suggested steps

To get learners to look carefully at the pizza diagram, ask them questions like this:
Does this man eat a lot of meat/vegetables?
Yes, he does. / No, he doesn't.

Learners make their own diagram dividing their circle into segments of appropriate sizes. They label the segments with food words.

Learners now use their personalised pizza diagram as the basis of their conversations with a partner.

2 Eight glasses of water ▭

Suggested steps

Learners read the text and list the drinks mentioned.
Elicit the answers.

Answer key

Six drinks are mentioned: *water, wine, coffee, beer, fruit
drinks, tea*

The class listens to the recording and repeats the
sections of the first question. This practice will help
with the next part of the exercise.

Tapescript

a day
drink a day
do you drink a day
of water do you drink a day
glasses of water do you drink a day
How many glasses of water do you drink a day?

Learners ask each other questions 1 – 5 and note
down answers.

This activity could be rounded off with a class
discussion about national and/or personal favourite
drinks.

REVIEW OF UNIT 9

1 Prices

Learners match the words with the pictures. Elicit the
answers.

Answer key

A T-shirt B necklace C wallet D camera
E CD   F shoes   G sunglasses

Individuals now decide on their own price for these
seven items, then use these prices as the basis of shop
conversations with a partner. Learners should take it
in turns to be the customer and the assistant.

2 Money and countries

Explain that learners work out the anagrams to
produce the names of five currencies. They then write
the appropriate countries.

Answer key

1. peseta   Spain
2. dollar   United States/Australia, etc.
3. yen   Japan
4. drachma   Greece
5. deutschmark   Germany

Unit 10 Worksheet

This is a simple information gap activity in which
learners match descriptions and exchange information
with a partner.

Suggested steps

Divide the class into pairs and give out A and B
worksheets.

Individually, learners match descriptions of six people
with their pictures and write sentences about each
person's job or weekend activities.

Finally in pairs they ask and answer questions to find
out more about the six people.

2 Eight glasses of water | How many? reading and speaking |

Read this. How many different drinks are there?

Some people say, 'Drink eight glasses of water a day; it's good for you'. Some people like wine, coffee, beer, fruit drinks and tea and they don't drink a lot of water.

▭ Listen and repeat the parts of question 1.

1. How many glasses of water do you drink a day?
2. How many cups of coffee do you drink a day?
3. How many cups of tea do you drink a day?
4. How many glasses of wine do you drink a day?
5. How many glasses/cups of .... (write a drink here) do you drink a day?

Ask two learners these questions. Talk about the answers you've got.

REVIEW OF UNIT 9

1 Prices | How much? speaking; vocabulary |

Match these words with the pictures.

| camera   CD   necklace   shoes   sunglasses   T-shirt   wallet |

How much do these things cost? Decide the price in dollars ($), pounds (£) or your currency. Don't show other people your prices.

In pairs make shop conversations, like this:

A: *Can I help you?*
B: *Yes. How much is the red T-shirt?*
A: *It's twenty-five dollars.*
B: *That's cheap/expensive!*

2 Money and countries | vocabulary |

Find the currencies and the right countries.

Example: undop = *pound* ....   *Britain* ....

1. tesepa   = ...
2. rolald   = ...
3. eyn   = ...
4. madarch   = ...
5. skuthracmed   = ...

11

ARE YOU THE RIGHT PERSON FOR YOUR JOB?

Language focus:	Vocabulary:
can, can't for ability	applying for jobs
question forms: *Why (not)?*	work skills
because	
What about ...?	
use of impersonal pronoun *you*	
apologies and excuses	

A YOU'VE GOT THE JOB!

1 I'm a TEN! | vocabulary; *can* for ability; *Why? Because ...* |

Give a score (between 1 and 10) for you for sentences 1–5.

1. I can write good business letters.   (..../10)

Report on Marketing
Trip to Vietnam

2. I can write good business reports.   (..../10)

3. I like people.   (..../10)   4. I can talk to people on the phone.   (..../10)   5. I can use computers.   (..../10)

Talk about your good scores, 6–10, like this:

A: *I think I'm a 6 for number 1.*
B: *Why?*
A: *Because I can write good letters. What about you?*

2 Yes, I can | dual listening; *can* questions; short responses |

⬛⬛ ⬛⬛ Listen to a woman answering questions from Exercise 1. Tick (✓) the things she can do. Cross (✗) the things she can't do.

business letters ☐   people ☐   computers ☐
reports ☐   phone ☐

Complete two of the *Can ...?* questions from the recording.

1. Can you ....?

2. Can you ....?

What is the answer to your two questions? Is it *Yes, I can* or *No, I can't*? Listen a second time and check.

ARE YOU THE RIGHT PERSON FOR YOUR JOB?

This is quite a challenging unit that has been developed in response to the demand for job or business-related material for low level learners. You may need to give additional support as some of the reading and listening material is more abstract than in other units. The new language forms and functions introduced are all highly relevant and useful to the learner starting English for the first time.

Lesson A introduces *can* and *can't* in the context of basic work skills. The question *Why?* and answers including *because* are also brought in and practised. The theme of Lesson B is working abroad and specific exercises focus on job applications and job adverts. There is further practice of *Why? Why not?* and *because*. Lesson C presents and provides practice in apologising and giving excuses for not being able to do things.

A YOU'VE GOT THE JOB

1 I'm a TEN!

Warm-up

To illustrate meaning of *can* for ability, bring in a mathematical puzzle or teaser using letters of the alphabet and say to learners: *Can you find the answer?* Let learners work in pairs. When the correct answer emerges, demonstrate the form:
X *can answer the puzzle question*
means
X *has got the ability to answer the puzzle question.*

Suggested steps

Model your own scores for one or two of the abilities described so that learners understand the task, hear some of the language and find out the difference between letters and reports.

> #### Language Point
> Indicate that Number 3. *I like people* does not need *can* because it is not an ability but a consistent attitude or expression of feeling. It therefore requires the question *Do you like people?*, whereas the others need *Can you ...?* questions, e.g. Number 1. *I can write good business letters* becomes in question form: *Can you write good business letters?*

Let learners answer individually first while you also finish the same task.

Give the learners your own scores and model *because ...* forms. Remember that *can* in sentences like *I can write good letters* is not stressed and native speakers use the schwa /ə/ in normal speed speech. This allows the meaning-carrying word (e.g. *write*) to stand out more clearly in the sentence.

Elicit one or two scores from learners. Ask: *Why?* to elicit *because ...*

Ask learners to exchange scores and reasons for scores in pairs. Monitor, assist and encourage the learners.

2 Yes I can ▢ ◾◾

Suggested steps

Elicit orally some of the questions that learners are likely to hear on the recording, e.g. *Can you write good business letters?*

Clarify the task: learners tick the things that the woman can do and cross the things she can't do. Play Version 1 of the recording.

Let the learners check their answers in pairs and write two of the *Can ...?* questions.

Play the recording again for pairs to supply the answers to their two questions.

Tapescript

See page 131.
Use Version 2 for an additional task, that is to say why she can write good letters and why she doesn't like computers. They can also listen for other new information.

Answer key

She can write good business letters, a good business report, talk to people on the phone.
Can ... ? questions:
Can you write good business letters?; Can you write a good report?; Can you talk to people on the phone?; Can you use computers?

3 Here's my report

Outline the writing task. Learners have to write two reports on other learners in the class.

Model the use of *can/can't* in the gapped report so that learners are quite clear about meaning.

Let learners walk around in search of their two respondents with note paper for taking down the necessary information.

Learners write their reports individually based on the outline.

Learners read their reports to the two people and ask each person if it is correct: *Is that correct?*

Quick Check
Answer key

A

1. Because   2. Why; you   3. do   Because; s

B

1. can   2. can't   3. Is   4. I can

Personal Study Workbook

1: vocabulary
2: questions/short answers with *can*

B WORK IN OTHER COUNTRIES

1 Jobs in other countries

Suggested steps

Elicit pronunciation of some of the jobs in the labelled photos by a word association game, e.g. *homework (student)*; *sick (doctor, nurse)*; *food (waiter)*.

Ask the learners to suggest which people can find jobs in other countries. Elicit examples of countries.

Talk about a friend of yours who is working in another country. Ask learners to ask you the four questions. Elicit an additional question.

Ask learners to write their own additional question individually; help where necessary.

Put learners in pairs for the short conversation about friends working in other countries.

Ask individual learners to report to the whole class on what they heard.

3 Here's my report [writing sentences with *can*]

Ask the same *can* questions and write a report for two people in your class.

Read your reports to the two people.

What about your teacher? Can she/he do some of these things?

> Quick report on ....
>
> .... *can/can't* write good
>
> business letters *and/but can/can't* write good
>
> reports. *He/She can/can't* use computers.
>
> .... *likes/doesn't* like
>
> people *and/but can/can't* talk to people on
>
> the phone.

✓ Quick Check

A Complete the questions or answers.

1. Why do you like your job? ....
   the money is good.
2. .... do .... like the phone?
   Because I like people.
3. Why .... you use a computer?
   .... it'..... quick.

B Complete the responses. Which *can* (1–4) has a different meaning from the other three?

1. Can you see my car?
   Yes, I .... It's over there.
2. Can you come on Saturday?
   No, I .... Sorry.
3. Can you open the window, please?
   Yes, sure. .... that OK?
4. Can you write in English?
   Yes, ...

B   WORK IN OTHER COUNTRIES

1 Jobs in other countries? [vocabulary]

In your country, which of these people can find good jobs in other countries?

student | soldier | manager | engineer | nurse | doctor | teacher | waiter | shop assistant

Have you got a friend with a job in another country?

Read these questions and write one more question.

With a partner, ask and answer the questions about your friend.

> Where is he/she?
> What's his/her job?
> Is he/she happy?
> Is the salary good?
> .... (Write your question.)

---

2 Change is good, because ...

reading; *Why (not)? because* responses

◀ John Grant works in an international bank. He's 25, not married, and lives in Geneva.

Mary O'Malley is 38 and teaches ▶ English part-time in Italy. She has a young son and her husband is a writer of travel books.

Which person likes change, do you think? John or Mary?

Read the things they say.

Today the world is small and many people work in other countries. Do they like change? John and Mary write:

> I like change, it's good. I like my job in Switzerland because in a new country I can learn new things. I can see new places and that's interesting. I can work with new technology, new ideas, new people. In today's world it's important to like change because change is everywhere – in work, in sport, in families. You can't live in the past because there isn't time.

> I don't like a lot of change. I'm a teacher and my students here in Italy are very important. I like time to understand my students – to learn about their lives and to be their friend and guide. I like to visit new countries because it's exciting, but I like lots of time to understand the life of the people in other countries. I haven't got a lot of things or a lot of money. I like to give time to the people in my life because they are my life.

Answer the questions. Choose *one* good reason (1–5) for John, and one good reason (1–5) for Mary.

Does John like change? .... Why?
1. Because it's interesting.
2. Because he's 25.
3. Because he isn't married.
4. Because he's a man.
5. .... (Write your reason.)

Does Mary like change? .... Why not?
1. Because she's a teacher.
2. Because she likes time to learn about people and places.
3. Because she's 38.
4. Because she has a young son.
5. .... (Write your reason.)

Talk about your two reasons, like this:

I think John likes change because ...
(Perhaps) Mary doesn't like change because ...

What about you? Do you like change? Why? Why not?

Is change exciting, interesting or difficult for you?

HELP	In your language?
It's hard to say.	....
It's difficult to know.	....

2 Change is good because ...

Warm-up

Put up two lists on the board with the headings 'old' and 'new'. Write or pin pictures of things under each heading, e.g. typewriter/computer; fast food/ traditional meal; new building / historical building. Ask learners to choose the list they prefer. Ask the 'new' and 'old' groups if they like change (explain change as things in your life that are new or different, not the same).

Suggested steps

Ask learners to read the introduction about John and Mary. Ask: *Who likes change? John or Mary?*

Divide the class into pairs; one reads about John, the other reads about Mary. The reading task is to say if John or Mary likes or doesn't like change and why. The pairs read and compare their ideas, then they try to answer the questions together. Encourage guessing of unknown items at this stage.

Help with any vocabulary problems from the reading but encourage learners to make sensible guesses wherever possible. This will help them to become more independent learners.

Model your own ideas on change; model and elicit: *Why? Why not?* from learners so that you can answer with *because ...* plus *exciting, interesting, difficult*. Ask each pair to join other pairs to discuss reasons in a similar way and their own reactions to change.

Monitor the conversations, giving assistance, feedback and encouragement.

Option

It may be easier to ask: *Are you a John?* or *Are you a Mary?* and follow that with *Why/Why not?* so that learners can repeat things from the text that they identify with.

3 International job applications 🕮

Suggested steps

It is a good idea to present some of the difficult vocabulary first, e.g. *interview, application form, salary, company, wait, get*. Try to use the pictures to illustrate meaning where possible.

Clarify the reading task: learners tick the boxes according to what happens with job applications in their country, as far as they know. Remember the Help box may provide useful, additional language.

Let learners complete the task individually and then share their answers with a partner.

Encourage individuals to share their answers with the whole class and elicit comment.

Establish the context for the listening, and the listening task. Two individuals are talking about what happens in their country with job applications. One is from Ecuador; the other from Australia. Encourage guesses as to likely differences between them.

The task is to write down three things they hear about what happens in each country. If you prefer, put learners in pairs and ask one of the pair to listen to the person from Ecuador and the other learner to listen to the person from Australia. They can compare answers after the recording, then listen to the other part to help their partner.

Play the recording. With less confident groups, play the recording in sections, allowing time to write after each section. Alternatively, if it is practical in your teaching situation, let learners control the recording in groups, using several cassette recorders.

Tapescript

A: In Australia, in my profession, you see an advert in a newspaper and you telephone the company to talk about the job and ask for an application form. Your job interview is very important. The interview can be with four or five people. You talk about salary at the interview because the salary is not in the advert.

B: When do you hear about the job?

A: You wait about two weeks or so and you get a letter. Some people wait a long time because they haven't got the job and the company forgets to write!

C: In my profession in Ecuador, you see a job advertisement in the newspaper and you write for an application form. You don't phone the company. You send a photo with your application form. For some jobs there isn't an interview, but for jobs with private companies there is an interview, maybe with two people. You don't talk about salary at the interview because the salary is in the advertisement, so you know the money you can get.

B: When do you hear about the job?

C: You get a letter after about one week. Some people wait a long time because the company doesn't write to everyone.

Answer key

In Australia:
You telephone to talk about the job and to ask for an application form.
The job interview is very important and can be with four or five people.
You talk about salary at the interview.
You wait about two weeks after the interview and you get a letter.
Some companies forget to write to people when they don't get the job.

In Ecuador:
You write for an application form.
You don't phone the company.
You have an interview maybe with two people.
You don't talk about salary at the interview.
You get a letter after about a week.
Some companies don't write to everyone.

4 Replying to a job advert

Suggested steps

Elicit as much information as you can about the two adverts, e.g. *Where are the jobs? Who gets the application? What is the job in A? What's the address for B?* etc. Explore some of the language in the letter, e.g. *I look forward to hearing from you; Yours faithfully.* Ask the learners to tell you what sorts of expressions could fill the spaces in the letter.

Let learners complete the letter individually and read out their letters to a partner. Monitor and assist where necessary.

Answer key

A
Please send me an application form for the position of **Senior Manager** as advertised in **The Australian** on **14th May**.

B
Please send me an application form for the position of **Lecturer** as advertised in **The Independent** on **28th August**.

3 International job applications

reading; listening for present tense; impersonal *you*

Think about job applications and interviews in your profession in your country. Tick the boxes and/or add words.

1. ☐ You see an advert in the newspaper.

2. ☐ You phone ![phone] to talk about the job and ask for an application form.

   ☐ You write ![pen and paper] for an application form.
   ☐ You write ...

3. You send the application form ... ![envelope]
   ☐ with a photo.   ☐ with no photo.   ☐ with ....

4. The company says ...
   ☐ no interview.   ☐ go for an interview.

5. You go for an interview with ... ![people]
   ☐ one or two people. ☐ four or five people. ☐ .... people.

6. In the interview ...
   ☐ you talk about salary. ![money]   ☐ you don't talk about salary.

7. You wait for ...
   ☐ a week.   ☐ two or three weeks.   ☐ .... weeks.

8. You get ...
   ☐ a letter.   ☐ a phone call.   ☐ ....

HELP	In your language?
usually	....
a long time	....

▭▭ Listen to two people, one from Australia and one from Ecuador. What happens in their countries? Write three things for each country. Talk with a partner about your three things.

4 Replying to a job advert   simple letter writing

Complete this letter for one of the adverts.

The Independent   28th August

LECTURER
required for computing faculty, private technical university, Bahrein.
Apply in writing to:
Secretary to the Dean,
Faculty of Computing,
Great Western University,
Saskatchewan, Canada.

THE AUSTRALIAN *14th May*

Senior Manager
required for import-export company in Hong Kong.
Apply to: Personnel Officer,
Position 145H, Global International,
Box 3421, Hong Kong.

Dear Sir/Madam,

Please send me an application form for the position of ....,

as advertised in the ....

on ....

I look forward to hearing from you,

Yours faithfully,

✔ Quick Check

A Study sentences a–d. Answer questions 1–4.

Sentences
a. Things change a lot.
b. They like change.
c. Change is good.
d. A quick change saves time.

Questions
1. In which sentences is change a noun?
   (Sentences ...., ... and ....)
2. In which sentence is change a verb?
   (Sentence ....)
3. In which sentence is change the object?
   (Sentence ....)
4. In which sentences is change the subject?
   (Sentences .... and ....)

B Write words for each definition.

1. You see a job advert and write a letter to get this. (an a................. f............)
2. A word for a job in formal letters. (a p........................)
3. Money you get month by month for professional work. (your s.................)
4. There are many in a newspaper – for jobs, for things in the shops for example. (a.................s)

C ▬ EXCUSES, EXCUSES

1 In conversation | saying why you can't do something; pronunciation: stressed syllables |

📼 Listen to the conversation and mark some of the strong sounds, like this:

Example: *Can you come to a pár̊ty on Sát̊urday év̊ening?*

A: Can you come to a party on Saturday evening?
B: Where?
A: Our place.
B: Is it your birthday?
A: No ... Eva's.
B: Oh, er, sorry, I can't. I haven't got the car.
A: What about the bus?
B: There aren't any buses on Saturday ... and I'm really busy with a job application.
A: Oh, OK. See you.
B: Bye. Say Happy Birthday to Eva.

How many excuses are there in the conversation?

Have conversations with a partner. Here is some help.

Partner A:
Can you come for a meal this evening?
What about Saturday evening?

Excuses for Partner B:
I'm sorry, I can't ...
          I'm very busy/tired.
          I haven't got time.
          my father is here.
          my daughter is ill.

2 Record and write | writing your recorded conversation |

Can you record your conversation?

Listen to your conversation and write all the words.

Ask your teacher for help.

Answer key

A
1. b; c; d   2. a   3. b   4. c; d
B
1. application form   2. position   3. salary
4. advertisements

Personal Study Workbook

3: questions and answers
4: reading adverts for jobs
5: question writing
6: listening

C EXCUSES, EXCUSES

1 In conversation ▭

Suggested steps

Look at the example to establish strong sounds on
particular syllables.

Explain that stress is often strong on words or parts of
words that carry information. Ask learners to read the
conversation and guess which words probably have
strong stress on one of their syllables. Let learners
discuss their ideas in pairs.

Clarify the listening task: learners should mark the
strongly stressed syllables.

Play the recording or let learners play the recording in
groups if you have several machines.

Check their answers in pairs or groups. Discuss any
unusual stress patterns. Elicit the number of excuses
mentioned.

Model the mini conversation with different learners
inviting you so that you can offer a variety of excuses
and they can try to overcome each excuse in some way.

Offer one or two variations for invitations, e.g. *come to
the cinema / come to the disco /come for coffee.*

Let learners move around the room, with some doing
the inviting and others giving excuses. Monitor and
encourage. This activity can act as preparation for the
next activity of recording conversations in pairs.

Answer key

2 excuses: no car; really busy
1 fact: no bus

2 Record and write

Suggested steps

Put learners in new pairs to prepare for conversation.

Explain your reasons for asking learners to record
their conversations: to enable them to assess their own
strengths and weaknesses, and to show them that they
are capable of having a short conversation in English.

Tell the learner who isn't the first speaker in the
conversation to press the record button on the cassette
recorder. Encourage the pairs to speak without
reading from a script if they can, and let them practise
before recording.

When conversations have been recorded, learners in
pairs try to transcribe them like a dictation. Offer
assistance as you monitor.

Ask learners to write comments on their
performance.

3 I'm sorry but ... 📖

Suggested steps

Elicit some of the vocabulary associated with the pictures, e.g. *What can you see in A? Can you see an old man? In which picture?*

Clarify the listening context and task. Learners will hear three conversations. A manager (Carlos) is trying to get staff to come to dinner on Sunday, but they are all busy and give excuses.

Learners have to tick the pictures that are related to the excuses. Not all pictures will be ticked.

Pre-teach other vocabulary if necessary: *idea, important, free, Linda's*. Play the recorded conversations one by one.

Tapescript

1. CARLOS: Hi, Sofia.
   SOFIA: Hi.
   CARLOS: Can you come to dinner?
   SOFIA: When?
   CARLOS: On Sunday.
   SOFIA: I'm sorry, Carlos, but it's Linda's birthday on Sunday. She's three.
   CARLOS: Mmm. OK.
   SOFIA: Phone Sven. Perhaps he's free.
   CARLOS: OK. Thanks, bye.

2. CARLOS: Sven, hi, it's Carlos. How are you?
   SVEN: Fine.
   CARLOS: Look can you come to dinner on Sunday?
   SVEN: On Sunday?
   CARLOS: Mmm.
   SVEN: I'm sorry, Carlos. My mother is ill ... and I'm very busy.
   CARLOS: Oh, I'm sorry about your mother.
   SVEN: What about Maria? Maybe she can go.
   CARLOS: Mmm, that's an idea. Thanks. Bye.

3. CARLOS: Maria, hi, how are you?
   MARIA: Fine, thanks, Carlos, how about you?
   CARLOS: Oh, I'm OK. Can you come for dinner on Sunday?
   MARIA: Oh, I'm very busy.
   CARLOS: Oh, really?
   MARIA: Yes. My son's at home from university. I'm really tired and I've got this report to finish ... for you!
   CARLOS: Oh, yes. Erm, what about Monday evening?

Let the learners compare their answers in pairs.

Option

For variety, put learners in groups of three. Assign conversation 1 to one learner, conversation 2 to a second, and conversation 3 to the third group member. Play the recording and let each learner tick the pictures for their conversation. Then the group compares their complete set of answers with those of another group.

Answer key

Excuses they talk about are: C, B, A, F

Quick Check

Answer key

A
1. Sorry, **she's** busy, and **her** son's ill.
2. Sorry, **he's** not well, and **his** car's in Barcelona.
3. Sorry, but **they're** in Oslo this weekend with (**John's/Mary's/his/her**) mother.

B
1. A: Can you come to a meeting at the office?
   B: When is the meeting?
   A: It's on Friday.
   B: I'm sorry but it's a holiday on Friday.
2. A: There's an important dinner on Friday.
   B: Where is it?
   A: At the Greek restaurant.
   B: I'm sorry but my mother is ill.

Personal Study Workbook

7: excuses; writing and listening
8: visual dictionary

3 I'm sorry but ...   listening for excuses

A   B   C

D   E   F   G

📖 Listen. Look at the pictures and tick the excuses they talk about.

Your manager asks:

– Can you work this evening?
– Can you come to the office on Sunday?

What do you say?

HELP	In your language?
I'm unemployed.	....
I am the manager.	....
I say *No*.	....

✔ Quick Check

A You are a secretary for Sofia, Carlos, John and Mary. Complete the excuses for them.

1. Can Sofia come to the party on Sunday?
   Sorry .... 's busy, and .... son's ill.
2. Can Carlos come to the office on Saturday?
   Sorry, ... ' s not well and .... car's in Barcelona.
3. Can John and Mary come to Sven's birthday party this evening?
   Sorry, but .... 're in Oslo this weekend with .... mother.

B Write the words for the two conversations in the right order.

1. A: you come at a meeting to the office Can?
   B: is meeting the When?
   A: Friday It's on.
   B: but I'm sorry it's a Friday on holiday.
2. A: an There's dinner on important Friday.
   B: Where it is?
   A: the Greek At restaurant.
   B: my mother is sorry but I'm ill.

PERSONAL STUDY WORKBOOK
- job and business crossword
- reading – job ads
- listening for *because* answers
- visual dictionary – offices and jobs
- reading – episode 11 of *Lost in time*

REVIEW OF UNIT 9

1 **On the phone** | vocabulary; speaking |

bike

You want to sell one of these things:

> your first computer   an old car   a bike

Write notes about: the colour, the age and the price.

Now work with another learner.

Partner A: You want to buy something from the other person. Ask questions about the colour, the age and the price. Find out B's address.
Partner B: Answer A's questions about your computer, your car or your bike. Ask when A can come and collect it.

Now change roles.

2 **Find the words** | vocabulary |

Fill the gaps in these sentences. Then put the answer words into the puzzle.

1. Can I pay by credit ....? (4)

2. How .... are those shoes? (4)

3. Fresh or cold food is here. (6)

4. One child, two .... (8)

5. You write with a .... (3)

6. Trousers. They are often blue. (5)

7. How much does this TV ....? (4)

8. Children play with .... (4)

9. A money word, for example, francs, pesetas. (8)

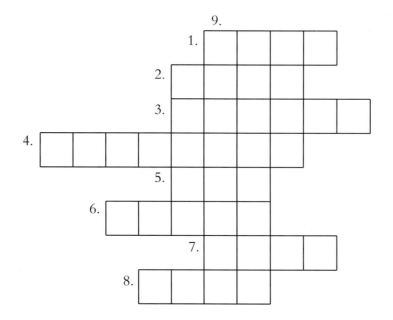

REVIEW OF UNIT 9

1 On the phone

Suggested steps

Use the picture to establish vocabulary and to introduce the context of selling old or unwanted things.

Hold up a picture of an old bike (your bike) but don't show the side with the picture on it. Tell learners it is a picture of a bike and elicit questions about colour, age and price.

Show the picture and ask: *Is it a good bike for the price?*

Ask the learners to write the colour, age and price for a bike, computer or old car. (You can distribute pictures of items if this helps.) Elicit and write up questions that the pairs will need for collection of item, e.g. address.

In pairs learners ask and answer questions. Change roles; ask and answer questions. Monitor, encourage and make a note of any points that need further practice later. If possible, record conversations for self-assessment.

2 Find the words

Suggested steps

This activity will make a good filler for learners who complete tasks before others; alternatively it could be used at the start of a lesson as a warm-up activity.

Answer key

1. card
2. much
3. fridge
4. children
5. pen
6. jeans
7. cost
8. toys
9. currency

3 Strong or weak sounds 💿

Suggested steps

Let learners guess answers to 1 – 4 in pairs before listening.

Play the recording and let learners check guesses or change them.

Help learners to deduce that generally, information words carry strong stress (except *for* in question 4 which is contrastive).

With the second set of discriminations, make sure the learners understand that it is similarity of vowel sounds that they are listening for. Again let them guess in pairs before listening as a check.

Answer key

1. a. W; b. S; c. W   2. W   3. W   4. a. S; b. W

1. phone – code; know   2. you – do; school
3. cost – boss; clock   4. your – floor; all
5. town – thousand; how

REVIEW OF UNIT 10

1 Your free time

Suggested steps

Review the meaning of the adverbs *always, sometimes* and *usually*, perhaps asking learners to suggest rough percentages for each adverb to distinguish level of frequency.

Let learners complete the table with a dictionary. Help them with verb forms.

Use the example to model the conversation, then let learners work in pairs.

Circulate, monitor and provide feedback, e.g. *Really? That's interesting*. A follow-up homework might ask learners to write a paragraph about their free time.

2 MORning 💿

Suggested steps

Try this as a pyramid activity. Put learners into pairs first and ask each pair to decide where the stress is in each of the eight words.

Put pairs together to form groups of four. Tell them to compare their answers and come to an agreement about one set of answers for that group.

Put the groups together to form a larger group of eight learners and repeat the process of negotiation. Listen to compare the recording with the single version eventually agreed upon by the class.

Tapescript

1. This is my office.
2. Do you like my new yellow jeans?
3. Where's the hotel?
4. Send me a postcard.
5. That train is too early.
6. Say it again, please.
7. The weather is terrible.
8. Can you repeat that, please?

Answer key

1. OFFice   2. YEllow   3. hoTEL   4. POSTcard
5. EARly   6. aGAIN   7. WEAther   8. rePEAT

Unit 11 Worksheet

Suggested steps

Photocopy and cut out two or three copies of each week's diary (12-18 in all). Mount each diary on to card for easy reuse.

Give each learner one card. Make sure that you give two copies of each card at least, so that learners are sure to find at least one 'partner' who can go out on the same day.

Each learner wants to go to the shops with a friend on their free day. They circulate asking different learners: *Can you go to the shops on (name of their free day)?*

Each learner looks at their diary and replies with an excuse or an agreement:
Sorry, I can't, I've got a/an …
or *Sorry it's …*
or *Yes OK, what time?*

Make sure you don't tell learners how many partners they will find so that they keep asking '*Can you …?*' questions to other learners even if they find a 'partner' with their first question.

3 Strong or weak sounds   pronunciation

A ☐☐ Do these words sound strong or weak? Listen and write *S* or *W*.

1. *Have*
a. **Have** you got a T-shirt?   b. Yes, we **have**.   c. Can I **have** these cassettes?

2. *Can*
Can I have this necklace please?

3. *There*
Is **there** a black T-shirt?

4. *For*
a. Who's it **for**?   b. It's a souvenir **for** my daughter.

B Which words sound like these words?

1. phone	....	....
2. you	....	....
3. cost	....	....
4. your	....	....
5. town	....	....

all   boss   clock
code   do   floor
how   know   school
thousand

☐☐ Listen and check your answers.

REVIEW OF UNIT 10

1 Your free time   present simple; frequency adverbs

What do you *always*, *usually* or *sometimes* do in your free time? Fill in the table. Follow the examples.

	always	*usually*	*sometimes*
1. in the evening	have dinner	watch TV	see friends
2. at the weekend	....	....	....
3. at parties	....	....	....
4. on holiday	....	....	....

Talk about your free time with another learner.

Example: A: *I usually watch television in the evenings. What about you?*
          B: *I sometimes watch television, but I usually see my friends.*

2 MORning   stress

These words all have two parts. Where is the stress? On the first part or the second part?

Example: *mor | ning – MORning*

1. off | ice   2. ye | llow
3. ho | tel   4. post | card
5. ear | ly   6. a | gain
7. wea | ther   8. re | peat

☐☐ Listen and check your answers.

12

LET'S HAVE A PARTY

> Language focus:
> suggestions: *Let's ... What about ...?*
> saying *yes* and *no* to suggestions
> *here/there*
>
> Vocabulary:
> parties

A   MAKING PLANS

1 Places for a party   `speaking; vocabulary`

Where is a good place for a party? Here are some ideas.

Write a list of good and bad things about these places, like this:

Place	Good things	Bad things
hotel	bar, disco, waiters	expensive, hot, small
garden	....	....
house or flat	....	....
beach	....	....

Where's the best place for a party? Tell another person your ideas.

2 Decisions   `making suggestions; listening and speaking`

A 📖 Listen to a conversation between two people. Answer the questions.

1. Who are the two people?   2. Why do they want a party?

B 📖 Listen to the rest of the same conversation. Answer the questions.

1. When do they decide to have the party? Which day? What time?
2. Where do they decide to have their party? Why? Choose one of these places: the beach, a hotel, a student's flat.
3. What is the problem with the other places?

Suggestions	Answers	
	Yes	*No*
Let's have a party.	Great/Good idea.	No.
What about the beach?	OK.	No, it's too cold.

12

LET'S HAVE A PARTY

This last unit is mainly skills-based, so little new language is introduced. The entire unit is devoted to the theme of parties.

Lesson A starts with the planning stage and includes the language of suggestions. Lesson B, which moves on to invitations, includes reading and writing party invitations and telephone conversations. Lesson C is the party itself which includes practice in listening, speaking, reading and writing.

Note: If the class is coming to an end after this unit, they might organise their own end-of-course party like Satoshi and Mayumi.

Warm-up

Before starting the unit, introduce the subject of parties with these questions, which could be discussed by pairs, groups or the class.

When do you have parties?   Do you like parties?   Why? Why not?   What do you do at parties?

A MAKING PLANS

1 Places for a party

Suggested steps

Get the class to look at the pictures and say which kind of place they would choose for a party; elicit reasons for their choices.

In pairs, learners now talk about and note down the pros and cons of each of the places illustrated. Possible answers:

Place	Good things	Bad things
hotel	bar, disco, waiters	expensive, hot, small
garden	not too hot, space, cheap	too cold, insects, dark
house or flat	cheap, comfortable, easy for music, food, no time limit	small, noise, neighbours
beach	not too hot, space, cheap	sand in food, cold?, gatecrashers

★ *gatecrashers* - people who come to a party even though they have not been invited

Elicit a few ideas, then get the class to vote on the most popular party venue.

2 Decisions 🔲

Suggested steps

Draw learners' attention to the two questions and tell them they are going to hear the conversation only once. Play the recording for the first time, allow learners time to compare ideas, then elicit answers.

Tapescript

SATOSHI: Do you like our English course?
MAYUMI: Yes, I do. It's very good and everyone's really friendly.
SATOSHI: When does it finish? Do you know?
MAYUMI: At the end of next week.
SATOSHI: Let's have a goodbye party.
MAYUMI: Great idea!

Answer key

1. Two students of English doing the same course.
2. It's the end of their course. It's a 'goodbye party'.

Read through Questions 1 – 3 with the class to check they understand, then play the next recording (an extended version of the one they have just heard).

Tapescript

SATOSHI   Do you like our English course?
MAYUMI: Yes, I do. It's very good and everyone's really friendly.
SATOSHI   When does it finish? Do you know?
MAYUMI: At the end of next week.
SATOSHI   Let's have a goodbye party.
MAYUMI: Great idea! Where?
SATOSHI   Our flat?
MAYUMI: No, it's too small. What about the beach?
SATOSHI   The beach is too cold at night.
MAYUMI: A hotel with a disco?
SATOSHI   That's a good idea. What about the New York Hotel? That's got a good disco.
MAYUMI: That sounds great. And when, Saturday?
SATOSHI   No, people often do other things on Saturdays. Let's have it on Friday.
MAYUMI: OK. Next Friday then – at ten o'clock?
SATOSHI   No, ten o'clock's too late. What about nine?
MAYUMI: Fine. So that's next Friday at nine o'clock. Let's write the invitations.

Play the recording again if necessary, give learners a chance to compare ideas, then elicit answers.

Answer key

1. At the end of next week. Friday. 9 o'clock.
2. The New York Hotel, because it's got a good disco.
3. The flat is too small and the beach is too cold.

Spend some time looking at the language of suggestions with the class before moving on to an exercise in which learners can practise this language in a different context.

3 Your plans

Suggested steps

Learners now have an opportunity to practise discussing plans, using the language of suggestions. Check that they understand the task: in groups of three or four they plan a business meeting. At the end of their discussion they should have decided on a place and a time.

Monitor conversations, listening for the correct use of the language of suggestions and replies to suggestions. If learners are not using this language, encourage them to do so.

Option

Instead of or as well as planning a business meeting, the class could plan a short holiday.

They could be asked to choose between these types of holiday: *beach, sightseeing, sports or activity*

Quick Check

Answer key

A

Possible answers:

1 – 3. Good idea! / Great! / OK!

4. No, it's too expensive/far.

5. No, it's too expensive. / it's not safe.

6. No, it's too hot.

B

1. idea   2. about   3. Let's   4. cold

5. interesting   6. where   7. when   8. early

C

1. in   2. with   3. at/of   4. at   5. for

1 Sending invitations

Suggested steps

Introduce this first task, by asking the class what this text is (an invitation). Explain the task: the invitation card should be filled in with information from Lesson A of the unit. Anyone's name can be used in the *To …* space.

Allow about 5 minutes for individual learners or pairs to fill in the invitation, then elicit answers.

Answer key

To **any name**
Bring a friend
Come to Satoshi's and Mayumi's end-of-course party
On **(Next) Friday**
Time **9 o'clock**
Place **New York Hotel**
Please bring something to drink or something to eat.
Can you come? Don't forget to tell us.
Phone Satoshi – 987891

In pairs, learners now write their own party invitations based on the one they have just completed. Monitor this writing task, helping and correcting where necessary.

3 Your plans   [speaking]

Work in groups of three or four. Plan a business meeting. Think about:

- the best place: a conference room in a hotel, a bar or café, a small office
- the best day and time

✔ Quick Check

A Say *yes* to these suggestions.

1. Let's have a party at the weekend.
2. What about a beach holiday?
3. Let's go to the swimming pool this afternoon.

Say *no* to these suggestions.

4. What about a holiday in the United States?
5. Let's fly.
6. What about a tour of Australia?

B Fill the gaps in this conversation with one of these words.

about   cold   early   idea   interesting   let's
when   where

A: Let's have a holiday together.
B: That's a good (1) .... Where?
A: What (2) .... the Bahamas?
B: No, that's too expensive for me. (3)
.... go to Norway.
A: No, the weather's too (4) .... in
Norway. What about Australia?

B: OK, there are lots of (5) ....
places to visit there. But (6) ....
in Australia? It's a very big country.
A: What about Tasmania?
B: OK. And (7) ....?
A: March?
B: No, that's too (8) .... Let's go
in May.
A: OK.

C Fill the gaps in these sentences with one of these words.

at   for   in   of   with

1. What about a holiday .... August?
2. I'd like a hotel .... a swimming pool.
3. Let's have a drink in the bar .... the hotel.
4. My university course finishes .... the end
of next month.
5. Summer in Istanbul is too hot .... me.

B   INVITATIONS

1 Sending invitations   [reading and writing]

Here is the invitation for Mayumi's and Satoshi's end-of-course party. Fill in the details.

Write an invitation to your party.
Copy this invitation or make your own.

To ....

Bring a friend.
Come to Satoshi's and Mayumi's
end-of-course party

On ....

Time ....

Place ....

Please bring something to drink or
something to eat.

Can you come?
Don't forget to tell us.
Phone Satoshi – 987891

---

2 Can you come? | listening |

A 📼 Listen to five phone conversations. Who can come to the party? Who can't come? Who doesn't know?

Write ✓, ✗ or ? next to the names.

1. Cecile ☐   2. John ☐   3. Peter ☐   4. Maria ☐   5. Lucy ☐

📼 Listen again. Who can bring a friend? What are the friends' names?

B Here are parts of the conversations. Fill the spaces with one of these words or phrases.

listen	a pity	perhaps	probably	sorry	sure

1. SATOSHI: John, this is Satoshi. Can you come to the party next Friday?
   JOHN: No, I can't. ....
   SATOSHI: Oh, that's ....

2. PETER: Mayumi! How are you?
   MAYUMI: I'm fine. ...., can you come to our party on Friday?
   PETER: I'm not .... I'm very busy this week. ....

3. MAYUMI: Can you come to the party on Friday?
   LUCY: I don't really know. ....

📼 Listen to these conversations again and check your answers.

3 On the phone | speaking |

Sit back to back with another learner and have phone conversations.

A
Ask: 'Can you come to my party?'
Say where.
Say which day.
Say what time.

B
Ask about the place.
Ask about the day.
Ask about the time.
Answer *yes*, *no* or *not sure*.

Now change roles.

4 Food and drink | speaking |

Talk to another person about things to get for the party. Think about:

– things to eat;   – things to drink;   – music;   – other things.

Which things have you got already? Write a shopping list of things you haven't got.

✔ Quick Check

A Answer these invitations.

1. Can you come to the party next weekend?
   (Say *yes*.)
2. Can you come to the cinema on Monday?
   (Say *no* and then say why you can't.)
3. Can you come for lunch tomorrow?
   (Say *not sure* and give a reason.)
4. Can you come to the international conference in Paris? (Say *yes*.)
5. Do you want to go on holiday in August?
   (Say *no* and give a reason.)

B Correct these expressions. Some have a word missing and some have an extra word.

1. Can I speak John, please?
2. Yes, in one moment.
3. Hello, Eva is speaking.
4. Hello, is Maria?
5. Hi, it Mayumi here.
6. Hello, Raymundo, is Mayumi.

---

2 Can you come? 🔲

Satoshi and Mayumi are now on the phone to some of the people who haven't replied to their party invitations. They need to know who is and who isn't coming. The names are listed in the order of the conversations on the cassette.

Suggested steps

Play the recording once or twice as necessary, allow time for learners to compare ideas, then elicit the answers.

Tapescript

See page 132.

Answer key

1. Cecile – ✓
2. John – ✗
3. Peter – ? (busy this week)
4. Maria – ✓
5. Lucy – ? (her father is not well)

Play the recording again. This time learners note whether each person can bring a friend, and if they can what the friend's name is.

Answer key

1. Cecile   Yes   Pascal
2. John   X
3. Peter   ?
4. Maria   Yes   Manuel (husband)
5. Lucy   ?

Explain the next exercise: learners fill the gaps in the extracts from three of the conversations with words from the list.

> ### Language Point
>
> Only two of these words, *a pity* and *probably* are new to the class. If you need to explain their meanings, mime a conversation for *That's a pity.*
>
> A: *Can you come to my party?*
> B: *No, sorry.*
> A: *That's a pity.* (sad voice, sad face)
>
> Contrast *probably* with *perhaps*, with a Yes/No chart, like this
>
> | | Yes | No |
> |----------|--------|---------|
> | | Yes | No |
> | perhaps | 50% | 50% |
> | probably | 80–90% | 10%–20% |

Finally, the class listens to the three conversations to check their answers.

Tapescript

See page 132.

Answer key

1. Sorry; a pity
2. Listen; sure; Perhaps
3. Probably

3 On the phone

Suggested steps

Learners sit back-to-back and have telephone conversations like the ones between Satoshi and Mayumi and their friends. There are suggestions about what learners should ask each other, but the language itself is not provided.

Allow learners a minute or two to prepare for the conversations, but discourage them from writing anything.

Monitor conversations, listening more for fluency than for accuracy. (Do learners sound natural and friendly?)

4 Food and drink

Suggested steps

As this is another speaking activity, suggest that learners work with new partners.

This activity involves more party decisions. Conversations can be quite free; learners can come up with their own ideas. They should write a shopping list of things that need to be bought for the party.

Monitor conversations discreetly, listening for suggestions. Are learners using suggestion language? Are they using it correctly?

Option

Round off this final activity in Lesson B with a quick class survey. Ask questions to find out the most popular food and drinks, the favourite music and what other things learners talked about.

Quick Check
Answer key

A
1. Yes, I can.
2. No, I can't. Sorry. I'm busy on Monday.
3. I'm not sure. / I don't know. I think I'm in London tomorrow.
4. Yes, I can.
5. No, I can't. Sorry. I work in August.

B
1. Can I speak **to** John, please?
2. Yes, one moment.
3. Hello, Eva speaking.
4. Hello, is **that** Maria?
5. Hi, **it**'s Mayumi here.
6. Hello Raymundo, **this** is Mayumi.

Personal Study Workbook

1: making suggestions   8: reading
2: listening and speaking   9: invitations
3: here or there

1 Conversations

This listening exercise simulates what it's like at a party for someone who is trying to work out what other people's conversations are about.

Suggested steps

Explain the task, then play the recording for the first time.

Tapescript

1. CECILE: Hi, Raymundo. How are you?
   RAYMUNDO: I'm fine, thanks. And you?
   CECILE: OK. This is my friend, Pascal.
   RAYMUNDO: Pleased to meet you. This is Karen. She's my girlfriend.
   CECILE: Hi. Where are you from?
   KAREN: I'm from Mexico. Are you from France, Pascal?
   PASCAL: Yes, I am. I'm from Normandy,
   KAREN: Normandy. That's famous for cheese, isn't it?
   PASCAL: That's right.
   KAREN: What do you do there?
   PASCAL: I buy all the cheese for a big French supermarket.

2. MAYUMI: Hi, Lucy, I'm pleased you're here.
   LUCY: It's nice to be here.
   MAYUMI: How's your father?
   LUCY: He's OK now, thanks. Oh, Mayumi, this is Tran.
   MAYUMI: Hi. Where are you from?
   TRAN: I'm from Vietnam. It's a great party.
   MAYUMI: Thanks. Do you like the music?
   TRAN: Yes, what is it?
   MAYUMI: It's Japanese.
   LUCY: It's very interesting. It's very different from American or European music. But I like it a lot.
   TRAN: Me too.

3. PETER: Hi.
   SATOSHI: Hello, Peter. What a surprise!
   PETER: It's a really nice party.
   SATOSHI: Thanks.
   PETER: The food looks fantastic.
   SATOSHI: There's something from everyone's country. Look this is our Japanese food.
   PETER: What's this?
   SATOSHI: That's French – from Cecile and Pascal. I think it's chicken in red wine.
   PETER: It looks wonderful. I haven't got anything, I'm afraid.
   SATOSHI: That's OK. Everyone knows you're too busy this week.

4. MARIA: Hi, Eva.
   EVA: Hi. It's a great party, isn't it?
   MARIA: Yeah. Eva, this is my husband, Manuel. He's Spanish.
   EVA: Pleased to meet you, Manuel. And this is my best friend, Nicole from Holland. She's here on holiday.
   MANUEL: Where are you from in Holland?
   NICOLE: I'm from Rotterdam, but I live in Washington now.
   MARIA: What do you do there?
   NICOLE: I'm a journalist for a Dutch newspaper.
   MANUEL: Do you like the States?
   NICOLE: Yes, I do. It's a really interesting place, but I would like to go back to Holland.
   MARIA: Really?
   NICOLE: Yes, I want to have children soon.

Allow learners a minute or two to compare ideas, play the recording a second time, then elicit the answers.

Answer key

Subjects	Conversation	1	2	3	4
home countries		✓	✓		✓
food or drink				✓	
music			✓		
jobs		✓			✓

Note: the speakers in the first conversation don't talk about food – cheese is only mentioned because Pascal comes from Normandy in France, which is famous for cheese.

Language Point

The words *here* and *there* are used in the conversations and are listed in the Help box. If learners do not already understand them or know the difference in meaning between them, present them like this:
Say: *This is my chair. It's here.*
That's your chair. It's there.

Write up the extracts of conversation where they are used and ask *Where?* questions.

MAYUMI: *Hi, Lucy, I'm pleased you're **here**.*
LUCY: *It's nice to be **here**.*
Where are Mayumi and Lucy now? At the same party.

NICOLE: *I'm from Rotterdam, but I live in Washington now.*
MARIA: *What do you do **there**?*
NICOLE: *I'm a journalist*
Where is Nicole now? At a party in England.
Where does she live? In Washington.
What does she do **there**? She's a journalist.

1 Conversations | listening |

📖 Here are some groups of people at Satoshi's and Mayumi's party. What are they talking about? Listen to their conversations. Tick the subjects.

Subjects	Conversation	1	2	3	4
home countries		....	....	....	....
food or drink		....	....	....	....
music		....	....	....	....
jobs		....	....	....	....

HELP	In your language?
famous for	....
different from	....
here	....
there	....

2 Party talk   `speaking`

Think of five questions to ask people at a party. Write them down.

Examples: *Where are you from?*
          What do you do there?

Give yourself a new character. Think of a new name, a new country, a new job, etc.

You are at a party. Talk to other learners. Ask your questions and answer their questions.

3 Hi from Mexico!   `reading and writing`

Two weeks after the end-of-course party, everyone is in their own country again. Here are two postcards to Satoshi and Mayumi.

Fill the gaps in the postcards with one of these words.

Postcard 1: come   country   fantastic   friends   home   music   party   thank

Postcard 2: course   friend   party   next   nice   number   write

1

> Hi from Mexico,
> We're (1) .... again after a great time.
> The English course was (2) ....
> We really miss all our (3) ....
> Your end-of-course (4) .... was wonderful – the food, the (5) ....,
> the people. (6) .... you for everything.
> Say a big hello to all our friends.
> (7) .... and see us when you are in our (8) ....
> Love from
> Raymundo and Karen

2

> To Satoshi, Mayumi and all our friends,
> How are you all? I start work again here tomorrow with my Dutch friends. It's
> (1) .... to see them, but I miss everyone on the English (2) ....
> My best (3) .... Nicole is in America again now, but she wants to come home
> (4) .... month.
> Please phone or (5) .... to me.
> You know my phone (6) .... and my address.
> Thanks again for the fantastic (7) ....
> See you soon.
> Love
> Eva

Write your own postcard like these to a friend in another country.

2 Party talk

Suggested steps

Clarify the task: learners think of five questions they might ask people (they don't know) at a party.
Examples:

> *Where are you from?*
> *Which town? Is it a big town?*
> *What do you do there?*
> *Do you like your job?*
> *Do you like music? / sport? / holidays?*
> *Do you play sports? Which sports?*
> *Where do you go for your holidays?* etc.

Now each learner thinks of a new character for him/herself including name, country, job, family background, etc.

With their new character, learners now work in groups or move around the classroom asking and answering their questions.

Monitor or join in with these conversations, but do not correct.

3 Hi from Mexico!

Suggested steps

Clarify the task, ask pairs of learners to fill the gaps in the postcards with words from the lists, then elicit answers.

Answer key

Postcard 1

1. home	2. fantastic	3. friends	4. party
5. music	6. Thank	7. Come	8. country

Postcard 2

1. nice	2. course	3. friend	4. next
5. write	6. number	7. party	

Option

Once the postcards have been completed, you could ask further comprehension questions about them.

Examples:

Postcard 1
Where are Raymundo and Karen? Who or what do they miss?

Postcard 2
Who is this postcard from? Who is Nicole? Where is she?

Finally each learner writes a postcard to a friend in another country. If this is done as classwork, monitor, giving help where necessary.

Quick Check
Answer key

A

1. I am; you are   2. How is   3. I have not; I am

B

1. Let's   2. Nicole's   3. you're   4. I'd

C

1.e   2.a   3.d   4.g   5.h   6.b   7.c

Answer f does not fit any of the questions.

D

	Short answers	*Longer answers*
a.	No.	No, I'm not. /No, I'm not Italian.
b.	Twenty-three.	I'm twenty-three.
c.	Twenty pounds	It's twenty pounds. / It costs twenty pounds.
d.	OK.	He's OK. / My brother's OK.
e.	Argentina	I'm from Argentina.
f.	/	/
g.	Italian	It's Italian. / It's Italian food.
h.	French wine.	It's French wine.

Personal Study Workbook

4: vocabulary   7: vocabulary
5: vocabulary   10: sounds
6: vocabulary   11: visual dictionary

D REVIEW AND DEVELOPMENT

REVIEW OF UNIT 10

1 Whose clothes?

This exercise revises the question *Whose …?* and clothes words.

Suggested steps

Learners decide for themselves which of the three people the clothes belong to, and write lists of clothes next to each name.

In pairs, they then have conversations like the example in the book. Since the three people could be male or female, there are no right or wrong answers to this exercise.

A Write the long forms.

1. I'm really pleased you're here.
2. How's your father?
3. I haven't got anything, I'm afraid.

B Write the short forms.

1. Let us go shopping.
2. My friend Nicole is in America now.
3. Come and see us when you are in Mexico.
4. I would like to come home soon.

C Match the questions with the short answers. There is an extra answer.

1. Where are you from?   a. No.
2. Are you Italian?   b. Twenty-three.
3. How's your brother?   c. Twenty pounds.
4. What kind of food is it?   d. OK.
5. What's this?   e. Argentina.
6. How old are you?   f. Probably.
7. How much is it?   g. Italian.
                                h. French wine.

D Now make the short answers longer.

Example: *Short*   *Longer*
          Argentina   *From Argentina* or
                         I'm from Argentina.

PERSONAL STUDY WORKBOOK

- listening to people organising a party
- reading and writing party invitations
- making telephone conversations
- pronunciation work
- visual dictionary – let's have a party
- reading – episode 12 of *Lost in time*

D **REVIEW AND DEVELOPMENT**

REVIEW OF UNIT 10

1 Whose clothes? | *whose; vocabulary* |

Whose clothes are these? You decide. Match the three people with the clothes.

Pat

Sam   Nicky

Now talk to another learner. Ask and answer questions, like this:

A: *Whose jeans are these?*   B: *I think they're Pat's.*

LESSON C THE PARTY   97

2 Compliments
[speaking]

Friends and people in your family have some new things. Say you like them.
Use *I like ...; ... suit(s) you; ... look(s) lovely.*

1. Your sister has a new white blouse.
2. Your best friend has a new necklace.
3. Your partner has some new green jeans.
4. Your boss has a new fast car.
5. Your mother has some new earrings.
6. Your teacher has some new shoes.

Talk to other learners. Tell them what you like.

REVIEW OF UNIT 11

1 Quick conversations
[listening; pronunciation]

A ⫐ Listen to six conversations. Do you hear *can, do* or *does*? Do you hear *she, he* or *they*?

	1	2	3	4	5	6			1	2	3	4	5	6
Can								he						
Do								she						
Does								they						

B ⫐ Listen to the two *Can ...?* questions again with short answers.
Has the *a* in *can/can't* got:

the sound /ə/?   the sound /æ/?   the sound /ɑː/?
1. Can he go to Barcelona? No, he can't.
2. Can she phone Monika at nine? Yes, she can.

Practise the questions and answers in pairs.

2 Can your mother drive?
[Can/Do/Does ...? speaking]

Which verbs in Box A go with *Can ...?* questions?

Box A	speak English	like Italian food	eat hot food
	eat meat	speak French	speak German
	sing well	drive	like holidays

Box B	your parents	your brother	your sister	your mother	your friends
	your father	your manager	your husband	your wife	you

Ask and answer *Can/Do/Does ...?* questions. Use language from *A* and *B*.

Examples: A: *Can (Do) your parents speak English?*
B: *Yes, they can./No, they can't./Yes, they can, a bit.*
(Yes they do, with English visitors.)
A: *Can your mother drive?*
B: *No, she can't./Yes, she can.*

HELP	In your language?
Yes, of course.	....
Yes, a bit.	....

2 Compliments

Suggested steps

Do one or two examples with the class, before pairs work through the rest of the exercise. Remind them to think about whether the objects they talk about are singular or plural.

Examples:

> That white blouse **suit<u>s</u>** you.
> but *Your green jeans* **suit** *you.*

Learners should take it in turn to compliment and be complimented.

When they have worked through the six sentences in the book, they could compliment each other.

Monitor the conversations, but do not interrupt.

REVIEW OF UNIT 11

1 Quick conversations 〇〇

Suggested steps

Model the differences in pronunciation between *Does she ...?, Does he ...?* and *Do they ...?* Write *she/he/they* on the board and ask learners which pronoun they heard. Try to model the question forms fairly rapidly so that the sound is similar to English conversation spoken at normal speed.

Clarify the listening task. Learners will hear six mini conversations; they have to tick the auxiliary (*Can, Do, Does*) and the pronoun (*he, she, they*) that they hear in each conversation.

Try the first conversation as a practice. Check the answers to the first one, then play the others. Check answers.

Option

Ask learners to practise one or two of the mini conversations themselves in pairs or to write and model new ones for other pairs to guess.

Answer key

	1	2	3	4	5	6		1	2	3	4	5	6
Can		✓		✓			he		✓			✓	
Do			✓				she	✓			✓		✓
Does	✓			✓	✓		they			✓			

For the second part of the exercise, which is sound discrimination, model the three individual sounds so that learners are aware of the differences.

Play the recording and let learners decide in pairs the sounds they hear. Check answers.

Let learners practise the questions and answers – monitor and encourage, but don't correct too much as it makes learners inhibited to speak.

Remind learners that in real conversations speakers often give different responses from the ones in the book to the *Can ...?* questions (e.g. *Can she phone Monika at nine?   Yes, OK / Yes, sure / Yeah all right.*) The *can/can't* response is there principally for sound discrimination and grammatical understanding, not necessarily as a set spoken model.

Tapescript

See page 132.

2 Can your mother drive?

Suggested steps

Explain the first part of this exercise: learners decide which expressions in Box A go with *can*. Elicit one or two examples, allow pairs to work together for a few minutes then elicit the rest of the answers.

Answer key

Can goes with: *speak English; eat hot food; speak French; speak German; sing well; drive*

Note: all of these expressions can also go with *Do/Does.*

Learners now combine the expressions in Box A with the people in Box B to form questions they can ask a partner.

Work through an example conversation with the class, then ask learners to make more conversations in pairs.

Unit 12 Worksheet

This is a general speaking activity which is not related specifically to the language content of Unit 12, but brings together and recycles language introduced in various earlier units.

Suggested steps

The key point for learners to realise is that they should not fill in the form as themselves but should create a new personality for themselves. As well as providing a fun element, this ensures that learners are asking *real* questions and finding out *real* information about each other.

Once this point is clear, hand out worksheets. Learners first complete the form individually, then ask each other questions and fill in the second form.

GRAMMAR REFERENCE
Useful lists

Alphabet

Aa	Bb	Cc	Dd	Ee	Ff	Gg
Hh	Ii	Jj	Kk	Ll	Mm	Nn
Oo	Pp	Qq	Rr	Ss	Tt	Uu
Vv	Ww	Xx	Yy	Zz		

Numbers

Cardinal numbers 1–10

one	1	six	6	zero	0 (or 'o')
two	2	seven	7		
three	3	eight	8		
four	4	nine	9		
five	5	ten	10		

Note:
We say *double* ... for two numbers in telephone numbers.
Examples:
double six = 66   double four = 44

Cardinal numbers 11–30

eleven	11	sixteen	16	twenty-one	21
twelve	12	seventeen	17	twenty-two	22
thirteen	13	eighteen	18	twenty-three	23
fourteen	14	nineteen	19	twenty-nine	29
fifteen	15	twenty	20	thirty	30

Cardinal numbers 31–100

thirty-one	31	seventy	70
forty	40	eighty	80
fifty	50	ninety	90
sixty	60	a hundred	100

Ordinal numbers: first – tenth

1	one	one man	the **first** man
2	two	two children	the **second** child
3	three	three letters	the **third** letter
4	four	four buildings	the **fourth** building
5	five	five floors	the **fifth** floor
6	six	six visitors	the **sixth** visitor
7	seven	seven stations	the **seventh** station
8	eight	eight mornings	the **eighth** morning
9	nine	nine days	the **ninth** day
10	ten	ten taxis	the **tenth** taxi

Large numbers: 100–1,000,000

100	**a** hundred/**one** hundred
135	**a**/**one** hundred **and** thirty-five
376	**three hundred** and seventy-six [NOT ~~three hundreds~~]
1,000	**a** thousand/**one** thousand
1,104	**one** thousand, **one** hundred and four [NOT ~~a thousand~~]
32,423	thirty-two thousand, four hundred and twenty-three
461,534	four hundred and sixty-one thousand, five hundred and thirty-four
1,000,000	**a** million/**one** million
1,000,017	**one** million and seventeen
1,547,982	one million, five hundred and forty-seven thousand, nine hundred and eighty-two

The time

08.00	eight o'clock (in the morning)
09.05	five past nine
10.10	ten past ten
11.15	a quarter past eleven/eleven fifteen
12.00	twelve o'clock/midday
12.20	twenty past twelve
13.30	half past one/one thirty
16.35	twenty-five to five (in the afternoon)
20.40	twenty to nine (in the evening)
22.45	a quarter to eleven (in the evening/at night)
23.50	ten to twelve (at night)/ten to midnight
00.00	twelve o'clock/midnight
03.00	three o'clock (in the morning)

Days of the week

Sunday	Monday	Tuesday	Wednesday
Thursday	Friday	Saturday	

Months

January February March April May June
July August September October November
December

Personal pronouns

1 PERSON THING	2 + PERSONS/THINGS
I	we
you	you
he	
she	they
it	

Pronouns with *be* (*am/is/are*)

SHORT FORM   LONG FORM

I'm ten (10).   I am ten.

You're ten.   You are ten.

He's ten.   He is ten.

She's ten.   She is ten.

It's ten.   It is ten.

We're ten.   We are ten.

They're ten.   They are ten.

Questions and answers with *are/am*

Are you John?	Yes, I am. (NOT ~~Yes, I'm.~~)
	No, I'm not.
Am I late?	Yes, you are. (NOT ~~Yes, you're.~~)
	No, you're not.

Questions and answers with *How ...?*

SHORT FORM	LONG FORM	ANSWER
	How are you?	I'm fine. (or Fine.)
How's Joanna?	How is Joanna?	She's fine.
How's she?	How is she?	She's fine.
How's he?	How is he?	He's fine.
	How is it?	It's fine.
	How are you?	I'm fine./We're fine.
	How are they?	I'm fine, how about you?
		I'm fine, thanks.
		They're fine.

This in introductions

*Hello. I'm John and **this** is Kate.*
*Hi. I'm Joanna and **this** is John.*

Mr/Ms/Mrs

married   not married   married or not married

Examples:
Mr Smith   *Ms Lopez*   *Mrs Tanaka*

Hello, goodbye and *thank you*

FORMAL	INFORMAL
Hello.	Hi.
Goodbye.	Bye./Bye bye.
Thank you.	Thanks.

2

Questions and answers with *is*

QUESTIONS		ANSWERS
SHORT FORM	LONG FORM	
What's this?	What is this?	It's a hotel.
What's that?	What is that?	It's the hotel.
Where's the hotel	Where is the hotel?	It's in New York.
	Is it a hotel?	Yes, it is.
		No, it isn't.

This and *that*

The plural words for *this* and *that* are *these* and *those*.

SINGULAR	PLURAL
this restaurant	**these** restaurants
that man	**those** men

Articles: *a* and *the*

*It's **a** hotel.* – We don't know which hotel. We don't know its name.
*It's **the** Hilton Hotel.* – We know the name of the hotel.

Plural nouns

1. noun + s	name/name**s**, student/student**s**
2. -x/-s/-ch/-sh + es	box/box**es**, bus/bus**es**
3. -y changes to -ies	city/cit**ies**, country/countr**ies**
4. irregular	man/**men**, woman/**women**, person/**people**

Possessive adjectives

I	**my**
you	**your**

3

Possessive adjectives

My/your (See Unit 2.)

his	It's **his** restaurant.	**His** restaurant is nice.
her	It's **her** restaurant.	**Her** restaurant is nice.
its	This is **its** drink.	**Its** drink is in the kitchen.

their	It's **their** restaurant.	**Their** restaurant is nice.

Note:
Its drink (possessive adjective)
It's my drink. (it is = it's)

Question forms with *is/are* and answers

QUESTIONS	ANSWERS
Is he busy?	Yes, he is. No, he isn't. (long answer: No, he is not.)
Is she popular?	Yes, she is. No, she isn't. (No, she is not.)
Is it nice?	Yes, it is. No, it isn't. (No, it is not.)
Are they nice?	Yes, they are. No, they aren't. (No, they are not.)

Where ... from? questions and answers

SHORT QUESTION	LONG QUESTION
Where's he from?	Where is he from?
SHORT ANSWER	LONG ANSWER
France.	He is from France.
	He's from France.
	From France.
SHORT QUESTION	LONG QUESTION
–	Where are they from?
SHORT ANSWER	LONG ANSWER
London.	They are from London.
	They're from London.
	From London.

How old ...? questions and answers

How old is he?	Fifteen. He's fifteen. He is fifteen.
How old are you?	Ten. I'm ten. I am ten.
How old are they?	Twenty. They're twenty. They are twenty.

Adjectives

Examples:
good   nice   popular   old   small

He is a good man.   He is good.
She is a good woman.   She is good.
They are good men.   They are good.
Good men are popular.

a and an

a
Examples:
a name   a man   a woman   a restaurant   a friend   a ring
a nice earring   a good address
an
Examples:
an address   an earring   an umbrella
an Indian ring   an old man
An is with words with a first letter: a, e, i, o, u.

there is/there are

LONG FORM
There is a restaurant in the hotel.
There are restaurants in the hotel.

SHORT FORM
There's a restaurant in the hotel.

QUESTIONS
Is there a restaurant in the hotel?

Are there restaurants in the hotel?

ANSWERS
Yes, there is. (~~Yes, there's.~~)
No, there isn't.

Yes, there are.
No, there aren't.

4

Is there ...?/Are there ...?

Singular
QUESTION
Is there a cinema in your town?

Plural
QUESTION
Are there any banks in your town?

SHORT ANSWERS
Yes, **there is.**
No, **there isn't.**

SHORT ANSWERS
Yes, **there are.**
No, **there aren't.**

Use *any* not *a/an* in questions.
Example:
*Are there **any** hotels in your town?*

Perhaps/I think

He's American.   I know this. I am sure.
Perhaps/I think he's American.   I don't know. I'm not sure.

5

has got/have got

SHORT FORM	LONG FORM	NEGATIVE
I've got	I have got	I haven't got
You've got	You have got	You haven't got
She's/He's/It's got	She/He/It has got	She/He/It hasn't got
We've/They've got	We/They have got	We/They haven't got

Examples:
I've got a car.   *They've got a coffee shop.*
It's got a kitchen.   *She hasn't got a sister.*

Note:
It's got = it has got (NOT ~~it is got~~)

Questions and answers with have got

Have you got a manager?   Yes, I have. (~~Yes, I've.~~)/
                          No, I haven't.

Has she/he got a car?   Yes, she/he has./
                          No, she/he hasn't.

Has it got an airport?   Yes, it has./No, it hasn't.
Have we/they got a drink?   Yes, we/they have./
                          No, we/they haven't.

What have you got?   I've got a coffee.
What has it got?   It's got a bedroom.
 (short form: What's it got?)
How many (brothers) have you got? I've got two.

some and any

any in questions
Have you got any coffee?   Have you got any tablets?

some in answers/statements
Yes, I've got some (coffee).   There's some coffee in the kitchen.

any in answers/statements
No. I haven't got any (coffee/tablets).   There isn't any coffee.

6

Imperative form of verbs

Examples:
Go to bed!
Come to Paris.
Tell your mother.
Call your manager.
Phone your sister.

Imperative: negative form

SHORT FORM	LONG FORM
Don't go to bed.	Do not go to bed.
Don't come to Paris.	Do not come to Paris.
Don't tell your mother.	Do not tell your mother.
Don't call your manager.	Do not call your manager.
Don't phone your sister.	Do not phone your sister.

Prepositions (i)

to: *Go to bed.*
at: *Stay at the hotel. Stay at home.*
for: *Stay for one day.*

Prepositions (ii)

7

Present simple verbs

Use present simple verbs for routines – what you do every day, every week, every month, etc.

STATEMENTS		NEGATIVE STATEMENTS	
I		I	
You	**work** here.	You	**don't work** there.
We		We	
They		They	
He		He	
She	**works** here.	She	**doesn't work** there.
(It)		(It)	

Wh- *questions*

Where	**do**	you they	**work**?
When	**does**	he she	**get up**?

Yes/No *questions*

Do	you they		
		work	in Istanbul?
Does	he she		

Short answers

	I/we		
Yes,	you	**do**.	
	they		
	he		
	she	**does**.	
	I/we		
No,	you/they	**don't**.	
	he/she	**doesn't**.	

Other verbs

Endings	I/you, etc.	he/she
-ly/-ry = + -ies	fly, carry	**flies, carries**
But	buy, stay, pay	**buys, stays, pays**
-ch/-sh/-s = + -es	watch, wash, guess	**watches, washes, guesses**
-o = + -es	go, do	**goes, does**

8

Verb tenses: Present simple

1 PERSON/THING	2 + PERSONS/THINGS
I like	We like
You like	You like
She/he/it likes	They like

Examples:
I like coffee.	*We like New York.*
She likes tea.	*They like their manager.*

SHORT FORM	LONG FORM
I don't like	I do not like
We don't like	We do not like
You don't like	You do not like
She/he/it doesn't like	She/he/it does not like
They don't like	They do not like

Examples:
I don't like hotels.	*They don't like tea.*
She doesn't like my sister.	

Questions and answers: present simple *like*

QUESTIONS	ANSWERS
Do you like ...?	Yes, I do./No, I don't.
Does she/he/it like ...?	Yes, she/he/it does./ No, she/he/it doesn't.
Do we like ...?	Yes, we do./No, we don't.
Do they like ...?	Yes, they do./No, they don't.

Agreeing

I like coffee.	*So do I./Me too.*
She/he likes tea.	*So does he/she.*
	So do we.
	So do they.

Question forms with *How long ...?* and *How many ...?*

How long is your course?
How many days are there in June?
How many men are there in this room?

The word after *How many ...?* is always a plural countable noun, for example day**s**, cit**ies**, restaurant**s**.

Conjunctions *and* and *but*

I like coffee and I like tea. (I like the two drinks – coffee/tea.)
I like coffee and tea.

I like coffee but I don't like tea. (I like one drink – coffee.)
I like coffee but not tea.

9

How much ...?

Use *How much ...?* to ask about prices.

QUESTIONS			ANSWERS
How much is	that wallet?		**It's** ten pounds.
are	those shoes?		**They're** three pounds.

How much does	that wallet	**cost**?	**It costs** five dollars.
do	those shoes		**They cost** thirty dollars.

Would like

I'd like/I would like = I want. It's polite.

STATEMENTS
I'd	**like**	a coffee,	please.
We'd		sandwiches,	

QUESTIONS	SHORT ANSWERS
Would you like a coffee?	Yes, (please) **I would**./ Yes, please. No, thanks./No, thank you.

10

Always, usually, often, sometimes, never

Use these words with present simple verbs. They answer the question *How often ...?*

I/you/we/they	**always** **usually**	go to work on Friday. get up early.
He/she	**often** **sometimes**	goes to work on Friday. gets up early.

always = 100% / every day
usually = 80–90% / 5–6 days a week
often = 50–80% / 4–5 days a week
sometimes = 20–50% / 1–3 days a week
never = 0%/0 days a week

Possessive 's

Use *'s* with names or nouns.

Examples:
John has got a car.   *This is **John's car**/his car.*
Jenny has got blue jeans.   *These are **Jenny's jeans**/ her jeans.*

The nurse has a uniform.   *This is the **nurse's** uniform/ her uniform.*

Whose?

Use *whose* to ask questions about possessions.

QUESTIONS	ANSWERS
Whose car is this?	It's John's car. It's John's.
Whose shoes are these?	They're Monica's shoes. They're Monica's.

Which?

Use *which* with nouns to ask about things or places.

QUESTIONS	ANSWERS
Which car is John's?	The red car (is John's).
Which shoes would you like?	I'd like the white shoes.

too

Use *too* with adjectives to describe nouns. Something is not right.

Example:
*This cap is **too small** for me.* (My head is big.)

Use *too* with adverbs to talk about verbs.

Example:
*Don't walk **too quickly**.* (I'm tired.)

can/can't (ability)

I can (write).   We can (write).
You can (write).
She/He/It can (write).   They can (write).

Note:
Can is used with the infinitive of the verb. Examples of infinitives: *write, eat, come, read.*

Examples:
I can write good letters.   She can read Spanish reports.
They can come to the meeting.

Negative

SHORT FORM   LONG FORM
I can't (write).   I cannot (write).
You can't (write).   You cannot (write).
She/he/it can't (write).   She/he/it cannot (write).
We can't (write).   We cannot (write).
They can't (write).   They cannot (write).

Examples:
He can't come to the restaurant.   They can't use a computer.
We can't write business letters.   I can't see your car.

Questions and answers with can

QUESTIONS	ANSWERS
Can you come?	Yes, I can./No, I can't.
Can she/he/it speak Turkish?	Yes, she/he/it can./ No, she/he/it can't.
Can we read Italian newspapers?	Yes, we can./ No, we can't.
Can they write good letters?	Yes, they can./ No, they can't.

Questions and answers with Why (not)? and because

QUESTIONS	ANSWERS
Why are you tired?	(I'm tired) because it's 12 o'clock at night.
You can't see the manager. Why not?	Because he's not in his office today.
I like France. Why?	Because French people are interesting.
Why do you like coffee?	Because it's tasty.
Why has he got your car?	Because his car is at the garage.

Impersonal you

> **What to do?**
>
> You phone the manager and leave your name, then you write an application.
>
> You get a reply in one week.

You here means any person or every person, NOT one person, for example YOU.

12

Suggestions

MAKING SUGGESTIONS	ANSWERING SUGGESTIONS	
	POSITIVE	NEGATIVE
Let's have a drink.	Great/Good idea.	No.
What about a coffee?	OK.	I'd like a tea.

Here and there

Here means this place. *There* means that place.

Examples:
*My house is **here**. **This** is my house.* (I am in or near my house.)
*Your house is **there**. **That's** your house.* (We are not near your house.)

Here and *there* also mean *to this place* and *to that place*.

Examples:
*Come **here**. I want to talk to you.*
*Don't go **there**. It's a terrible school.*

I'm here and you're there.

No, **I'm** here and **you're** there.

WORKSHEETS

WORKSHEET 1

★ = man's name

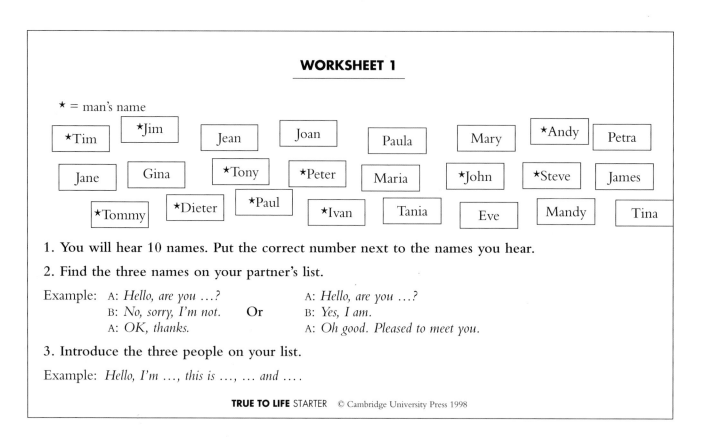

| ★Tim | ★Jim | Jean | Joan | Paula | Mary | ★Andy | Petra |

| Jane | Gina | ★Tony | ★Peter | Maria | ★John | ★Steve | James |

| ★Tommy | ★Dieter | ★Paul | ★Ivan | Tania | Eve | Mandy | Tina |

1. You will hear 10 names. Put the correct number next to the names you hear.

2. Find the three names on your partner's list.

Example: A: *Hello, are you …?*   A: *Hello, are you …?*
          B: *No, sorry, I'm not.* **Or** B: *Yes, I am.*
          A: *OK, thanks.*   A: *Oh good. Pleased to meet you.*

3. Introduce the three people on your list.

Example: *Hello, I'm …, this is …, … and ….*

TRUE TO LIFE STARTER   © Cambridge University Press 1998

WORKSHEET 2A

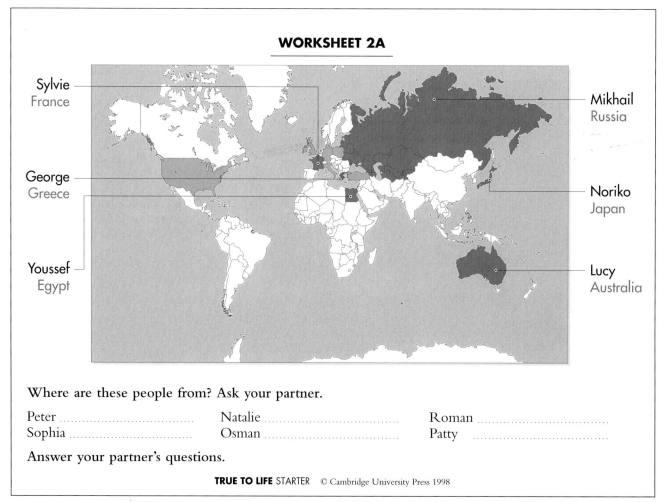

Sylvie
France

Mikhail
Russia

George
Greece

Noriko
Japan

Youssef
Egypt

Lucy
Australia

Where are these people from? Ask your partner.

Peter .... Natalie .... Roman ....
Sophia .... Osman .... Patty ....

Answer your partner's questions.

TRUE TO LIFE STARTER   © Cambridge University Press 1998

WORKSHEET 2B

Natalie
Britain

Patty
USA

Sophia
Italy

Peter
Germany

Roman
Poland

Osman
Turkey

Where are these people from? Ask your partner.

Lucy ....
Noriko ....

Youssef ....
George ....

Sylvie ....
Mikhail ....

Answer your partner's questions.

WORKSHEET 3

Choose one item (from Box 2) for one person (from Box 1).
Write down your choice, e.g. *The big cup of coffee for the old man.*

Take turns to ask and answer questions.
Find out what your partner has written down.

Example:	A: *Is it a watch?*	B: *No*
	A: *Is it a mobile phone?*	B: *No*
	A: *Is it a cup of coffee?*	B: *Yes*
	A: *Is it for a woman?*	B: *No*
	A: *For a man?*	B: *Yes*
	A: *Is it for a young man?*	B: *No*
	A: *A man in his sixties?*	B: *Yes*
	A: *It's a big cup of coffee for C?*	B: *Yes*

WORKSHEET 4A

What are the buildings in this city? Some buildings have names already. Write words in all the buildings. Use ten words from this box:

> police station   cinema   library   nightclub
> post office   opera house   bank   hotel
> restaurant   station   museum   theatre

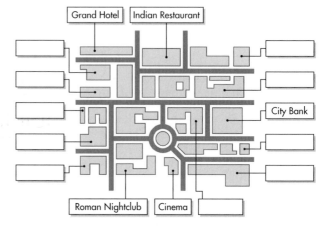

Ask your partner about his or her town.
Ask questions like this:
Is there a cinema in your town?
Are there any banks in your town?

Write your partner's answers like this:
bank ___ ✓ 2 ___ or bank ___ ✗ ___

bank	cinema	library	nightclub	police station	post office ......
theatre	opera house	hotel	restaurant	station	museum ......

Answer your partner's questions like this:
Yes, there are two cinemas in my town.
No, there aren't any cinemas in my town.

TRUE TO LIFE STARTER   © Cambridge University Press 1998

WORKSHEET 4B

What are the buildings in this city? Some buildings have names already. Write words in all the buildings. Use ten words from this box:

> police station   cinema   library   nightclub
> post office   opera house   bank   hotel
> restaurant   station   museum   theatre

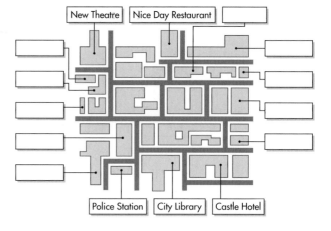

Ask your partner about his or her town.
Ask questions like this:
Is there a cinema in your town?
Are there any banks in your town?

Write your partner's answers like this:
bank ___ ✓ 2 ___ or bank ___ ✗ ___

bank	cinema	library	nightclub	police station	post office ......
theatre	opera house	hotel	restaurant	station	museum ......

Answer your partner's questions like this:
Yes, there are two cinemas in my town.
No, there aren't any cinemas in my town.

TRUE TO LIFE STARTER   © Cambridge University Press 1998

WORKSHEET 5A

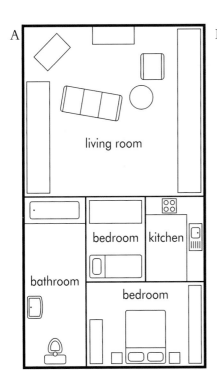
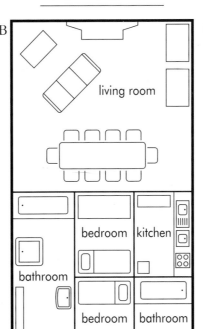

Describe the houses to your partner. Don't look at your partner's Worksheet. Which two houses are the same?

WORKSHEET 5B

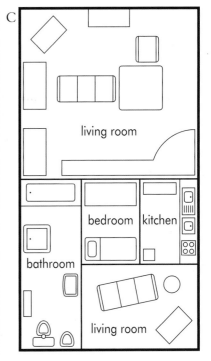

Describe the houses to your partner. Don't look at your partner's Worksheet. Which two houses are the same?

WORKSHEET 6A

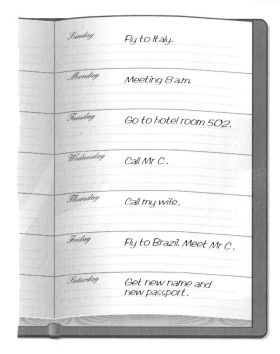

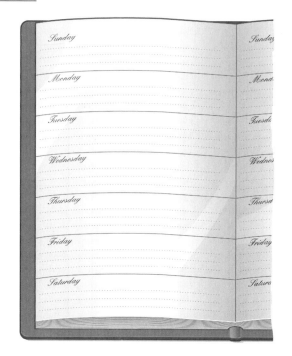

Take it in turns to read out your diary entries and to write down your partner's diary entries.

TRUE TO LIFE STARTER   © Cambridge University Press 1998

WORKSHEET 6B

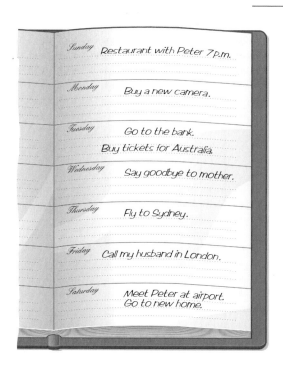

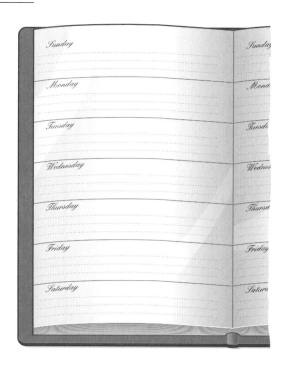

Take it in turns to read out your diary entries and to write down your partner's diary entries.

TRUE TO LIFE STARTER   © Cambridge University Press 1998

Write the times in the clocks. Write the times for you and for someone in your family, like this:

Example: *Me*

My wife

Ask your partner about his or her times. Ask questions like this:

What time do you get up?
What time does your brother, husband, son, etc. get up?

Write your partner's answers here:

he/she	his/her ...
Example: *He gets up at half past six.*	*His wife gets up at seven o'clock.*
1.	....
2.	....
3.	....
4.	....
5.	....
6.	....

TRUE TO LIFE STARTER   © Cambridge University Press 1998

Survey A: I like

Name ....

Do you like ...?	Yes, I do.	It's OK.	No, I don't.	I don't know.
... bread?	☐	☐	☐	☐
... meat?	☐	☐	☐	☐
... fruit?	☐	☐	☐	☐
... salad?	☐	☐	☐	☐
... vegetables?	☐	☐	☐	☐
... rice?	☐	☐	☐	☐
... fish?	☐	☐	☐	☐
... pasta?	☐	☐	☐	☐

TRUE TO LIFE STARTER © Cambridge University Press 1998

Survey B: I eat

Name ....

Do you eat ... ?	Yes, a lot.	Sometimes.	Now and again.	No, never.
... bread?	☐	☐	☐	☐
... meat?	☐	☐	☐	☐
... fruit?	☐	☐	☐	☐
... salad?	☐	☐	☐	☐
... vegetables?	☐	☐	☐	☐
... rice?	☐	☐	☐	☐
... fish?	☐	☐	☐	☐
... pasta?	☐	☐	☐	☐

TRUE TO LIFE STARTER © Cambridge University Press 1998

WORKSHEET 9A

Choose presents for **five friends** from the **left-hand page** of this catalogue. Write a list like this:

	Friend	Present	Price
Example:	Mike	clock	....
1.	....	....	....
2.	....	....	....
3.	....	....	....
4.	....	....	....
5.	....	....	....

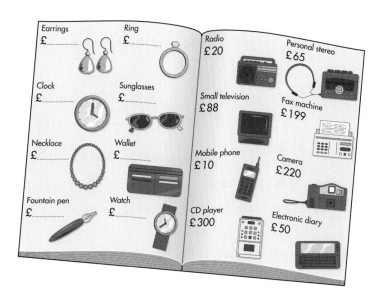

Find out how much the five things cost.
Ask your partner questions like this: *How much is the clock?*

Write the prices in the table.
Then have a shop conversation. You are the customer. Your partner is the shop assistant. Ask him or her for two of the presents.

TRUE TO LIFE STARTER   © Cambridge University Press 1998

WORKSHEET 9B

Choose presents for **five friends** from the **right-hand page** of this catalogue. Write a list like this:

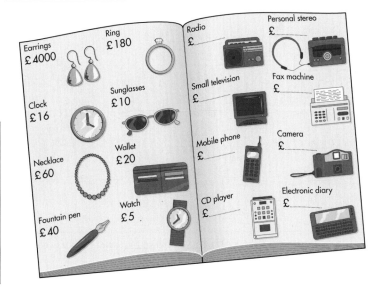

	Friend	Present	Price
Example:	Sue	camera	....
1.	....	....	....
2.	....	....	....
3.	....	....	....
4.	....	....	....
5.	....	....	....

Find out how much the five things cost.
Ask your partner questions like this: *How much is the camera?*

Write the prices in the table
Then have a shop conversation. You are the customer. Your partner is the shop assistant. Ask him or her for two of the presents.

TRUE TO LIFE STARTER   © Cambridge University Press 1998

WORKSHEET 10A

Example: *Steve's a shop assistant.*

Match the six people with these descriptions. Write their names and jobs under their pictures.

- *Fran usually wears a short skirt, a sweatshirt and sports shoes.*
- *Steve usually wears a dark suit, a white shirt and a tie.*
- *Natalie works in many places. She often wears a jacket, jeans and boots.*
- *Bridget always wears a blue skirt, a white blouse and flat shoes.*
- *Tom always wears jeans, a T-shirt and sunglasses.*
- *Joe always wears shorts, a T-shirt and boots.*

What do they wear at the weekend? Ask your partner.

TRUE TO LIFE STARTER   © Cambridge University Press 1998

WORKSHEET 10B

Example: *Steve plays football.*

Match the six people with these descriptions. Write their names and what they do at the weekend under their pictures.

- *Fran usually wears a short dress and high-heeled shoes.*
- *Steve wears shorts, a T-shirt and boots.*
- *Natalie sometimes wears shorts, a T-shirt and a cap.*
- *Bridget wears a short skirt, a white blouse and trainers.*
- *Tom wears jeans and a T-shirt and sunglasses.*
- *Joe always wears jeans, a T-shirt and old sandals.*

What do they wear at work? Ask your partner.

TRUE TO LIFE STARTER   © Cambridge University Press 1998

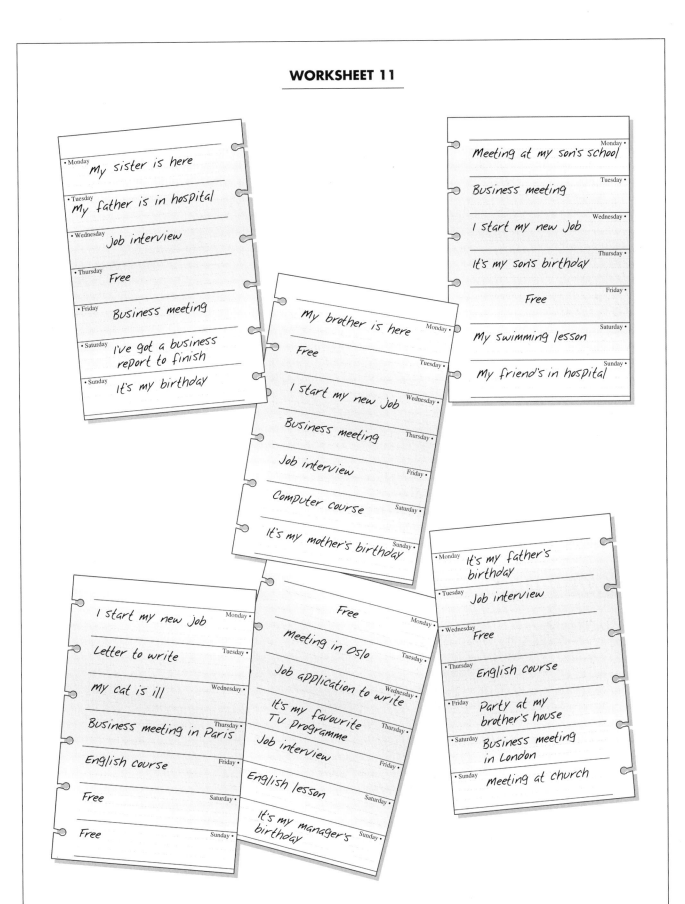

Diary 1 (top left):
- Monday — My sister is here
- Tuesday — My father is in hospital
- Wednesday — Job interview
- Thursday — Free
- Friday — Business meeting
- Saturday — I've got a business report to finish
- Sunday — It's my birthday

Diary 2 (top right):
- Monday — Meeting at my son's school
- Tuesday — Business meeting
- Wednesday — I start my new job
- Thursday — It's my son's birthday
- Friday — Free
- Saturday — My swimming lesson
- Sunday — My friend's in hospital

Diary 3 (centre):
- Monday — My brother is here
- Tuesday — Free
- Wednesday — I start my new job
- Thursday — Business meeting
- Friday — Job interview
- Saturday — Computer course
- Sunday — It's my mother's birthday

Diary 4 (bottom left):
- Monday — I start my new job
- Tuesday — Letter to write
- Wednesday — My cat is ill
- Thursday — Business meeting in Paris
- Friday — English course
- Saturday — Free
- Sunday — Free

Diary 5 (bottom centre):
- Monday — Free
- Tuesday — meeting in Oslo
- Wednesday — Job application to write
- Thursday — It's my favourite TV programme
- Friday — Job interview
- Saturday — English lesson
- Sunday — It's my manager's birthday

Diary 6 (bottom right):
- Monday — It's my father's birthday
- Tuesday — Job interview
- Wednesday — Free
- Thursday — English course
- Friday — Party at my brother's house
- Saturday — Business meeting in London
- Sunday — meeting at church

Choose one of these diaries. You want to go to the shops with a friend on your free day.
Take it in turns to ask: *Can you go to the shops on* (name of your free day)?

Look at your diary and reply with an excuse or an agreement:
Sorry, I can't, I've got a/an … or *Sorry it's …* or *Yes, OK, what time?*

TRUE TO LIFE STARTER   © Cambridge University Press 1998

Give yourself a **new personality**. Fill in this form about yourself.

You

NAME:
....

AGE: .... JOB: ....

ADDRESS:
....

TELEPHONE NUMBER: ....

Your family

BROTHERS/SISTERS: .... Names: ....

....

MARRIED   Yes ☐   No ☐   Wife's / husband's name: ....

CHILDREN   Yes ☐   No ☐   Names: ....

....

Interview your partner. Ask questions and fill in this form with information about his or her new personality.
Useful questions:
How do you spell that?   Could you say that again, please?

Your partner

NAME:
....

AGE: .... JOB: ....

ADDRESS:
....

TELEPHONE NUMBER: ....

Your partner's family

BROTHERS/SISTERS: .... Names: ....

....

MARRIED   Yes ☐   No ☐   Wife's / husband's name: ....

CHILDREN   Yes ☐   No ☐   Names: ....

....

TRUE TO LIFE STARTER   © Cambridge University Press 1998

TESTS

1 Greetings 5 marks

Fill the gaps.

1. A: Hello, ... Peter.
   B: Hi, ... to meet you, Peter. I'm Tina.
2. A: How .... you?
   B: Fine, ..., and .... ?
   A: I'm OK, thanks.

2 Questions and replies to be 5 marks

Complete the questions and replies.

A: Are .... Martin?
B: Yes I ....
A: Good. I'm your teacher, Anna.
B: .... late?
A: Yes, you ....
B: Sorry.

3 Pronouns 5 marks

Write the pronouns.

A: How's Maria?
B: ....'s fine, thanks.
A: And Alain and Elsa?
B: Fine. ....'re in Berlin.
A: Are they? What about your new coffee shop?
B: ....'s busy, very busy.
A: Good, good. How about ....?
B: ....'m busy.

4 Alphabet and numbers 1–10 10 marks

Write the missing letter on each line.

1. A B D E   (............)
2. F G H J   (............)
3. K L N O   (............)
4. P Q R T   (............)
5. U V W Y Z   (............)

Write the numbers in the correct way.
Example: wot two (2)

6. einn   .... ( )
7. vnees   .... ( )
8. herte   .... ( )
9. tigeh   .... ( )
10. rofu   .... ( )

5 Negative answers to to be questions 5 marks

Complete the phone conversations with negative forms.

1. A: Hello, is Gloria there?
   B: Sorry, no she ....

2. A: Is Bill in today?
   B: No, he ....
3. A: Hi, Steve here. Are John and Mike there?
   B: Hi, Steve. No, they ....
4. A: Hello .... Katerina? Is the meeting at four?
   B: Oh, hi, Elisabeth, no, it ....
5. A: Hi, I'm not late, am I?
   B: No, you ....

6 Vocabulary and plurals 5 marks

What are they? Write the plural.
Example: restaurant, hotel, station   buildings

1. Rio, New York, Moscow   ....
2. Brazil, France, Italy   ....
3. tea, coffee, beer   ....
4. 6, 20, 13, 23, 11   ....
5. 3, York Avenue, Sydney
   112, Albert Street, London
   26/2 Rue Molière, Paris   ....

7 Vocabulary – places 5 marks

Circle the five places.

family	fine	gym	guide
tea	busy	visitor	classroom
bar	swimming pool	name letter	
late	number	restaurant	

8 Question words 10 marks

Write the question words.

1. ....'s this?
   It's an e-mail.
2. ....'s Istanbul?
   In Turkey.
3. .... can I help?
   A beer, please, room 223.
4. .... are they?
   In the hotel.
5. .... about a drink ?
   Yes, great. Thanks.
6. ....'s your name?
   Paul.
7. ....'s 'arrigato' in English?
   'Thank you'.
8. ....'s your wife?
   She's fine, thanks.
9. ....'s the restaurant?
   On the fifth floor.
10. ....'s your phone number?
    8223 75641.

9 Numbers 11–30 5 marks

Write the numbers as words.

....

....

....

....

....

10 Prepositions 5 marks

Write in the prepositions.

Dear Jorge
We're .... London, ... the
Grand Hotel.
The hotel is .... the city centre
and our room is .... the twenty-
eighth floor!
Our tourist guide is .... Liverpool.
She's great.
Love
Carolina and Sam

11 Plurals 5 marks

Write the plurals.

Singular	Plural
1. city	....
2. guide	....
3. address	....
4. hotel	....
5. visitor	....

12 Numbers 5 marks

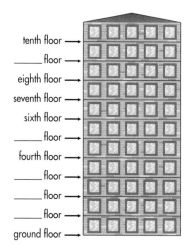

tenth floor →
_____ floor →
eighth floor →
seventh floor →
sixth floor →
_____ floor →
fourth floor →
_____ floor →
_____ floor →
_____ floor →
ground floor →

13 Questions 5 marks

Rewrite the questions in the conversation.

A: is this who? (1)
B: A friend.
A: from she where's? (2)
B: Moscow.
A: is she old how? (3)
B: About thirty.
A: nice she is? (4)
B: Mm, very nice.
A: cat that her is? (5)
B: Mm, it's really old.

14 Possessive adjectives 5 marks

Complete the possessive adjectives.

1. O...... friends are in France.
2. There's a picture of m...... wife.
3. Richard's in Paris and h...... father's in London.
4. The key is in t...... car.
5. Lisa is in h...... bedroom.

15 Vocabulary 10 marks

Write the words under the right heading.

park   visitor   husband   colleague   shop   friend
ring   letter   key   bedroom

Thing	Place	Person

16 A or an? 10 marks

Write *a* or *an* in each space.

1. ..... earring   2. ..... day
3. ..... car   4. ..... address
5. ..... old cat   6. ..... husband
7. ..... mobile phone   8. ..... room
9. ..... office   10. ..... home

Total = 100 marks

1 Numbers 100+ 5 marks

Write the numbers.

1. 567 ....
2. one thousand and ten ....
3. 10,001 ....
4. four hundred and twenty eight ....
5. 933 ....

2 Is/Are there ...? questions 5 marks

Write *Is there* or *Are there* in the questions.

1. .... a theatre in town?
2. .... any banks open today?
3. How many cinemas .... in the city centre?
4. .... one library or two in the university?
5. .... offices on the third floor?

3 Short answers 5 marks

Answer the questions. Use: *there is/isn't; there are/aren't; they are/aren't.*

1. Is there any coffee in the kitchen?
   No, ...

2. Are there any nightclubs in the town?
   Yes, ...

3. Are José and Juan in Tokyo?
   No, ...

4. Is there a police station in this street?
   Yes, ...

5. Are the English students late?
   Yes, ...

4 Vocabulary 10 marks

Write the words in the box under the correct heading.

post office	sports centre	picture	clock
toilet	bank	library	bathroom
theatre	kitchen		

Rooms   *Buildings*   *Things on the wall*

5 Finding mistakes 10 marks

Circle 5 mistakes and correct them.

1. I'm got an apartment in the city. It's   ....
2. got two bedroom, a living room and   ....
3. a nice bathroom. My friends has got   ....
4. a apartment in London. They've got a   ....
5. Picasso on the wall of there living room.   ....

6 Some/any 5 marks

Write *some* or *any*.

1. A: I'd like .... candles, please.
   B: What colour?
   A: Red.

2. B: We haven't got .... red ... sorry.
3. A: Have you got .... blue?
   B: No, sorry. How about green?
4. A: No thanks, I've got .... green candles at home.
5. B: There are .... candle shops in the city centre.
   A: OK, thanks.

7 Prepositions 4 marks

Look at the picture. Answer the questions with a different preposition for the first word of each answer.

1. Where's the camera?   ....
2. Where are the flowers?   ....
3. Where's the bin?   ....
4. Where are my sunglasses?   ....

8 Imperatives 6 marks

Put the verbs into the gaps.

| go | phone | stay | forget | take | have |

MOTHER: Don't .... to the USA, ... in Canada with your brother. Is your plane late?

DAUGHTER: No it's at 4.

MOTHER: .... your sunglasses, it's hot in Canada at the moment, and don't .... your camera.

DAUGHTER: No, OK.

MOTHER: .... a great time.

DAUGHTER: Mm OK. .... me tomorrow. Have you got the number?

MOTHER: Yes, it's in my bag.

9 Days of the week 5 marks

Write the days correctly.

1. Satuday   ....
2. Tuseday   ....
3. Wenesday   ....
4. Thirsdag   ....
5. Freday   ....

10 Pronunciation 10 marks

Mark the main stress on each word.

Example: wŏnderful

1. popular
2. interesting
3. fantastic
4. beautiful
5. international
6. computer
7. headache
8. envelopes
9. postcards
10. cathedral

11 Countries and nationalities 10 marks

Write the nationalities.

Example: England *English*

1. Turkey   ....
2. France   ....
3. Spain   ....
4. Greece   ....
5. India   ....
6. Germany   ....
7. Japan   ....
8. Brazil   ....
9. Hungary   ....
10. Italy   ....

12 Question words 5 marks

Write the question words.

1. A: .... old is this building?
   B: About a hundred years old.
2. A:........................ rooms has it got?
   B: Ten or eleven, I think.
3. A: .... is the man in the car?
   B: He's my manager.
4. A: .... is the toilet, please?
   B: On the second floor.
5. A: .... is the name of the theatre?
   B: The Grand.

13 Vocabulary – family 5 marks

Complete the family names.

Husband and ....

Brother and ....

Mother and ....

Daughter and ....

It's a boy! It's a ....

14 Vocabulary 10 marks

Put the words into pairs.

Example: tea and coffee; library and book

letter	tablets	photo	envelope	camera
green	key	classroom	east	drink
door	headache	today	white	student
south	weekend	bar	wall	picture

1. .... and ....
2. .... and ....
3. .... and ....
4. .... and ....
5. .... and ....
6. .... and ....
7. .... and ....
8. .... and ....
9. .... and ....
10. .... and ....

15 Responses and reactions 5 marks

Fill the gaps with a good response from the box.

see you	really?	that's fine	I think	lots

1. A: I've got a million dollars in my bag!
   B: Wow, ...
2. A: I'm sorry, but I'm really tired. Goodnight.
   B: Goodnight, ... in the morning.
3. A: Come about eight. Is that OK with you?
   B: Yes, ...
4. A: Is their number 81 or 82?
   B: Er ... 82, ...
5. A: Have you got any CDs?
   B: Yes, ...

Total = 100 Marks

1 Present simple 10 marks

Fill the gaps with the correct form of the verb in brackets.

1. Where .... you ....?   (live)
2. .... she .... in London?   (work)
3. No, she .... in London.   (work)
4. She .... in New York.   (work)
5. When .... your sister .... work?   (start)
6. No, we .... coffee.   (like)
7. .... you .... Thai food?   (eat)
8. How much .... that shirt ....?   (cost)
9. When .... you .... breakfast?   (have)
10. His mother .... work at 10 o'clock.   (finish)

2 Short answers 10 marks

Finish these short answers to the questions.

1. Do you get up early?   No, I ....
2. Is your name Peter?   Yes, it ....
3. Are you a teacher?   No, ...
4. Are you a doctor?   Yes, ...
5. Is Ed your brother?   Yes, ...
6. Does he go to university?   No, ...
7. Do your friends like Italian food? Yes, ...
8. Does your mother go to work?   Yes, ...
9. Are your parents American?   No, ...
10. Do you like Coca-Cola?   Yes, ...

3 Question words 10 marks

Choose the right question words.

1. .... time do you get home?
2. A: .... do you go for your holiday?
   B: I go to Florida.
3. ....'s your address?
4. .... does your flight go?
5. A: .... are you?
   B: Fine, thanks.
6. .... brothers have you got?
7. A: .... are those earrings?
   B: They're $50.
8. ....'s your family name?
9. A: .... is this shirt for?
   B: It's for Pat.
10. .... are you from?

4 Times 10 marks

Write the times in words and use one of these time phrases:

in the morning, in the afternoon, in the evening, at night.

1. 10.00 ....
2. 15.25 ....
3. 22.10 ....
4. 06.30 ....
5. 19.45 ....

Now write the times in numbers.

6. twenty-five to four in the afternoon. ....
7. half past seven in the morning. ....
8. five to two in the afternoon. ....
9. twenty past nine in the morning. ....
10. a quarter to eleven at night. ....

5 Likes and dislikes 5 marks

Fill the gaps in this conversation with words from the box.

| do | do | don't | so | too |

JOHN: I love coffee.
1. SUE: .... do I.
2. PAUL: Me ....
3. SUE: .... you like black coffee?
4. JOHN: Yes, I ....
5. PAUL: I .... I like white coffee with lots of sugar.

6 Correct the mistakes 10 marks

a There is one wrong word in these sentences. Cross out the wrong word and write the correct word in the space.

1. I'd like a umbrella, please. ....
2. How much are that red T-shirt? ....
3. It cost seven dollars. ....
4. My brother doesn't likes chicken. ....
5. I love India food. ....

b There is a word missing from these sentences. Mark the place in the sentence and write the missing word in the space.

1. That car very cheap. ....
2. How many names you got? ....
3. When your birthday? ....
4. I go out with my friends the weekends. ....
5. I start work half past eight in the morning. ....

7 Prepositions 10 marks

Fill the gaps in these sentences with one of these prepositions:

about   at   for   from   in   of   to

1. These earrings are .... my mother. It's her birthday.
2. In my holidays I work .... a French restaurant.
3. I have lunch .... one o'clock.
4. My father is the manager .... a German bank.
5. What do you do .... the evening?
6. Do you go .... work on Saturday?
7. When do you get back .... Australia?
8. I'm a sports journalist. I write .... football and tennis.
9. I start work at seven o'clock .... the morning.
10. CDs cost £20 .... three.

8 Vocabulary: Jobs

a 5 marks

Find pairs of words that go together. Choose a word from List A and a word from List B.

	A	B
Example:	journalist	holiday
1.	teacher	café
2.	travel agent	newspaper
3.	waiter	laboratory
4.	scientist	hospital
5.	doctor	school

b 10 marks

Now add words and make 5 sentences using the pairs of words.

Example: A journalist writes in a newspaper.

1. ....
2. ....
3. ....
4. ....
5. ....

9 Vocabulary: Countries and nationalities 10 marks

Fill the gaps with a country word or a nationality word.

	Country	Nationality
1.	China	....
2.	....	Spanish
3.	....	Thai
4.	Greece	
5.	Italy	....
6.	....	French
7.	the USA	....
8.	Japan	....
9.	India	....
10.	....	British

10 Vocabulary: Food 5 marks

Look at all the words in the box. Circle the 5 words for different kinds of meat.

bacon	bread	burger	cheese	chicken
fruit	fish	fruit	ham	hamburger
jam	jelly	rice	salad	sugar

11 Vocabulary: Money 5 marks

Fill the gaps in these sentences with a money word from the box.

cost	credit card	pay	price	wallet

1. The .... of these shoes is £49.
2. A: How do you want to ....?
3. B: Is a .... OK?
   A: Yes. What's the number?
4. How much does that necklace ....?
5. Where's my ....? My money is in it.

Total = 100 Marks

1 How often? 10 marks

a Put these 5 words in order.

1 = 100% and 5 = 0%

often   usually   never   always   sometimes

1. ....
2. ....
3. ....
4. ....
5. ....

b Now add the five words to these sentences:

6. I play football at the weekend.
7. Paul watches TV in the evenings.
8. You go out with your friends on Monday.
9. Ed and I work at home at the weekend.
10. Sue, Jeff and Emma watch TV in the morning.

2 Questions 10 marks (2 each)

Here are some answers. What were the questions?

1. No, not French, but I can speak Italian.
2. They're Paul's shoes.
3. It's me, Paul. Can I come in?
4. Yes, I like America very much.
5. I'm seventeen.

3 Short answers 10 marks

Finish the short answers to these questions.

1. Are you from Russia?   Yes, ...
2. Can you swim?   No, ...
3. Do you like coffee?   No, ...
4. Can your brother play tennis? Yes, ...
5. Does your father play golf?   No, ...
6. Are your parents at home?   No, ...
7. Is Paul at school?   Yes, ...
8. Can they speak English?   No, ...
9. Is she French?   No, ...
10. Can I watch TV?   Yes, ...

4 Match the questions and the short answers 10 marks

1. How many?   a. Fine.
2. Why?   b. On Friday.
3. How old?   c. Twenty pounds.
4. Whose?   d. Thirty next week.
5. Where?   e. My friend.
6. When?   f. Half past six.
7. How much?   g. Because I like it.
8. Who?   h. Laura's.
9. How?   i. About 200.
10. What time?   j. At the supermarket.

5 Prepositions 10 marks

Fill the spaces with one of these prepositions:

at	for	from	in	on	to	with

1./2. .... the weekend I often go out .... my friends.
3. Thank you .... the birthday present.
4. The party is .... Jo's house.
5. Can you write .... Spanish?
6./7. Let's go .... the cinema .... Friday.
8./9. My best friend is .... Japan, but she works .... Canada.
10. He's the best person .... the job.

6 Vocabulary 10 marks

Write the words in the correct spaces:

| boots   cap   high-heeled shoes   jacket   jeans |
| shirt   suit   T-shirt   trainers   trousers |

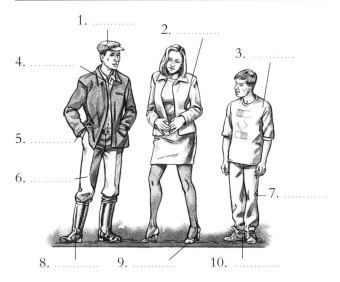

1. ....
2. ....
3. ....
4. ....
5. ....
6. ....
7. ....
8. ....
9. ....
10. ....

7 Vocabulary: verbs and nouns 10 marks

Find two nouns from Box B to go with each verb in Box A.

A *Verbs*
drink   eat   go   have   open   play   visit
watch   wear   write

B *Nouns*
children   city   coffee   door   film   food
friends   fun   games   letter   meal   report
shopping   swimming   tennis   tie   TV
uniform   window   wine

8 Apostrophe or not? 5 marks

Choose the correct words.

1. My shirts / shirt's white.
2. Is that Eds / Ed's jacket?
3. Her shoes / shoe's are black.
4. This hat is Helens / Helen's.
5. These jeans are Jeans / Jean's.

9 *Vocabulary: opposite adjectives* 10 marks

Fill the gaps in the answers with one of the words from the list:

awful	bad	big	cold	expensive
high-heeled	ill	late	modern	short

1. A: Do you like flat shoes?
   B: No, I don't. I like .... shoes.
2. A: Have you got a small car?
   B: No, my car's ....
3. A: Are you OK?
   B: No, I'm .... today.
4. A: Do you like hot weather?
   B: Yes, but I don't like .... weather.
5. A: Is it a long meeting?
   B: No, it's very ....
6. A: Is your house very old?
   B: No, it's ....
7. A: Is it a good film?
   B: No, it's very ....
8. A: Do you go to bed early?
   B: No, I usually go very ....
9. A: Is that a cheap supermarket?
   B: No, it isn't. It's very ....
10. A: It's a wonderful party.
    B: No, it isn't. It's ....

10 **Here *or* there? This *or* that?** 5 marks

Write *here, there, this* or *that* in the spaces in these sentences:

1. Come .... I want to talk to you.
2. Hi Jane. .... is my friend Bianca.
3. A: Do you like Spain?
   B: Yes. Let's go .... for our holidays.
4. A: Is your phone number 223111?
   B: ....'s right.
5. Hello, Dave .... Can I help you?

11 *Conversations* 10 marks

Write these conversations in the right order.

a A: come can to my you party?
   B: is when it?
   A: on it's Sunday.
   B: my friend bring I can?
   A: course can you of.

b A: evening eat let's a this restaurant in.
   B: good a idea is that.
   A: you like Chinese do food?
   B: love it yes I.
   A: I do so.

Total = 100 Marks

TESTS ANSWER KEYS

TEST 1

1 Greetings
1. I'm; pleased
2. are; thanks/thank you; you

2 Questions and replies to be
you; am; Am I; are

3 Pronouns
She; They; It; you; I

4 Alphabet and numbers
1. C   2. I   3. M   4. S   5. X
6. nine (9)   7. seven (7)   8. three (3)   9. eight (8)
10. four (4)

5 Negative answers to to be questions
1. isn't   2. isn't   3. aren't   4. isn't   5. aren't

6 Vocabulary and plurals
1. cities   2. countries   3. drinks   4. numbers
5. addresses

7 Vocabulary – places
gym; classroom; bar; swimming pool; restaurant

8 Question words
1. What   2. Where   3. How   4. Where
5. How/What   6. What   7. What   8. How
9. Where   10. What

9 Numbers 11–30
1. twenty-eight   2. fifteen   3. twenty   4. eighteen
5. twenty-five

10 Prepositions
in; at; in; on; from

11 Plurals
1. cities   2. guides   3. addresses
4. hotels   5. visitors

12 Numbers

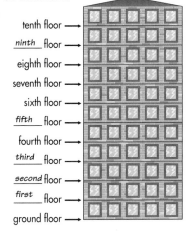

tenth floor →
ninth floor →
eighth floor →
seventh floor →
sixth floor →
fifth floor →
fourth floor →
third floor →
second floor →
first floor →
ground floor →

13 Questions
1. Who is this?   2. Where's she from?   3. How old is she?   4. Is she nice?   5. Is that her cat?

14 Possessive adjectives
1. Our   2. my   3. his   4. their   5. her

15 Vocabulary
Thing: ring; letter; key
Person: visitor; husband; colleague; friend
Place: park; shop; bedroom

16 A or An?
1. an   2. a   3. a   4. an   5. an   6. a   7. a   8. a
9. an   10. a

TEST 2

1 Numbers 100+
1. five hundred and sixty-seven
2. 1010
3. Ten thousand and one
4. 428
5. nine hundred and thirty-three

2 Is/Are there …? questions
1. Is there   2. Are there   3. are there   4. Is there
5. Are there

3 Short answers
1. there isn't   2. there are   3. they aren't   4. there is
5. they are

4 Vocabulary
Rooms: toilet; bathroom; kitchen
Buildings: post office; sports centre; bank; library; theatre
Things on the wall: picture; clock

5 Finding mistakes
1. I've   2. bedrooms   3. have   4. an   5. their

6 Some/any
1. some   2. any   3. any   4. some   5. some

7 Prepositions
1. on the table   2. under the table   3. by the flowers/table   4. in the bin

8 Imperatives
go; stay; Take; forget; Have; Phone

9 Days of the week
1. Saturday   2. Tuesday   3. Wednesday   4. Thursday
5. Friday

10 Pronunciation
1. po̱pular
2. i̱nteresting
3. fanta̱stic
4. bea̱utiful
5. interna̱tional
6. compu̱ter
7. he̱adache
8. e̱nvelopes
9. po̱stcards
10. cathe̱dral

11 Countries and nationalities
1. Turkish   2. French   3. Spanish   4. Greek
5. Indian   6. German   7. Japanese   8. Brazilian
9. Hungarian   10. Italian

12 Question words
1. How   2. How many   3. Who   4. Where
5. What

13 Vocabulary – family
wife   sister   father   son   girl/twin

14 Vocabulary
1. envelope; letter
2. tablets; headache
3. photo; camera
4. green; white
5. key; door
6. classroom; student
7. east; south
8. drink; bar
9. today; weekend
10. wall; picture

15 Responses and reactions
1. really?   2. see you   3. that's fine   4. I think
5. lots

TEST 3

1 Present simple
1. do; live   2. Does; work   3. doesn't work
4. works   5. does; start   6. don't like   7. Do; eat
8. does; cost   9. do; have   10. finishes

2 Short answers
1. don't   2. is   3. I'm not   4. I am   5. he is   6. he
doesn't   7. they do   8. she does   9. they aren't
10. I do

3 Question words
1. What   2. Where   3. What   4. When / What
time   5. How   6. How many   7. How much
8. What   9. Who   10. Where

4 Times
1. ten o'clock in the morning
2. twenty-five past three in the afternoon
3. ten past ten at night
4. half past six in the morning
5. a quarter to eight in the evening
6. 15.35
7. 07.30
8. 13.55
9. 09.20
10. 22.45

5 Likes and dislikes
1. So   2. too   3. Do   4. do   5. don't

6 Correct the mistakes
a *Wrong words*
1. a = an
2. are = is
3. cost = costs
4. likes = like
5. India = Indian

b *Missing words*
1. car **is** very
2. names **have** you
3. When **is** your
4. friends **at** the
5. work **at** half

7 Prepositions
1. for/from   2. in/at   3. at   4. of   5. in   6. to
7. from/to   8. about   9. in   10. for

8 Vocabulary: Jobs
a *Pairs*
1. teacher; school
2. travel agent; holiday
3. waiter; café
4. scientist; laboratory
5. doctor; hospital

b *Make sentences*
1. A teacher works/teaches in a school.
2. A travel agent sells holidays.
3. A waiter works/serves in a café.
4. A scientist works in a laboratory.
5. A doctor works / helps people in a hospital.

9 Vocabulary: Countries and nationalities

1. Chinese   2. Spain   3. Thailand   4. Greek
5. Italian   6. France   7. American   8. Japanese
9. Indian   10. Britain

10 Vocabulary: Food

bacon; burger; chicken; ham; hamburger

11 Vocabulary: Money

1. price   2. pay   3. credit card   4. cost   5. wallet

TEST 4

1 How often?

a
1. always   2. usually   3. often   4. sometimes
5. never

b
6. I always play football at the weekend.
7. Paul usually watches TV in the evenings.
8. You often go out with your friends on Monday.
9. Ed and I sometimes work at home at the weekend.
10. Sue, Jeff and Emma never watch TV in the morning.

2 Questions

1. Can you speak French?
2. Whose shoes are they/these?
3. Who's that? / Who is it?
4. Do you like America?
5. How old are you?

3 Short answers

1. I am   2. I can't   3. I don't   4. he can   5. he doesn't   6. they aren't   7. he is   8. they can't
9. she isn't   10. you can

4 Match the questions and the short answers

1. i   2. g   3. d   4. h   5. j   6. b   7. c   8. e   9. a
10. f

5 Prepositions

1. At   2. with   3. for   4. at   5. in   6. to   7. on
8. from   9. in   10. for

6 Vocabulary

1. cap
2. suit
3. T-shirt
4. shirt
5. jacket
6. trousers
7. jeans
8. boots
9. high heeled shoes
10. trainers

7 Vocabulary: verbs and nouns

1. drink – coffee, wine
2. eat – food, meal
3. go – shopping, swimming
4. have – children, fun
5. open – door, window
6. play – games, tennis
7. visit – city, friends
8. watch – film, TV
9. wear – tie, uniform
10. write – letter, report

8 Apostrophe or not?

1. shirt's   2. Ed's   3. shoes   4. Helen's   5. Jean's

9 Vocabulary: opposite adjectives

1. high-heeled   2. big   3. ill   4. cold   5. short
6. modern   7. bad   8. late   9. expensive   10. awful

10 Here *or* there? This *or* that?

1. here   2. this   3. there   4. That   5. here

11 Conversations

a
A: Can you come to my party?
B: When is it?
A: It's on Sunday.
B: Can I bring a friend?
A: Of course you can.

b
A: Let's eat in a restaurant this evening.
B: That is a good idea.
A: Do you like Chinese food?
B: Yes, I love it.
A: So do I.

TAPESCRIPTS

Exercise 2

1.
RECEPTIONIST: What's your address, please, Mr Jones?
MAN: It's 25, York Avenue, Liverpool, L14 2PR.
2.
RECEPTIONIST: What's your first name please, Mrs Smith?
WOMAN: Julie, that's J-U-L-I-E.
RECEPTIONIST: Thank you, and what's your address?
WOMAN: It's 24, Exeter Gardens, Manchester.
RECEPTIONIST: Can you spell Exeter, please?
WOMAN: Yes, that's E-X-E-T-E-R.
RECEPTIONIST: Thank you, and what's your post code?
WOMAN: It's M17 2AG.
RECEPTIONIST: M7 2AG?
WOMAN: No, M17.
RECEPTIONIST: Thanks.
3.
RECEPTIONIST: What's your address, please, Mr Procter?
MAN: Sixteen, New Road, Melbourne.
RECEPTIONIST: Sixteen?
MAN: Yes. Sixteen, New Road, Melbourne, 3001, Aus …
RECEPTIONIST: Three O O one.
MAN: Yes, that's Australia, of course.
RECEPTIONIST: Oh, and can you tell me your first name, please?
MAN: Yes, it's Simon.
RECEPTIONIST: Is that S-I-M-O-N?
MAN: Yes, that's right.
4.
RECEPTIONIST: What's your address, please, Ms Harriman?
WOMAN: It's 21, Central Avenue, Washington, DC.
RECEPTIONIST: Twenty-nine, Central Avenue, Wash . . .
WOMAN: Not 29, 21.
RECEPTIONIST: Sorry.
5.
RECEPTIONIST: Can you tell me your address, please, Miss Collins?
WOMAN: Of course, it's 28, Barrack Street …
RECEPTIONIST: Barrack Street? Can you spell that, please?
WOMAN: Yes, it's B-A-R-R-A-C-K Street.
RECEPTIONIST: 18, Barrack Street.
WOMAN: No, 28.
RECEPTIONIST: Sorry, 28, Barrack Street …
WOMAN: Cape Town, eight O O O, South Africa.
RECEPTIONIST: Thank you.

6.
RECEPTIONIST: Can you tell me your first name, please, Mr Charles?
MAN: Yes, of course, it's William.
RECEPTIONIST: Can you spell that, please.
MAN: Yes, W-I-L-L-I-A-M.
RECEPTIONIST: Thank you. And your address?
MAN: 18 Park Road, Perth 6026, Western Australia.
RECEPTIONIST: Perth 18?
MAN: No, Perth 6026. It's 18 Park Road.
RECEPTIONIST: Right. Thanks.

Exercise 3

A
Version 1
Tenth floor   Ninth floor   Eighth floor   Seventh floor
Sixth floor   Fifth floor   Fourth floor   Third floor
Second floor   First floor   Ground floor

Version 2
LIFT VOICE: Tenth floor.
MAN 1: Hi.
WOMAN 1: Good morning.
LIFT VOICE: Ninth floor. Eighth floor.
MAN 2: Morning. Nice day.
MAN 1: Hi.
WOMAN 1: Hello.
LIFT VOICE: Seventh floor. Sixth floor. Fifth floor.
WOMAN 2: Hi, Sue. How are you?
WOMAN 1: Fine, thanks. And you?
WOMAN 2: I'm fine.
LIFT VOICE: Fourth floor.
MAN 3: Morning.
OTHERS: Hi. Morning. Hello.
LIFT VOICE: Third floor. Second floor. First floor. Ground floor.
VOICES: Bye. Goodbye. Bye.
B
RECEPTIONIST: OK, Mrs Smith. You're in Room 232.
MRS SMITH: Where's that?
RECEPTIONIST: It's on the second floor.
MRS SMITH: Thanks very much.

RECEPTIONIST: Here's your key, Mr Procter.
MR PROCTER: Where's my room?
RECEPTIONIST: It's on the fourth floor. Room 473.
MR PROCTER: Thank you.
RECEPTIONIST: You're welcome.

RECEPTIONIST: You're on the fifth floor, Ms Harriman.
MS HARRIMAN: The fourth floor?

RECEPTIONIST: No, the fifth floor. You're in Room 591. Here's your key.
MS HARRIMAN: Ah, 591, thank you very much.
RECEPTIONIST: Here's your room key, Miss Collins.
MISS COLLINS: Thank you. Ah, I'm on the seventh floor?
RECEPTIONIST: That's right – Room 740.
MISS COLLINS: That's fine – thanks a lot.
RECEPTIONIST: Here's your key, Mr Charles. You're in Room 193.
MR CHARLES: Is that on the first floor?
RECEPTIONIST: Yes, it is.
MR CHARLES: Thank you very much.
RECEPTIONIST: You're welcome.

Unit 3 Lesson D

Review of Unit 2

Exercise 2

A
1. A: What's your e-mail address?
   B: It's Maria.Suarez, that's m-a-r-i-a dot s-u-a-r-e-z@v-i-r-t-u-a-l dot n-e-t dot c-o-m dot b-r.

2. A: What's your e-mail address?
   B: It's Angela dot Collins ...
   A: Can you spell it, please?
   B: Yes, OK. A-n-g-e-l-a dot C-o-l-l-i-n-s @ S-i-m-e-x dot d-e-m-o-n dot c-o dot u-k.

B
A: Are you on e-mail?
B: Yes. my address is John, that's j-o-h-n, dot, Smythe, that's s-m-y-t-h-e @ unisa (that's u-n-i-s-a) dot e-d-u dot a-u.
A: OK, so that's John dot Smythe at unisa dot e-d-u dot a-u.
B: Correct.
A: Great. Thanks very much.
B: You're welcome.

Unit 4 Lesson A

Exercise 2

Version 1

1. Satoshi
INTERVIEWER: Satoshi, is there a cinema in your town?
SATOSHI: Yes, there are three cinemas.
INTERVIEWER: And are there any nightclubs?
SATOSHI: No, there aren't.
INTERVIEWER: Is there a sports centre?
SATOSHI: Yes, there's a big sports centre.
INTERVIEWER: And is there a theatre?
SATOSHI: Yes, there is. It's very old.

2. Raymundo
INTERVIEWER: Raymundo, is there a nightclub in your town?
RAYMUNDO: Yes. There are four nightclubs in my town.
INTERVIEWER: Four? And is there a cinema or a theatre?
RAYMUNDO: There's a cinema, but there isn't a theatre.
INTERVIEWER: Is there a sports centre?
RAYMUNDO: Yes, there is, there's a small sports centre.

3. Paloma
INTERVIEWER: Hello, Paloma. Is there a cinema in your town?
PALOMA: Yes, there is, but there isn't a theatre.
INTERVIEWER: Is there a sports centre?
PALOMA: Yes, there's a new sports centre. It's fantastic!
INTERVIEWER: Are there any nightclubs?
PALOMA: There is one nightclub. It's very good.

Version 2

1. Satoshi
INTERVIEWER: Satoshi, can I ask you about your town?
SATOSHI: Yes, OK.
INTERVIEWER: Thanks. First, is there a cinema in your town?
SATOSHI: Yes. In fact there are three cinemas.
INTERVIEWER: And are there any nightclubs?
SATOSHI: No, there aren't, unfortunately.
INTERVIEWER: What about a sports centre?
SATOSHI: Yes, there's a really big sports centre. It's new.
INTERVIEWER: And what about a theatre?
SATOSHI: Yes, there's a theatre. It's a very beautiful old theatre.
INTERVIEWER: Thanks a lot.

2. Raymundo
INTERVIEWER: Raymundo, can I ask you about your town?
RAYMUNDO: Yes, of course.
INTERVIEWER: Thanks. First of all, is there a nightclub in your town?
RAYMUNDO: Yes, there are four. Two of them are really good.
INTERVIEWER: Really? What about cinemas and theatres?
RAYMUNDO: Well, there's a cinema, but I'm afraid there isn't a theatre.
INTERVIEWER: And is there a sports centre?
RAYMUNDO: Yes, there is, but it's not a very big one, unfortunately.
INTERVIEWER: Thanks very much.

3. Paloma
INTERVIEWER: Hello, Paloma. Do you think I could ask you some questions about your town?
PALOMA: Yes, OK.
INTERVIEWER: Is there a cinema in your town?
PALOMA: Yes, there is, but there isn't a theatre.
INTERVIEWER: And a sports centre?
PALOMA: Yes, there's a new sports centre. It's great!
INTERVIEWER: Are there any nightclubs?
PALOMA: There's one. It's good but it's very expensive!

Exercise 1

1. A: Have you got the time, please?
   B: Yes, it's half past seven.
   A: Is it really?

2. A: Excuse me, what time is it, please?
   B: It's five to one.
   A: Thanks.

3. A: What's the time?
   B: It's one o'clock.
   A: Thanks very much.

4. A: What's the time?
   B: A quarter past four!
   A: Oh no!

5. A: Excuse me, have you got the time, please?
   B: Erm, yes, it's a quarter to eleven.
   A: Thank you.

6. A: What's the time, please?
   B: It's twenty past five.
   A: Twenty past?
   B: Yes.

7. A: Steve, have you got the time?
   B: Yes, five past two.
   A: Thanks a lot.

8. A: Clare, what time is it, please?
   B: It's twenty to ten.

Exercise 2

1. A: What do you do?
   B: I'm a businesswoman.
   A: Oh, really? Where do you work?
   B: I work in two places. I've got offices in New York and London.

2. A: What's your job?
   B: I'm an engineer.
   A: Where do you work?
   B: I work in a small laboratory at home, but I also go to other countries.

3. A: What do you do?
   B: I'm a doctor.
   A: Where do you work?
   B: Most of the time, I work in a large hospital.

4. A: What's your job?
   B: I'm a waiter.
   A: Where do you work?
   B: In a Greek restaurant in the town centre.
   A: Which restaurant?
   B: The Apollo.
   A: Oh, really? That's a good restaurant.

5. A: What do you do?
   B: I'm a shop assistant.
   A: Where do you work?

B: In a department store in the town.
A: Which department store?
B: D & A.
A: That's interesting. I buy all my clothes there.

6. A: What's your job?
   B: I'm a teacher.
   A: Do you work in a university?
   B: No, I work in a school.

Exercise 2A

A

1. MAN: Excuse me.
   ASSISTANT: Yes.
   MAN: Have you got a T-shirt with *I love Australia* on it, please?
   ASSISTANT: Yes, we have. What colour would you like?
   MAN: Have you got a dark blue T-shirt?
   ASSISTANT: Yes, we have.

2. ASSISTANT: Good morning.
   WOMAN: Hi. Can I have this necklace, please?
   ASSISTANT: Yes, of course. Is it a present?
   WOMAN: Yes, it is.

3. ASSISTANT: Hello, can I help you?
   MAN: Yes, I'd like a small television, please.
   ASSISTANT: This one?
   MAN: No, a very small one – the size of a camera.
   ASSISTANT: Ah, yes. What colour would you like?
   MAN: Have you got black?
   ASSISTANT: Yes, we've got black, white or red.

4. WOMAN: Hi. Can I have these CDs, please?
   ASSISTANT: Thank you.
   WOMAN: And have you got the new Phil Collins CD?
   ASSISTANT: Yes, we have.
   WOMAN: Can I have two, please?

5. ASSISTANT: Good morning. Can I help you.
   MAN: Yes, I'd like a teddy bear, please.
   ASSISTANT: Yes, of course. A big one or a small one?
   MAN: Oh, not too big.

Exercise 2B

B

1. MAN: Excuse me.
   ASSISTANT: Yes.
   MAN: Have you got a T-shirt with *I love Australia* on it, please?
   ASSISTANT: Yes, we have. What colour would you like?
   MAN: Have you got a dark blue T-shirt?
   ASSISTANT: Yes, we have.
   MAN: Good.
   ASSISTANT: And size? Large, medium or small?
   MAN: Small, please – it's for my wife.

2. ASSISTANT: Good morning.
   WOMAN: Hi. Can I have this necklace, please?
   ASSISTANT: Yes, of course. Is it a present?
   WOMAN: Yes, it is.
   ASSISTANT: Who's it for?
   WOMAN: It's a souvenir for my daughter.

3. ASSISTANT: Hello, can I help you?
   MAN: Yes, I'd like a small television, please.
   ASSISTANT: This one?
   MAN: No, a very small one – the size of a camera.
   ASSISTANT: Ah, yes. What colour would you like?
   MAN: Have you got black?
   ASSISTANT: Yes, we've got black, white or red.
   MAN: White, please. It's a present for my girlfriend.

4. WOMAN: Hi. Can I have these CDs, please?
   ASSISTANT: Thank you.
   WOMAN: And have you got the new Phil Collins CD?
   ASSISTANT: Yes, we have.
   WOMAN: Can I have two, please? One for my sister and one for my husband. It's his birthday tomorrow.

5. ASSISTANT: Good morning. Can I help you?
   MAN: Yes, I'd like a teddy bear, please.
   ASSISTANT: Yes, of course. A big one or a small one?
   MAN: Oh, not too big. It's for my grandson – he's only ten weeks old.

Exercise 2A

1. A: Good holiday?
   B: Yeah, wonderful. Italian people are so friendly.
   A: I like your shoes.
   B: They're from Rome.

2. A: Hi.
   B: Jill! Come in.
   A: How was America?
   B: Fantastic!
   A: And New York?
   B: Busy!
   A: Hey, I like the painting! It's very modern.
   B: That's from New York.

3. A: Paul! You're back!
   B: Hi.
   A: Nice time in England?
   B: Yes, great.
   A: And the weather?
   B: Not so good.
   A: I like your umbrella.
   B: Thanks – it's from London.

4. A: I love your sunglasses.
   B: They're Spanish.
   A: Oh yeah. How was the holiday?
   B: Wonderful.

Exercise 2B

1. A: Hello, can I help?
   B: Yes, how much is that painting?
   A: The large, modern one?
   B: Yes.
   A: It's 200 dollars.
   B: That's very cheap.

2. A: How much are these sunglasses, please?
   B: They're eight hundred pesetas.
   A: That's not bad and they're very nice.

3. A: I really like these shoes. How much are they?
   B: They're two hundred thousand lire.
   A: Phew! That's very expensive.
   B: They're Gucci shoes.

4. A: How much is this umbrella?
   B: This week it's fifteen pounds.
   A: That's cheap for a large umbrella.

Exercise 2

Version 1

A: OK ... first question. Can you write good business letters?
B: Mm, yes, I can.
A: OK. Erm, what about reports? Can you write a good report?
B: Mm, I can. I like writing.
A: Do you like people?
B: Yes, of course, I like people ... I've got no problem with people from any country.
A: Right. Can you talk to people on the phone?
B: Oh, yes, I can talk on the phone. I'm good.
A: What about computers? Can you use computers?
B: No, I can't. I don't like computers.

Version 2

A: OK ... first question. Can you write good business letters?
B: Mm, yes, I can. I can write any sort of letter. I'm a good writer because I write a lot.
A: OK. Erm, what about reports? Can you write a good report?
B: Mm, I can. I'm a good writer ... letters, reports, I can write anything.
A: Do you like people?
B: Yes, of course I like people. I've got no problem with people from any country, and I can speak French and Italian.
A: Right. Can you talk to people on the phone?
B: Oh, yes, I can talk on the phone. I'm good with people and they like me ... I think.
A: What about computers? Can you use computers?
B: No, I can't, I'm afraid. I don't like computers because I've got a bad back.

Exercise 2A

1. CECILE: Hello.
   SATOSHI: Hi, Cecile, it's Satoshi.
   CECILE: Satoshi. How are you?
   SATOSHI: I'm fine. Listen, can you come to our party?
   CECILE: Yes, I can.
   SATOSHII: Can you bring a friend?
   CECILE: Yes, he's called Pascal – he's French.

2. A: Hello.
   SATOSHI: Hello. Can I speak to John, please?
   A: Yes, of course. One moment.
   JOHN: Hello, this is John.
   SATOSHII: John, this is Satoshi. Can you come to the party next Friday?
   JOHN: No, I can't. Sorry.
   SATOSHI: Don't worry. That's OK.
   JOHN: Have a good time.

3. PETER: Hello.
   MAYUMI: Hi, Peter, it's Mayumi.
   PETER: Mayumi! How are you?
   MAYUMI: I'm fine. Listen, can you come to our party on Friday?
   PETER: I'm not sure. I'm very busy this week. Perhaps.

4. MARIA: Hello.
   SATOSHI: Is that Maria?
   MARIA: Yes, it is, who's that?
   SATOSHI: It's Satoshi from school.
   MARIA: I'm sorry, I can't come to your party on Saturday.
   SATOSHI: It isn't on Saturday. It's on Friday.
   MARIA: Oh, great! I can come on Friday.
   SATOSHI: Wonderful! Can you bring a friend?
   MARIA: Yes, of course. Manuel – he's my husband.
   SATOSHI: Oh, good.
   MARIA: See you on Friday.
   SATOSHI: OK. Thanks. Bye.

5. LUCY: Hello.
   MAYUMI: Hi, Lucy – it's Mayumi.
   LUCY: Oh, hi.
   MAYUMI: Can you come to the party on Friday?
   LUCY: I don't really know. Probably.
   MAYUMI: That's OK.
   LUCY: I want to come, but my father is not very well.
   MAYUMI: I'm sorry. Try to come.
   LUCY: OK.

Exercise 2B

1. A: Hello.
   SATOSHI: Hello. Can I speak to John please?
   A: Yes, of course. One moment.
   JOHN: Hello, this is John.
   SATOSHI: John, this is Satoshi. Can you come to the party next Friday?
   JOHN: No, I can't. Sorry.
   SATOSHI: Oh, that's a pity.

2. PETER: Peter here.
   MAYUMI: Hi Peter, it's Mayumi.
   PETER: Mayumi! How are you?
   MAYUMI: I'm fine. Listen, can you come to our party on Friday?
   PETER: I'm not sure. I'm very busy this week. Perhaps.

3. LUCY: Hello.
   MAYUMI: Hi Lucy – it's Mayumi.
   LUCY: Oh hi.
   MAYUMI: Can you come to the party on Friday?
   LUCY: I don't really know. Probably.

Exercise 1

A
1. A: Does she go to work on Saturdays?
   B: No, I don't think so.

2. A: Can he go to Barcelona this morning?
   B: No, he can't, there's a meeting at 10.
   A: Oh, OK.

3. A: Do they come from Hungary?
   B: Yes, from Tblisi.

4. A: Can she phone Monika at nine, please?
   B: I think so. Mmm, that's fine.
   A: Thanks. Bye.

5. A: Does he like the new job?
   B: Mm, very much.
   A: That's good.

6. A: Does she like Italian food?
   B: Italian? I don't know. I think so.

B
1. A: Can he go to Barcelona?
   B: No, he can't.

2. B: Can she phone Monika at nine?
   B: Yes, she can.

ACKNOWLEDGEMENTS

Authors' acknowledgements

We would like to thank the other series authors Ruth Gairns, Stuart Redman and Joanne Collie for their professionalism and continuing support as the *True to Life* series grows. Special thanks to Joanne Collie for her valuable feedback on early drafts of this material.
At Cambridge University Press our special thanks go to our commissioning editor, Kate Boyce, who has been a patient, courteous and constant professional guide throughout the writing, feedback, revision and production process. To our editor, Helena Gomm, we are grateful for her tireless excellence in ensuring economy, consistency and accuracy. We are grateful also to Frances Amrani for editing the Teacher's Book, to Martin Williamson of Prolingua productions and the staff at Studio AVP for producing the recordings, and to the design team, Samantha Dumiak and Gecko Limited. Stephen Slater is grateful to his family for their patience and to the family dog for her unconditional enthusiasm for life, which has transferred valuable, positive energy to him when he really needed it.

The authors and publishers would like to thank the following individuals and institutions for their help in testing the material and for the invaluable feedback which they provided:
Laura Renart, T. S. Eliot Institute, Buenos Aires, Argentina; Pat MacRitchie, Hawthorn English Language Centre, Victoria, Australia; Judy D'All, Centre d'Anglais d'Angers, Angers, France; Don Ward, Centre d'Étude des Langues, Évry Cedex, France; Miriam Zeh-Glöckler, Sprachwerkstatt Glöckler, Leipzig, Germany; Kerry Flanagan, Regent Italia, Milan, Italy; Suzanne Wragge, Buckingham School, Rome, Italy; Michelle Hug, Rothrist, Switzerland; Canan O'Flynn, Bilgi University, Istanbul, Turkey.

The authors and publishers are grateful to the following illustrators and photographic sources:
Illustrators: David Axtell: pp 5 *b*, 9 *b*, 36, 76; Kathy Baxendale: pp 7, 26, 46, 63; Lee Ebrell: pp. 8, 16, 20, 22, 25, 39, 41, 39, 58 *t*, 107 *r*, 118 *l*, 119 *t*; Martin Fish: pp. 9 *tr*, 38, 43, 66, 80 *t*, 81, 83 *t*, 90, 98, 111; Steve Lach pp. 6, 24, 62, 97; Mark McLaughlin: pp. 5 *t*, 37, 52, 68, 84, 87, 112; Tracy Rich: pp. 14, 23, 30, 40, 46, 60, 70, 71, 83 *b*; Martin Sanders: pp. 28, 32, 47, 58 *b*; Jamie Sneddon: pp. 7, 8, 9, 11, 15, 16, 17, 21, 23, 25, 26, 28, 31, 32, 34, 40, 41, 43, 46, 51, 65, 75, 81, 84, 85, 88, 96, 103, 106, 107 *t*, 108, 109, 110, 113, 115, 118 *b*, 125; John Storey: pp. 107 *l*, 114, 118 *r*, 119 *b*, 120, 123; Kath Walker: pp. 44, 64, 80 *b*, 82, 88, 89, 100, 101, 102, 104, 105; Rosemary Woods: p. 29.

Photographic sources: Action-Plus photographic: p. 78 (racer); Peter Adams: p. 85 (nurse); Tick Ahearn: p. 13 (all except Statue of Liberty & World Trade Center); Ancient Art & Architecture Collection: p. 30 *br* (G. T. Garvey); Paul Beard: pp. 38, 50; The Bell Educational Trust: p. 19 *cl*; Bord Failte – Irish Tourist Board: p. 33 *b* (Bryan Lynch); Collections: p. 85 (engineer: R. J. Davis); E. T. Archive: p. 7 *c*; Malcom Fife: p. 32; Leslie Garland: p. 44 *r*; Hulton Getty Collection: p.7 *b*; courtesy of ICI: p. 53 *bc*; Image Bank: p.4 *c* (Steve Niedorf); Joel Photography: p. 30 *bcl*; Melvyn P. Lawes: p.30 *tr*; Life File: pp. 12 *br*, 35 *c* (Emma Lee), 12 *tr*, 35 *br* (Jeremy Hoare), 13 (Statue of Liberty: Su Davies), 19 *cr* (Mike Maidment), 31 *bl* (Andrew Ward), 33 *l* (Arthur Jumper), 33 *t* (Nigel Shuttleworth), 37 *t* (Barry Mayes), 78 (nun: Paul Fisher); Nigel Luckhurst: pp. 21 *bl*, *br*, 22 *t* (jewelry courtesy of Cellini, Cambridge), 21 *bc*, 22 *cl*, *cr*, *br*, *bl*; Popperfoto: pp. 78 (UN), 79 (Mandela, Pope, Lennon); 79 (Reuters: Woods, Hingis, Crawford); David Simson: pp. 4 (all except *c*), 7 *t*, 8, 10, 11, 12 *tl*, *bl*, 13 (World Trade Center), 14, 15, 16, 17, 19 *l*, *r*, 20, 21 *tl*, *tr*, 25, 30 *tl*, *bl*, *bcr*, 31 *t*, *br*, *bc*, 35, *t*, *bl*, 37 *bl*, *br*, 39, 40, 42 *r*, 44 *l*, 48, 49, 51, 53 (all except *bc*), 54, 55, 56, 57, 61, 63, 64, 70, 73, 75, 78 *l*, 78 (fireman), 78 *r*, 81, 85 (all except doctor, nurse, engineer), 86, 88, 92, 95; Mike Wyndham Picture Collection: p.78 (nurse), 85 (doctor).

t = top, *b* = bottom, *c* = centre, *l* = left, *r* = right

Design and production by Gecko Ltd, Bicester, Oxon.
Picture research by Callie Kendall.
Sound recordings by Martin Williamson, Prolingua Productions, at Studio AVP, London.